future park

Imagining Tomorrow's Urban Parks

Amalie Wright

© Amalie Wright 2013

All rights reserved. Except under the conditions described in the *Australian Copyright Act 1968* and subsequent amendments, no part of this publication may be reproduced, stored in a retrieval system or transmitted in any form or by any means, electronic, mechanical, photocopying, recording, duplicating or otherwise, without the prior permission of the copyright owner. Contact **CSIRO** PUBLISHING for all permission requests.

National Library of Australia Cataloguing-in-Publication entry

Wright, Amalie, author.

Future park : imagining tomorrow's urban parks / by Amalie Wright.

9780643100336 (paperback)
9780643106611 (epdf)
9780643106628 (epub)

Includes bibliographical references and index.

Urban parks – Economic aspects – Australia.
Urban parks – Environmental aspects – Australia.
Urban parks – Social aspects – Australia.

333.7830994

Published by
CSIRO PUBLISHING
150 Oxford Street (PO Box 1139)
Collingwood VIC 3066
Australia
Telephone: +61 3 9662 7666
Local call: 1300 788 000 (Australia only)
Fax: +61 3 9662 7555
Email: publishing.sales@csiro.au
Website: www.publish.csiro.au

Front cover photography: **Landschaftspark Duisburg Nord** *Amalie Wright.*
Photography throughout: *Amalie Wright* unless credited.

Set in Clarendon LT and Corona Lt Std.
Edited by Anne Findlay
Cover and text design by Nicole Arnett Phillips
Typeset by Nicole Arnett Phillips
Printed in China by 1010 Printing International Ltd

CSIRO PUBLISHING publishes and distributes scientific, technical and health science books, magazines and journals from Australia to a worldwide audience and conducts these activities autonomously from the research activities of the Commonwealth Scientific and Industrial Research Organisation (CSIRO). The views expressed in this publication are those of the author(s) and do not necessarily represent those of, and should not be attributed to, the publisher or CSIRO. The copyright owner shall not be liable for technical or other errors or omissions contained herein. The reader/user accepts all risks and responsibility for losses, damages, costs and other consequences resulting directly or indirectly from using this information.

Original print edition:
The paper this book is printed on is in accordance with the rules of the Forest Stewardship Council®. The FSC® promotes environmentally responsible, socially beneficial and economically viable management of the world's forests.

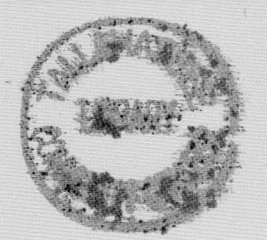

Contents

Introduction **p.1**

01 . *Linkages* **p.31**

02 . *Obsolescences* **p.113**

03 . *Co-locations* **p.169**

04 . *Installations* **p.255**

Where to from here? **p.311**

Endnotes **p.323**

Appendix **p.339**
Project distribution p.340

Index **p.343**
Places p.348
Projects p.350
People p.352

Acknowledgements

This book has been a long journey, and I acknowledge with deep gratitude those who have travelled the road with me.

Firstly I thank Rosemarie Kennedy and the Centre for Subtropical Design in Brisbane, Australia. In 2007 I was the lucky recipient of a travel scholarship awarded by the CSD, which enabled me to visit the first of many parks in Colombia and the United States that feature in these pages.

Thanks also go to Ted Hamilton at CSIRO Publishing. Ted heard me interviewed about my scholarship travels and kindly offered the opportunity to develop a book. Ted later passed the baton to Tracey Millen and her team, who guided the book through to publication.

I am deeply humbled and grateful for the amazing generosity of design firms, local authorities, photographers, both professional and amateur, and other wonderful individuals all around the world, who have granted permission to use their photographs to illustrate the parkland projects.

To my family and friends who have lived this project for more years than should surely be reasonable, I thank you for your endless encouragement despite well concealed scepticism that it would ever be completed.

Thank-you Nicole Arnett Phillips, for creating such a wonderful house for my words to inhabit. The 'k' is indeed a delight.

Lastly to Richard – backstop, sounding board, site visit accompanist and head cheerleader – thank-you. Your support makes everything seem like a walk in the park.

The Author

Amalie in the Landscapology design studio (Michael Clarkson)

Amalie Wright is an award-winning landscape architect and architect, passionate about achieving positive change through great design.

She is the director of Landscapology, a design studio established to help passionate and curious people create beautiful, contemporary and sculptural landscapes that are responsible and resilient. She has over 16 years' prior experience in multidisciplinary practices, working on significant public realm projects in Australia and abroad.

In 2007 Amalie won the mecu travel bursary awarded by Queensland's Centre for Subtropical Design. She travelled to Colombia and the United States studying the changing role of city parks, and parks as agents of social change. These investigations formed the starting point for this book, and for an ongoing fascination with the way cities and communities imagine, use and value their parks and people places – the places where everyday life happens.

www.landscapology.com.au

For my parents, Marilyn Ann Charlesworth and Keith Samuel Wright.

Introduction

Introduction

What do a vacant lot in Philadelphia and a water treatment plant in central Colombia have in common? Cops? Cocaine? How about the Sydney Harbour Bridge and a sixteenth century Dutch fort? The answer: seen through my eyes, they are all places that have been transformed by parks.

We Westerners have a fairly consistent image of what a park is. There's definitely some lawn, usually some trees and plants, often paths, and maybe somewhere to sit. In our cultural consciousness a park looks like this…

'Park'

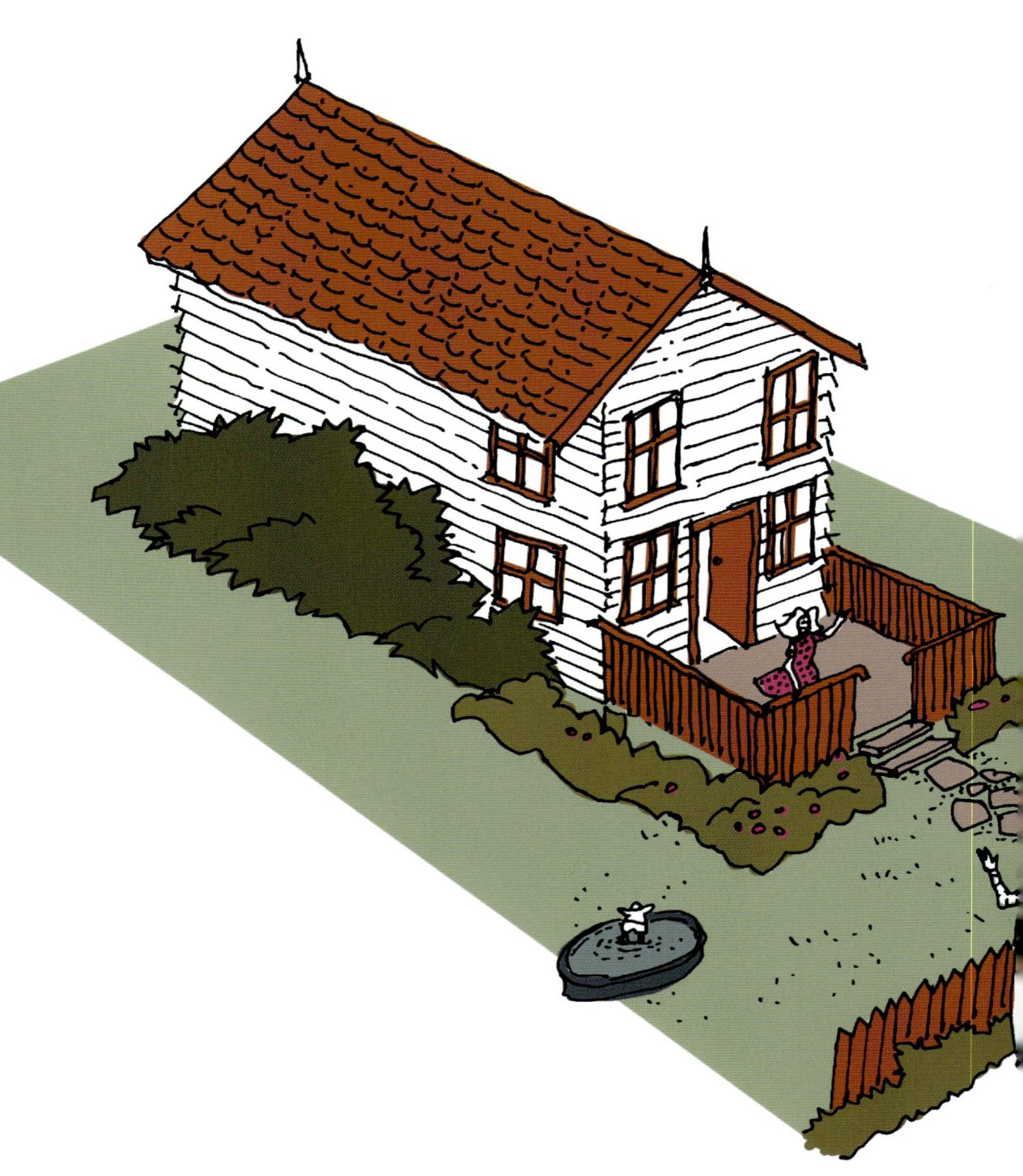

'House'

...in the same way that a house looks like this, even though very few of us actually live in, or walk our dogs in places that look like either of these two images. Beyond the stereotype, things can start to get complicated.

Introduction

For some, a park is definitely a place where kids can play, or people can run around and kick a football. For this group an ideal park has lots of things to 'do', and there are facilities like cafés and bicycle hire stations, and events like outdoor zumba classes and multicultural festivals to provide variety and keep interest levels high. You know who you are.

A park with lots of things to see and do. Portland Farmers Market, South Park Blocks, Portland State University.

Reading alone in the middle of a city of 7.5 million people. Potters Field Park, London.

For other people, this is a description of sheer hell. Shrieking and hollering and frisbees and family reunions with fold-out chairs are all likely to have them running for cover as quickly as they can manage. They think a park should be a place of quiet and calm.

Rules.

Then there are those who believe that parks should be very well maintained and manicured, with signs advising what sorts of activities are allowed, fences separating the dogs from the walkers from the children, and preferably uniformed staff around to make sure that adherence to the rules is scrupulously observed.

Anything goes: local men unself-consciously enjoy a day by the river at Jiuzhan Park in Harbin, northern China.

Many other people feel a park like this is akin to a shop window display, sterile and unwelcoming. They instead prefer a place where it is possible to set up some chairs under a canopy and enjoy a beer, or let a dog run freely. This type of person might sneak to a favourite secluded corner to canoodle. They are more than happy for the lawn to be mowed, but otherwise they prefer the park, like themselves, to be left to its own devices.

The further we delve, the further away we move from the prototypical park idea.

If there are remnants of past use – crumbling walls, rotting wharf piles – some of us think they should be retained and given special treatment, while others counsel demolishing and starting afresh.[1]

Spread over 300 ha, part of the new Chenshan Botanical Garden is built in a former Shanghai quarry. Steps and paths traverse the steep sides of the cuttings. (Nev Connell)

No trace remains today of the farm that gave New Farm Park its name. The 'new farm' was established to supplement produce from the Botanic Gardens, necessary to feed the population of the convict colony. The farm displaced the indigenous population from the riverfront land, then became a racetrack in 1846, and finally a public park when the Brisbane City Council purchased the land in 1913.

Introduction   **11**

Roma Street Parkland, Brisbane: dense, naturalistic planting.

Some of us strongly believe that parks provide a 'connection with nature', and they must always be heavily planted and as 'naturalistic' as possible.

1. Director Park, Portland: hard paving, furniture, water and very little vegetation. (Richard Buchanan)
2. Robert F Wagner Jr Park, New York: live music and children's activities at Battery Point, near the ferry to the Statue of Liberty.
3. A sign warns park users away from this revenue-generating part of Roma Street Parkland.
4. Callan Park: the former Mental Hospital building, now part of the Sydney College of the Arts. (Adam.J.W.C. via Wikimedia Commons)

Many others would argue that it is possible to create a successful park without a single blade of grass. Commercial activity is another bellwether for public opinion. Some argue that parks need commercial activity – cafés, food carts, spaces rented for weddings – to attract visitors and help defray costs. Opponents believe, equally as strongly, that the voice of commercial interest speaks louder than public interest. Once the door is open it's hard to close, and parks risk becoming quasi-private enclaves.

In the face of so many options, many park owners and managers now use public surveys to define community preference. In 2008, Leichhardt Municipal Council in Sydney's inner west used a two-page survey to generate input into a planned redevelopment of Callan Park. Question 3 asked 'What were your main reasons for going to Callan Park on recent visits?' There were 24 possible responses, ranging from 'running or jogging' through to 'mental health services', 'picnic or social gathering', 'heritage gardens', 'drug or alcohol services' and 'peaceful enjoyment'.

For those not familiar with Callan Park's location and history, the thought of some of these uses might be confusing and confronting.[2] Some might wonder, perhaps not unreasonably, whether those visiting a park for drug or alcohol services would be likely to fill out an online survey. The lead consultants, McGregor Coxall stress that the website created specifically for the project enabled the widest cross-section of the community to participate and have their voices heard.[3] Others might hope that the only reason a council might want to know the numbers would be to discourage 'undesirable' park visitors. The realities, of course, are never that simple.

The Wellington Park Management Trust in Hobart, Tasmania, took a slightly different approach in its 2010 Community Values Survey. All Tasmanians were invited to comment, and the survey contained mainly blank space, where members of the public could respond in their own words. The survey formed part of a larger Landscape Study that included a Historical Landscape Values study and a Visual Quality study.

In the words of the Trust:

'The results from these studies will be combined to provide a comprehensive statement on the landscape values of the Park. This new, detailed information will be used to help manage the important landscape and cultural values of Wellington Park, and enable the Trust to better meet its management obligations under the Wellington Park Act.'[14]

The dispassionate way in which the surveys were introduced could have implied that the Trust viewed Wellington Park primarily as an asset to be managed, rather than a place to be visited, enjoyed or even loved.

It is illuminating that so much of the Wellington Park study focused on 'values'. In contemporary society there are few decisions that are made, few dollars that are spent, without at least some analysis of the 'value' that will be delivered by the proposed expenditure. Parks have not escaped this focus. Making parks takes time, money and space. Keeping them going requires additional time and money. Yet parks contribute to our cities in ways that are often difficult to measure using traditional accounting benchmarks. Cities benefit from parks in three main ways: socially, environmentally and economically.

Parks contribute socially by providing opportunities for different types of leisure and recreation, by enhancing the amenity of cities and neighbourhoods, and by incorporating cultural and heritage values. Parks provide a setting for cross-cultural differences to be negotiated – we can learn to get along in parks. In Brooklyn, researchers found that different cultural groups used Prospect Park in different ways. Locals from Hispanic or West Indian backgrounds, for example, visited in large, extended family groups, and stayed in the park for a whole day. They would hang hammocks from trees, cook barbecues, and generally occupy large areas of space. White visitors rarely barbecued or picnicked. Many white locals jogged or walked dogs, which few visitors from other ethnic backgrounds did. Park managers found that, in many cases, the way keen park-users actually wanted to use the park was in conflict with the original design intent of Frederick Law Olmsted and Calvert Vaux: attracting a large West Indian drumming gathering was probably not what was intended by 'uplifting recreation' in the park, and some well-meaning contemporary managers felt it risked tree damage by overcompaction of the root zone. In the midst of such diversity, attracting visitors remains very important for Prospect Park.

Unlike its more famous Manhattan counterpart, Central Park, Prospect Park does not benefit from wealthy neighbours willing to contribute millions of dollars annually to a conservancy that helps manage and maintain the park on behalf of the City. Prospect Park has to make every dollar count, so managing and maintaining the park to accommodate its cross-cultural constituency is as important as managing and maintaining its cultural legacy.[5]

Prospect Park, Brooklyn: the Drummer's Circle. (Jen Robinson via Flickr)

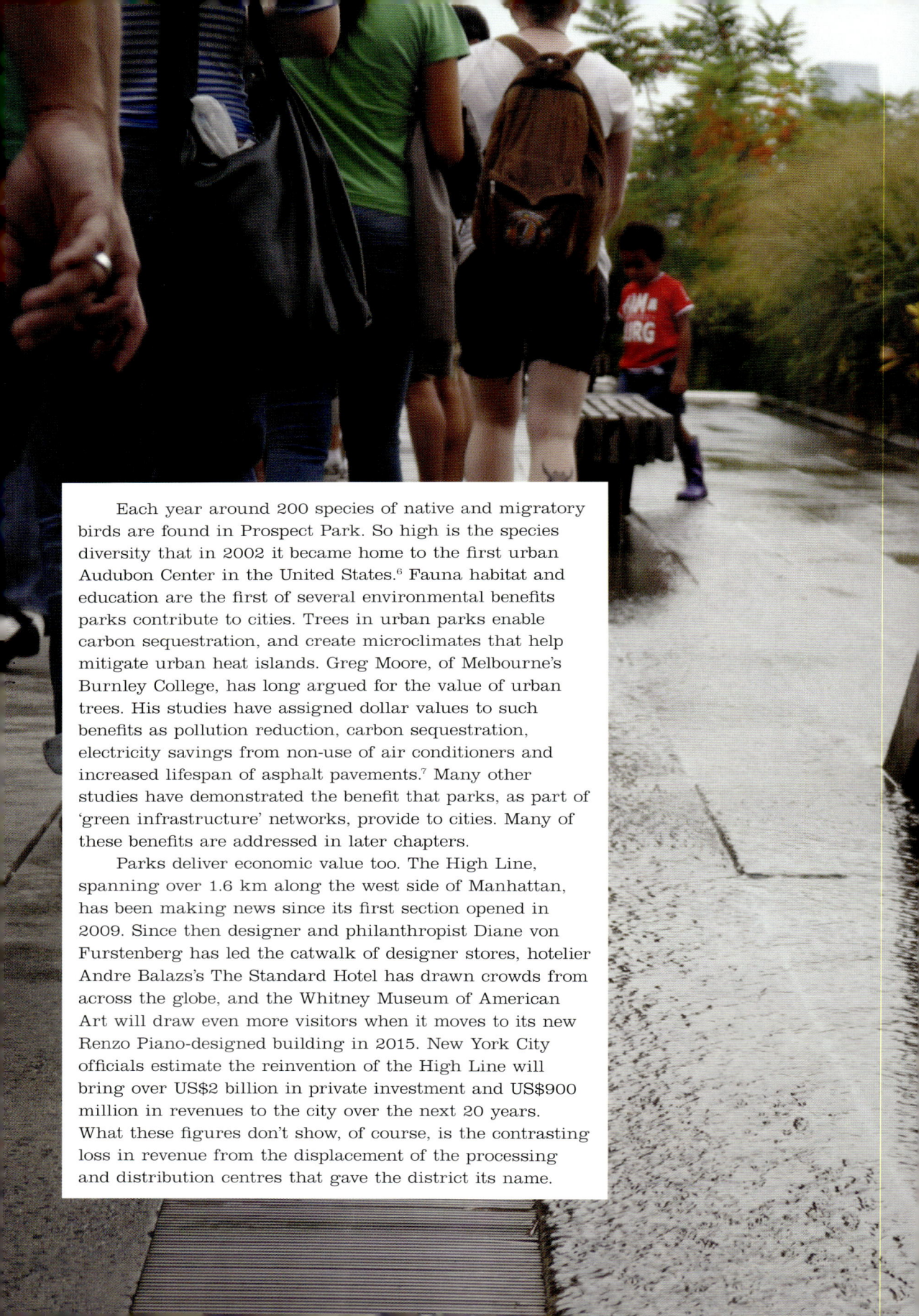

Each year around 200 species of native and migratory birds are found in Prospect Park. So high is the species diversity that in 2002 it became home to the first urban Audubon Center in the United States.[6] Fauna habitat and education are the first of several environmental benefits parks contribute to cities. Trees in urban parks enable carbon sequestration, and create microclimates that help mitigate urban heat islands. Greg Moore, of Melbourne's Burnley College, has long argued for the value of urban trees. His studies have assigned dollar values to such benefits as pollution reduction, carbon sequestration, electricity savings from non-use of air conditioners and increased lifespan of asphalt pavements.[7] Many other studies have demonstrated the benefit that parks, as part of 'green infrastructure' networks, provide to cities. Many of these benefits are addressed in later chapters.

Parks deliver economic value too. The High Line, spanning over 1.6 km along the west side of Manhattan, has been making news since its first section opened in 2009. Since then designer and philanthropist Diane von Furstenberg has led the catwalk of designer stores, hotelier Andre Balazs's The Standard Hotel has drawn crowds from across the globe, and the Whitney Museum of American Art will draw even more visitors when it moves to its new Renzo Piano-designed building in 2015. New York City officials estimate the reinvention of the High Line will bring over US$2 billion in private investment and US$900 million in revenues to the city over the next 20 years. What these figures don't show, of course, is the contrasting loss in revenue from the displacement of the processing and distribution centres that gave the district its name.

The High Line, New York: Sunday afternoon peak hour at the Sundeck Preserve

Just up the road from the High Line is another, bigger piece of green space. This is a park that started with a competition. This is also a park that removed some 17 000 potential building sites from the market when its 340 ha were designated for public use. It sits on a piece of land that is worth approximately US$529 billion, according to a 2007 study. And this is a park that is so desirable that, even in today's economic climate, a three-bedroom apartment nearby can be confidently marketed for US$14.5 million.[8] This, of course, is Central Park.

Central Park, New York: highrise apartment buildings overlook the park.

A report commissioned by the Central Park Conservancy estimated that 'spending by Central Park enterprises and visitors to the Park directly and indirectly accounted for US$395 million in economic activity in the city in 2007, and that this activity, along with the increase in real property values attributable to proximity to the Park, generated US$656 million in tax revenues to the City in the same year'.[9] Years before, Frederick Law Olmsted had already recognised the difference his creation had made. Olmsted reportedly 'tracked the value of land around Central Park and found the city's US$13 million investment had led to an astounding US$209 million increase in just seventeen years'.[10] Central Park's value to New York's economy reflects both the foresight of its creators but also the cumulative impact of investment in its renovation, maintenance, management and continuous improvement.

Value is a contentious concept. Landscape architects today, caught in the midst of an earnest debate (with what are now called 'stakeholders') about whether there should be one or two rubbish bins next to the park entry, may regretfully remind themselves that Olmsted and Vaux weren't required to participate in 'value management' workshops,[11] nor did they feel the need to survey the residents of upper Manhattan before submitting their competition-winning entry for Central Park. Nor were the residents of Paris's 6th arrondissement asked by Napoleon to formulate a 'community vision' for how they would like to use the Jardin de Luxembourg. Today the designers wouldn't make it past the proposal stage if they failed to describe how their consultation process would work. Yet these parks remain among the most beloved and visited in their respective cities, as do many more that were created without input from the people who would eventually end up using them. Is this due to the way we define 'parks'?

Dictionaries are of little help. Australia's *Macquarie Dictionary* offers this:

> 'an area of land within a town, often with recreational or other facilities, which is set aside for public use'.[12]

Think for a moment about your favourite park in the world. Does this definition, these 20 words, come even close to capturing what is special about your favourite park – how the low light paints everything in a golden haze on winter mornings; how the new growth blushes onto the lilly pillies in spring; how the smell of barbecuing sausages wafts from the prize picnic spot next to the lake?

In their 2010 book for the *Basics Landscape Architecture* series, Ed Wall and Tim Waterman defined 'park' as: 'In urban terms, an often green and pleasantly landscaped area of land set aside for public use, in particular sports, recreation and relaxation, and also valuable for its ecological functions.'[13]

Using this definition a place could be 'not green', and 'not pleasantly landscaped', and still be a park, as long as it is 'set aside for public use'. Either way, it's not much more evocative, nor more definitive than the dictionary effort.

Thirty years before them, pioneering teacher of landscape studies John Brinckerhoff Jackson argued that,[14] through our misunderstanding of history, we now associate the word almost exclusively with the picturesque, structured and deliberately contrived park passed down to us through a lineage of aristocratic hunting and pleasure grounds. This park provides 'urban amenity' and opportunities for 'passive recreation', a term Jackson viewed nearly as dimly as 'open space'. What we have forgotten, he argued, is that until well into the nineteenth century, every town also contained 'sizeable areas of land where the common people, and particularly adolescents, could exercise and play and enjoy themselves, and at the same time participate in community life'. Those places, near churches, on riverbanks, in forests, outside city walls, do not exist anymore, killed off by the expansion of settlements, changes in our recreation preferences and societal abhorrence of risk.

The first type of park has become the default setting, and we build more of the same to validate our belief that, 'what the public wants (or ought to have) is "contact with nature" in a professionally designed park'. Our belief is tested though, by the continued presence of the people disenfranchised by this type of park. Teenagers in particular ride bikes down stairs, parkour over walls and skateboard along rails and seats. I suspect that part of the magic world of Harry, Hermione and Ron so appealing to children is that, as well as the flying broomsticks, they also get to clamber their way through forests, and schlep through mud, and **do battle,** rather than climb to a safe distance, in carefully calibrated and age-appropriate heights, on a stable and secure piece of 'play equipment', encircled by impact-cushioning 'softfall'. For our teenagers we have responded with things like 'skate parks', often crude and unlovely places where we corral them until they have 'grown up' enough to be let back into the real thing.

About the same time Jackson was making his argument, the beloved design touchstone *A Pattern Language* was published. Although it included 253 'patterns' for 'an entirely new approach to architecture, building and planning', there was no pattern for 'park'. Instead a range of different patterns – 'accessible green', 'common land', 'connected play', and so on – described elements or qualities that might be combined at different scales to create many different types of outdoor or green spaces.[15]

Even as recently as 2007, Julia Czerniak described urban parks as 'an increasingly hard-to-define landscape type'.[16]

Rather than fighting to define parks, we could embrace a multitude of possibilities.

Maybe therein lies a clue: it's so hard to move the definition of parks beyond the dryness of the dictionary and the stereotype of the picturesque because we are still figuring out what we mean by 'landscape'.[17] As Anne Whiston Spirn reminds us, we see landscape very much through the filter of our own position and expectation: for ecologists, a landscape is a habitat; for planners it's a zone – Brinckerhoff's dreaded 'open space'; for architects, a landscape is often a view, or a site for intervention. Given this, it seems entirely possible that we are always going to fall short by trying to position and define parks within their broader context of something else we find hard to agree on – landscape.

I prefer to leave the definitions to others. Instead of trying to map the parkland equivalent of the human genome project, I would rather embrace the 'Pandora's Box' possibilities of parks.

Introduction **23**

The varied ways people already think about and make parks shows us just how much latitude there is in the idea of what a park can be. The open-ended or absent definition admits the possibilities of moving beyond our fixed cultural norms and allowing an exploration of diversity, in culture, use, needs and much more. It creates freedom in the many edges and adjacencies created, the boundaries that can be pushed and pulled. The Pandora's Box approach also grants the freedom to think transformationally about what parks might become in the future. By acknowledging that the term 'park' admits a very broad church of places, spaces and uses, we open the door to thinking of parks as ways of providing solutions to a much broader range of current and future challenges. As Galen Cranz emboldens us,

> 'those with an interest in the character of urban life should seize on parks as one of the vehicles for the realization of their particular visions, and debate around parks should revolve around those visions', even to the extent that parks can become 'a perfect world in miniature, one that provides norms for the larger world to live up to'.[18]

With great freedom, so the saying goes, comes great responsibility. This book started with a voracious consumption of a vast array of projects and proposals that have been undertaken, generally, in the last 15 years. As a landscape 'outsider' I have no formal training in my adopted profession, but rather a convert's passion to read, see and learn about the many ways we can, and have, shaped our landscape. In recent years a couple of types of stories seemed to appear time and time again. 'Green' stories, for example, were popular, featuring skyscrapers garlanded in vines, walls awash in verdant foliage and aerial shots of cities with all the roofs painted green. Just as popular were stories about overcrowded cities, and ones about bicycles. It seemed that many of these stories and projects were exploring similar themes. It also seemed that individuals, communities and leaders were responding to some of the great paradoxes of our time in a very deliberate way, through the creation of landscapes and parks – parkscapes.

Globalisation is the first contemporary paradox. Maligned by some, embraced by others, globalisation encourages reaching out and retreating in equal measure. With everyone nominally participating in the same global marketplace, competition rises between different countries and different cities, but also between cities and states, states and regions, cities and suburbs and so on. Globalisation challenges borders, and recent parks have responded by exploring ways to create Linkages.

Urbanisation is the second contemporary paradox. More than half the world's population now lives in its cities, a percentage that is expected to rise. More people also live on our planet than ever before. Cities throughout the world are struggling to deal with the constant influx of new residents. The counterpoint to rising population and urbanisation is shrinkage, and many places are exploring the ways in which parks can form part of a response to urban Obsolescence.

The third contemporary paradox concerns segregation, safety, silos and space. Many cities are now finding that separating functions, land uses, and governmental departments into ever-increasing silos is hindering rather than helping cities progress – it takes longer, is more expensive and more difficult to get things done. Recent parks have explored responses of sharing, through Co-location.

The fourth and final contemporary paradox is global financial crisis in an economy of consumption. While many wait confidently for things to 'bounce back to normal', a growing minority questions whether or not we are seeing instead the birth of a 'new normal'. Parks have expressed both ends of the continuum, and have responded to impermanence and uncertainty with Installations.

These paradoxes, and the park-like responses, are not necessarily new topics, but they are ones that are seldom reflected upon by the wider community in this country, despite the appearance here of most of the paradoxes in some form or another. Where local project examples are available they are included. Absence in many cases reflects the fact that Australia has not been a park-making place for very long.

While the original inhabitants of this continent shaped the landscape as surely as humans have done the world over, they did not build cities, with all the elements we expect to find in the settlements of 'sophisticated' cultures.[19] Once Europeans arrived, they wasted no time in making their mark on the country.

Uluru, Northern Territory. Australia: a country with an ancient landscape, and a short history of park-making.

Driven by a need to exert control over the unfamiliar landscape, new Australians began gardening with a vengeance. Gardens evoked old memories and created new ones. They represented absolute need and blinding hope. They marked places of happiness, domesticity, death and survival. Gardening was practised by all members of the new society, from well-to-do colonial gentlemen who corresponded with Kew Gardens, to the convicts who cleared the land and planted the first crops with stock carefully nursed across the sea from southern Africa.[20]

Early authority figures also took it upon themselves to impart the civilising influence of parks on the new towns of Australia. Despite lofty intentions, historians suggest that the early use of The Domain in Sydney for such activities as quarrying, grazing and timber-getting, not to mention lewd and disorderly behaviour, point to it being treated by the public as a sort of public 'common', rather than the edifying and educational facility Governor Macquarie had in mind. Others remind us that all gardening in Australia takes place on contested ground, and that the creation and designation of early 'public parks' was in fact an act of exclusion, with Aboriginal people neither admitted to such parks, nor in fact regarded as part of the public.[21]

The love of gardening persists. In 2011, *Better Homes and Gardens* was the second-biggest-selling magazine in Australia.[22] When *The Sydney Morning Herald* newspaper commissioned a 2005 survey of the most popular individual television programs 'of the century', gardening show *Backyard Blitz* made the cut, coming in at Number 33, ahead of the Athens Olympic Games Opening Ceremony.[23]

Presenters of our television gardening shows have become much-loved public figures, paving (literally) the way for celebrity chefs, dancers and music judges.

Hyde Park, Sydney: Australia's oldest public park, gazetted in 1810. (Adam J.W.C. via Wikimedia Commons)

Jamie Durie, the former Manpower dancer and original host of *Backyard Blitz*, went on to publish books, found a successful landscape design consultancy based in Sydney, develop his own line of outdoor furniture products, and become a regular guest on the Oprah Winfrey show. Before Jamie was Don Burke, famous for a dazzling array of violently patterned and textured jumpers. His show, *Burke's Backyard*, virtually pioneered the genre, regularly drawing 2 million viewers each week. Before both of them was Peter Cundall, passionate host of the ABC's *Gardening Australia* program until the age of 81. In 2008 he was voted the eighth most trusted Australian out of a list of 100.[24] Both Burke and Cundall have been recognised for their services to both media and the environment with Medals of the Order of Australia.

These television gardening shows tend to follow one of two paths. The first is more horticulturally based, and focuses on the 'stuff' of gardening; compost, seasons, climate zones. The second is more 'lifestyle' focused; gardens can be created 'instantly', and in a variety of 'themes'. Although they have critics, both contribute to the national conversation. It is not a bad thing for 'everyday Australians' to be interested in aspects of design, just as it's not a bad thing for city dwellers to value soil.

What is curious is the fine line these shows walk between the realm of the everyday and the expert. Costa Georgiadis, Peter Cundall's gregariously hirsute replacement on *Gardening Australia*, is identified as a landscape architect on the show's website, as he was when he hosted *Costa's Garden Odyssey* on SBS. Sometimes the subtlety is lost, as when *The Sydney Morning Herald* reported that his interest in environmental issues emerged when he studied 'landscape gardening' at university.[25] As a group, Costa's fellow *Gardening Australia* presenters have qualifications in landscape architecture, horticulture, environmental science, aboriculture and agricultural science, among their many other notable accomplishments.

Introduction **27**

Despite this, their professional and educational backgrounds are scrupulously downplayed, in the same way that our political leaders talk up their ordinary, suburban upbringings rather than their Rhodes scholarships. And frustratingly for the landscape architects and designers responsible for many of the projects showcased on the program, they are very rarely named.

If few landscape architects are household names in Australia, word about some is getting out. In 2009 Sydney firm McGregor Coxall won the International Landscape Architecture Practice of the Year, awarded every second year by international landscape and urban design journal *Topos*. Among the exquisitely conceived and executed projects that helped nab the trophy were two waterfront parks: Carradah Park, and Ballast Point Parkland.

Given our relatively late start, most Australian parks have emerged as either green parks or brown parks. Green Parks vary in many ways but share one purpose: to provide a place of refuge away from the everyday. Refuge is articulated by creating the park as a piece of 'nature'; sanitised, well-maintained nature, but undeniably 'not city'. The desire for a park comes first, and the land needed for its establishment identified, often before a supporting population exists. Brown Parks are distinguished by their existence in locations where parkland use was neither contemplated nor planned. As cities have depleted their green landbanks, Brown Parks have emerged opportunistically, on the parts of cities that have outgrown their previous role and usefulness. In her 2002 book *New Conversations with an Old Landscape* (Images Publishing Group, Mulgrave, Victoria), Catherin Bull argues that as Australian society has matured, so too has our relationship with our landscape. With conquering no longer the goal, landscape architects have instead focused on repairing and reinstating landscapes, treasuring water and embracing the challenges of Australia's diverse ecosystems as opportunities to explore. Even within this context, nearly all of our parks, whether well-established or newly made, contain a germ of the picturesque model, although newer ones do attempt to reposition the ecological functions.

Responding to contemporary complexities and contradictions of creating inclusive, accessible, resilient urban places surely demands more than two ways of making parks. This book, therefore, presents recent proposals and projects that coalesce around four broad themes – linkages, obsolescences, co-locations and installations – that can be regarded as at least partial attempts to respond to the four contemporary paradoxes described earlier. Linkage park-making creates continuous parkland systems at a citywide, regional, national or even international scale. Parks may be the driver for the initiative, or one of the outcomes. A hallmark of urban obsolescence and shrinkage is vacant land. Reconsidering the role of parks and landscape is one way shrinking cities can respond to their surplus buildings, land and infrastructure. Co-locations parks are the result of creating new parks in conjunction with other land use functions; and Installation parks explore and demonstrate alternative typologies by creating seasonal or temporary parks.

Carradah Park, Sydney (formerly the BP Site Parkland) is built around the circular shapes that were blasted out of the sandstone headland to accommodate fuel storage tanks.

The themes, and the projects presented, are by no means intended to provide a comprehensive understanding of the myriad histories, complexities and possibilities of that aspect of the cultural landscape. Many detailed studies have already been made, by eminently knowledgeable individuals, of the details and intricacies of the contributing elements or particular aspects of each theme. For now, there is much work still to be done in understanding the paradoxes of contemporary life. And looking ahead, it will be many years before we get a sense of how we as a species respond to those paradoxes with the landscapes we make. These themes also represent my own observations and interpretations. Some may look at the projects and find only aesthetic appeal or repulsion, or a practical way to resolve a current challenge, or a clever way to detail a concrete seat. These are all valid responses, and indeed many times I have scoured the pages of books looking for exactly those particular things. Others may find in these projects the encouragement to pause, step back from the quotidian pressures of budgets and timelines, and to reflect on the amazing complexity and potential of one of the most-loved building blocks of our cities – their parks.

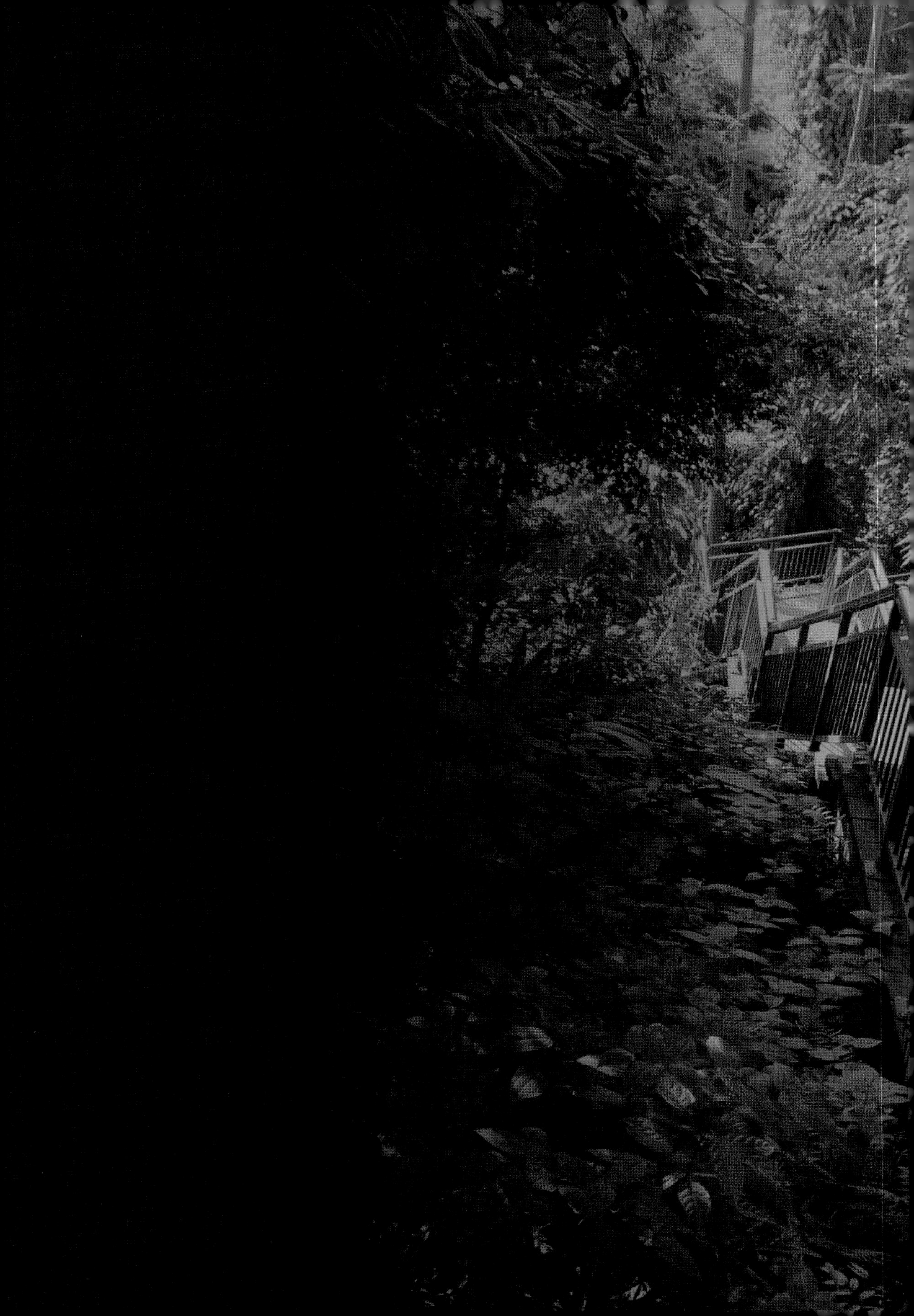

01
Linkages

Linkages

Linking previously disconnected places.
Before

After

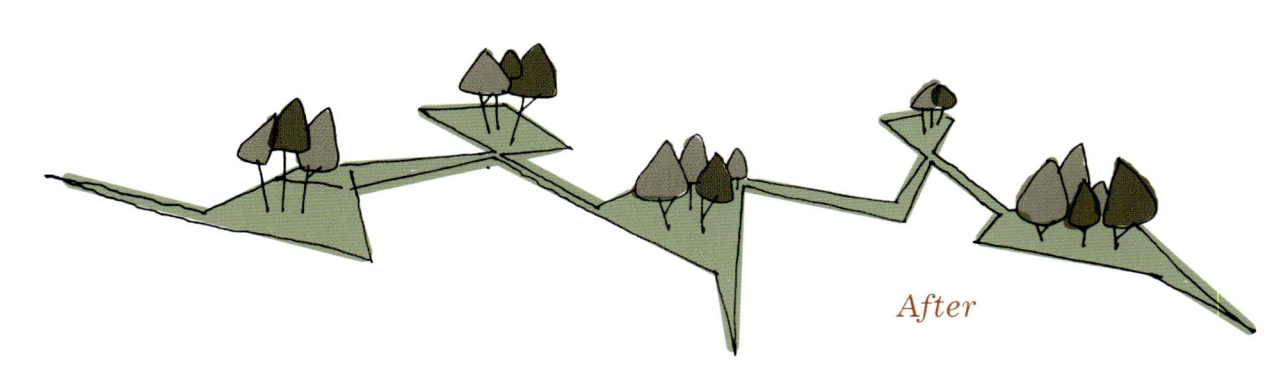

Linkage park-making creates continuous parkland systems at city or regional scale. Parks may be the driver for the initiative, or one of the outcomes, and they can vary considerably in size.

The first type of Linkage Park project is one that connects existing, separate parks.

The Southern Ridges project in Singapore is a National Parks initiative connecting 10 km of diverse 'green' spaces at the south of the country. Once visitors have passed the first test – leaving the MRT station via an adjacent labyrinthine shopping centre – they are, within minutes, enveloped in dense shade and flourishing plantlife. In some places, walls of vegetation thrust skyward in all directions.

This page – The Henderson Waves at Singapore's Southern Ridges.

Occasional breaks reveal gasp-inducing views of the city skyline and harbour, or vertiginous glimpses of the motorways far below. Southern Ridges uses a grab-bag of solutions – skinny roadside footpaths, tortuous staircases, hovering walkways, sculptural bridges – to connect existing parks with places that were previously more isolated. In beastly Sunday afternoon humidity, groups gather under the bridge canopies, children ride scooters, and everyone except the joggers seems to be photographing.

Linkages **33**

The Henderson Waves at Singapore's Southern Ridges.

The next type of Linkage creates new and well-connected public realm, park and landscape outcomes through transit-led urban regeneration. In such cases, parks are generally an outcome, rather than a primary reason for the project. Many European light rail projects from the 1990s onwards illustrate this type of Linkage park-making, and Paris's T3 light rail is a good example.

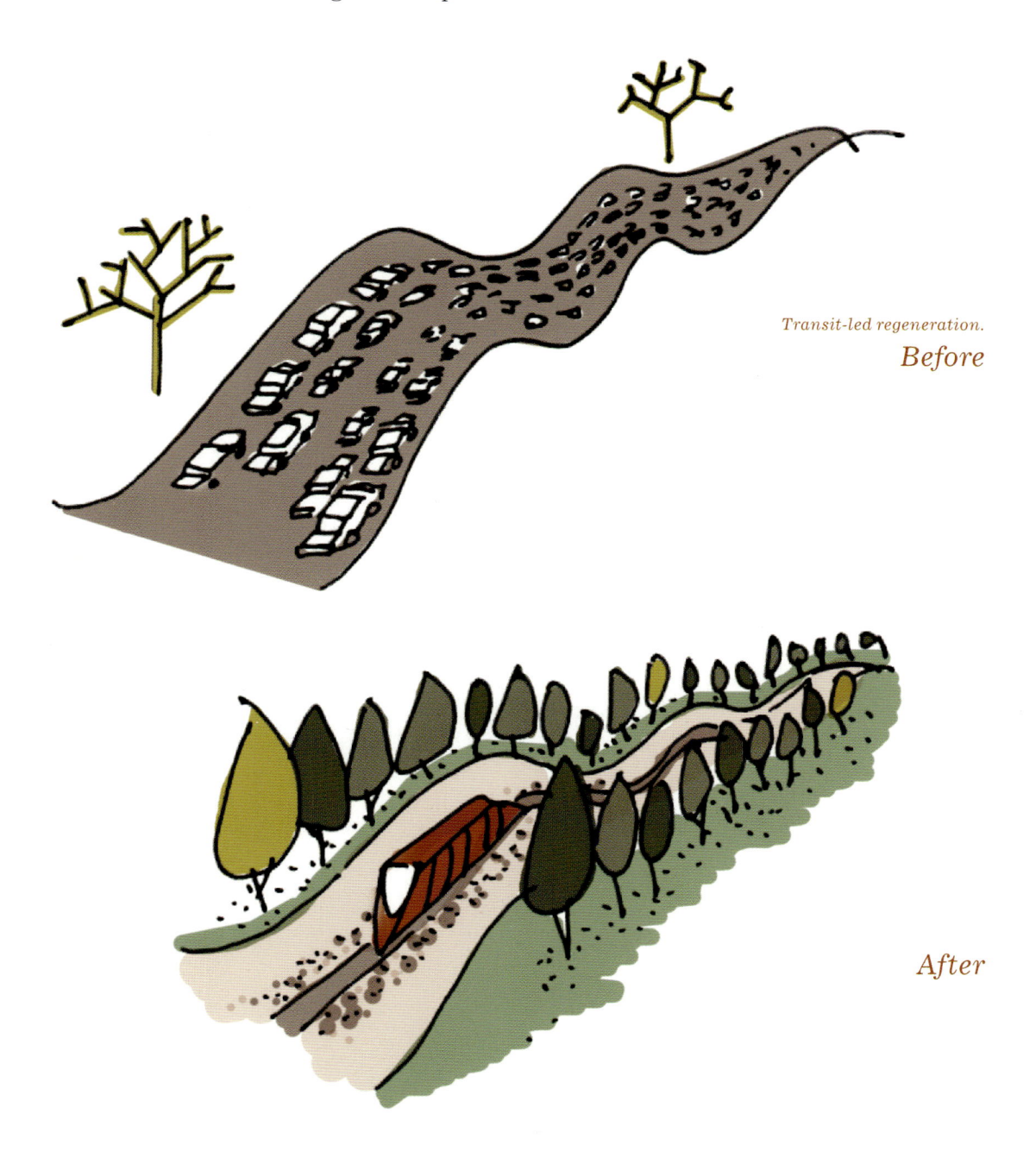

Transit-led regeneration.
Before

After

Linkages   **35**

Trains on the turf-lined T3 route. (Nxenara via Wikimedia Commons)

Above – Dusseldorf: a stretch of turfed track in the inner city, surrounded by very dense screening vegetation.

Left – Paris: T3 light rail, with turfed track area, reduced vehicle pavement and street tree planting. (Kirikou via Wikimedia Commons)

Stage 1 of the T3 light rail was completed in 2006. It follows the route of three boulevards named after Napoleon's First Empire Marshals. They in turn follow the line of a nineteenth century fortification on the southern boundary of the city. The 7.9 km route was created within existing city streetscapes by reducing the amount of space available for vehicular traffic. The project's urban designers aimed to reclaim the boulevard as a public place.[26] Nearly three-quarters of the track length is turfed, and significant tree planting and public realm upgrades were completed. Overall the project has created a setting along the boulevards Brune, Jourdan, Kellermann and Massena that is indisputably park-like.

Light rail projects in Nice, Bordeaux and Dusseldorf wove similar green threads through the existing urban fabric of those cities, while Houston's light rail terminated in a blue line, at a dramatic inner-city stop where the tracks run through water and spray jets shower alongside in full Texan exuberance.

Linkages

The third type of Linkage Park results from the development and reconsideration of existing corridors. These corridors can be either natural or manmade, and include rivers, roads, rail lines, and military or political corridors. The edges of river corridors are most commonly 'unlocked' for public use in one of two ways: through deindustrialisation, or through stormwater-based initiatives such as flood mitigation or waterway health schemes.

Before

Unlocking river corridors.

After

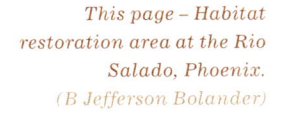

*This page – Habitat restoration area at the Rio Salado, Phoenix.
(B Jefferson Bolander)*

The Rio Salado (or Salt River) Project in Phoenix restored 8 km of degraded riverbank, improving flood mitigation capacity, and creating an environmentally improved waterway and habitat combined with linear parkland to the south of the CBD. The Salt River and its tributaries have been the lifeblood of the south-west desert region since pre-Columbian times, when the Hohokam tribe constructed an elaborate canal system to support its agricultural community. Subsequent years of dam-building, water extraction and neglect eventually depleted the river, with the city reaches being visited only by the homeless, or by those dumping rubbish – 1000 tonnes of tyres alone were removed during construction of the Rio Salado Project.[27]

To ensure environmental outcomes were achieved, maintained and valued, within the setting of a positive community asset, the multidisciplinary project team established strong guiding design principles, including the use of recycled materials, use of local materials and building techniques, and integration of strong interpretive elements. Prosaic engineering elements such as stormwater outfall trash racks are integrated, but they are honestly displayed, not concealed. Significant community infrastructure is located on axes with major streets leading from the CBD, to help knit the river into the fabric of the city. In wide shallow floodplains like the one through Phoenix, this is always going to prove the most difficult challenge for urbanists: when the river needs space so it can meander and flood, how does it remain an active, integrated part of city life? Riverside locations that do not experience high tidal ranges or severe inundation allow for a different type of river edge experience.

40 future**park**

The Main Riverside Promenade in Frankfurt, Germany, is a classic demonstration of this type of post-industrial riverfront Linkage Park. The Riverside Promenade was substantially completed in 2006, and involved the 'renewal of existing green systems' along the river, as well as the extension of a portion of riverfront promenade that was constructed in the 1860s, the result of the vision of the then city gardener.[28] At 7 km the promenade covers a similar linear distance to Rio Salado, but deals with entirely different context and conditions. This time, continuing the existing promenade and extending the linear parkland was the major driver for the project, not just a happy by-product.

Many projects of this nature have been created in cities worldwide, as long-neglected riverfronts have been reclaimed from their former industrial uses. Brisbane, for example, now includes an extensive and well-used system of riverfront cycleways, paths, picnic areas and parkland fringing West End, Kangaroo Point, New Farm, South Brisbane and beyond, the centrepiece of which is South Bank Parklands, created on the site of the city's former shipyards.

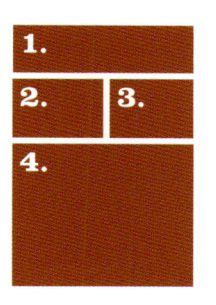

Images 1. 2. & 3. – Main Riverside Promenade.
1. The Promenade in 2010. (Mylius via Wikimedia Commons)
2. By night. (Mylius via Wikimedia Commons)
3. The Promenade in 1900. (Photographer Unknown via Wikimedia Commons).
4. South Bank Parklands, on former shipping and industrial land, is now part of Brisbane's riverfront park and path network.

The Cheonggyecheon River Park in Seoul involved not just the creation of a 5.8 km long linear riverfront park, but the daylighting of the actual river itself. Buried since the mid-1970s, the restored river and new park were cornerstones of an ambitious electoral campaign program by mayoral candidate Lee Myung-bak to implement a Bus Rapid Transit system, decrease vehicular traffic and congestion, demolish an ageing elevated freeway and improve urban regeneration opportunities in the area.

All images this spread – Cheonggyecheon River Park.
1. *The buried river flows again. (Brian Nolan)*
2. *Families enjoying seasonal celebrations. (LWY via Wikimedia Commons)*
3. *Remnant structure from the former Cheonggye freeway retained in the park. (Bcody80 via Wikimedia Commons)*
4. *Elaborate river edge treatment, with steps, seats, fountains and changes in level. (riNux via Wikimedia Commons)*
5. *Simple riverside pathway. (w00kie via Wikimedia Commons)*

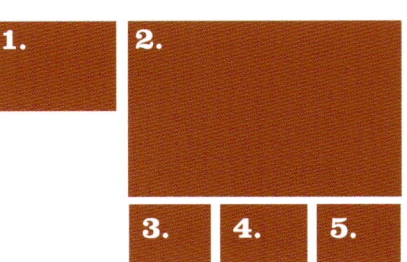

Linkages 43

The removal of roadways has also been the method for achieving Linkage Parks in other cities. The 43 km long Madrid Rio project included the undergrounding of a major metropolitan motorway, which unlocked 6 km of riverfront access as part of a significant new parkland and public realm system. Three initial strategic projects on the newly reclaimed land formed the foundation for additional development. Nearly 50 of these additional subprojects have since been completed, including the Avenida de Portugal, featuring West 8's contemporary interpretation of the cultural landscape along a major avenue connecting into the city centre, and the Parque de Arganzuela, a 40 ha linear water park.[29]

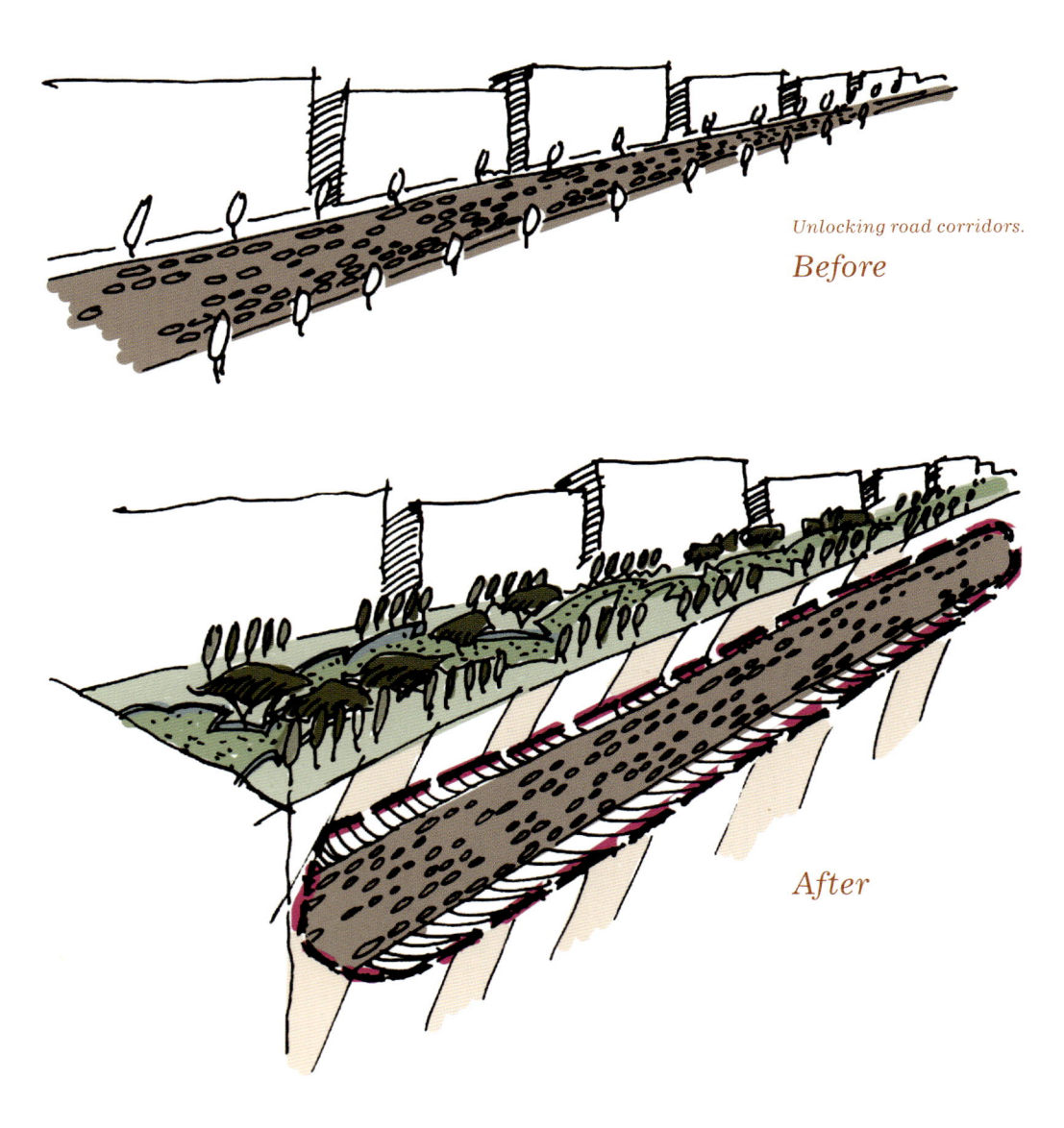

Unlocking road corridors.
Before

After

Above – Madrid Rio: aerial view looking back towards the Palacio Real. (bgaa via Wikimedia Commons)

Right – Madrid Rio: aerial view of the Parque de Arganzuela. (Photographer Unknown, via Wikimedia Commons)

Linkages   **45**

On a hot September morning the park throngs with life. Cyclists of all ages and cruising speeds negotiate an equally diverse battalion of foot-powered traffic. Tiny children, attracted by the reflecting pools, grow emboldened and set out on their own to explore, but fly back on pin-wheeling arms when the pop jets come on. A student reads, and groups of women share lunch in a shady grove. Other women are lured by the sun – crackling their skin so intently they could be served up with apple sauce. The banks are laced together by a heroic collection of new bridges. The Puentes Cascara arch is like a pair of upturned canoes. As visitors draw closer, their crude silhouettes are revealed as cast concrete shells, the sun barking off the rough texture. Inside it is sleek and cool, the surface covered in an extraordinary mosaic depicting skateboarders launching, grinding, mid-olly. In contrast the Arganzuela Bridge is a tautly coiled silver toothpick that has been snapped in two and placed down again with its broken spine gaping upwards.

All images this spread – Madrid Rio.

Linkages 47

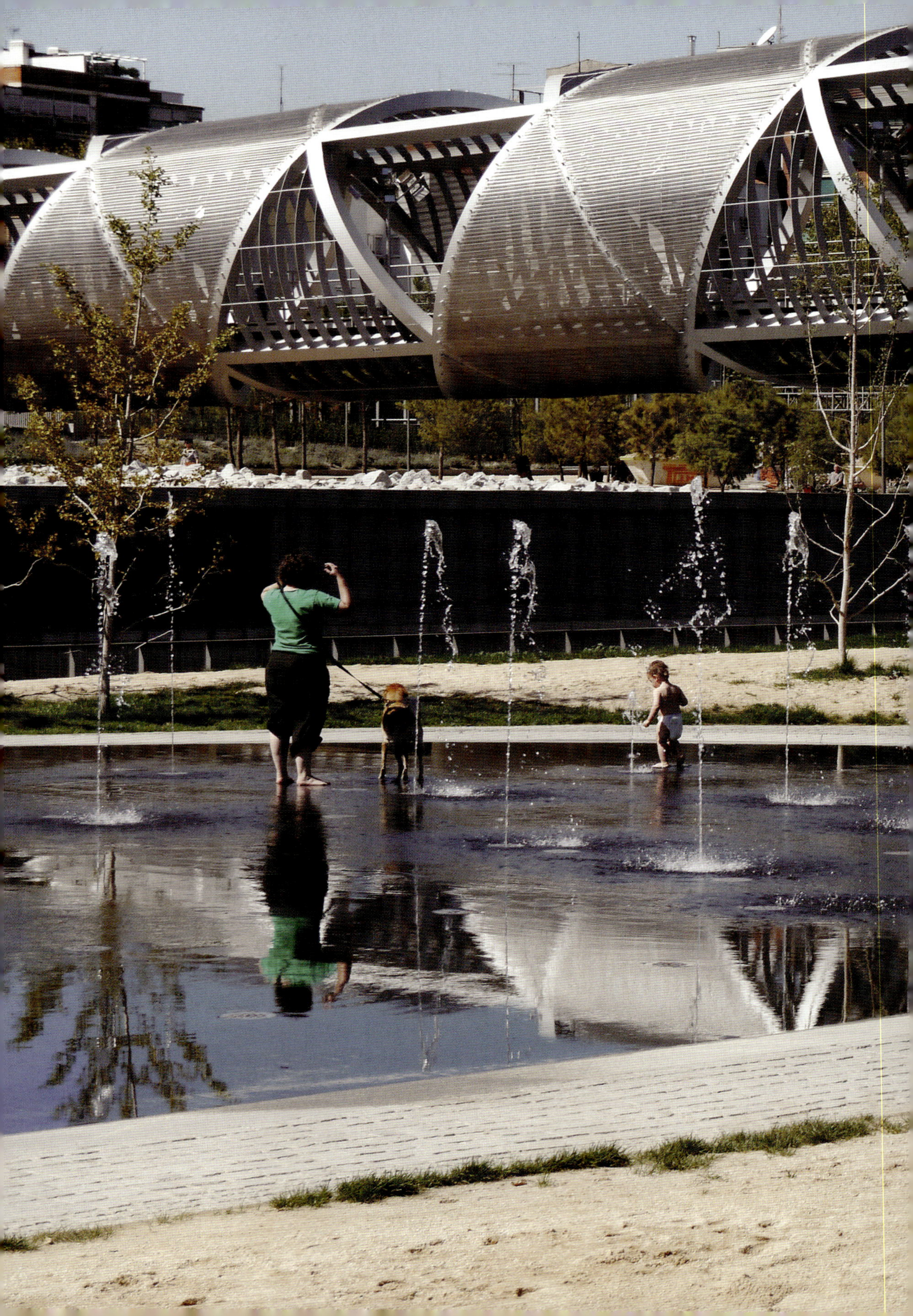

Images this spread – Madrid Rio.

Madrid Rio. (Jeroen Musch via Wikimedia Commons)

Along with unlocking land along rivers and roads, the redevelopment of former rail corridors is a well established method of creating Linkage Parks.

Before
Unlocking rail corridors.

After

New York: Sunday afternoon peak hour on the High Line.

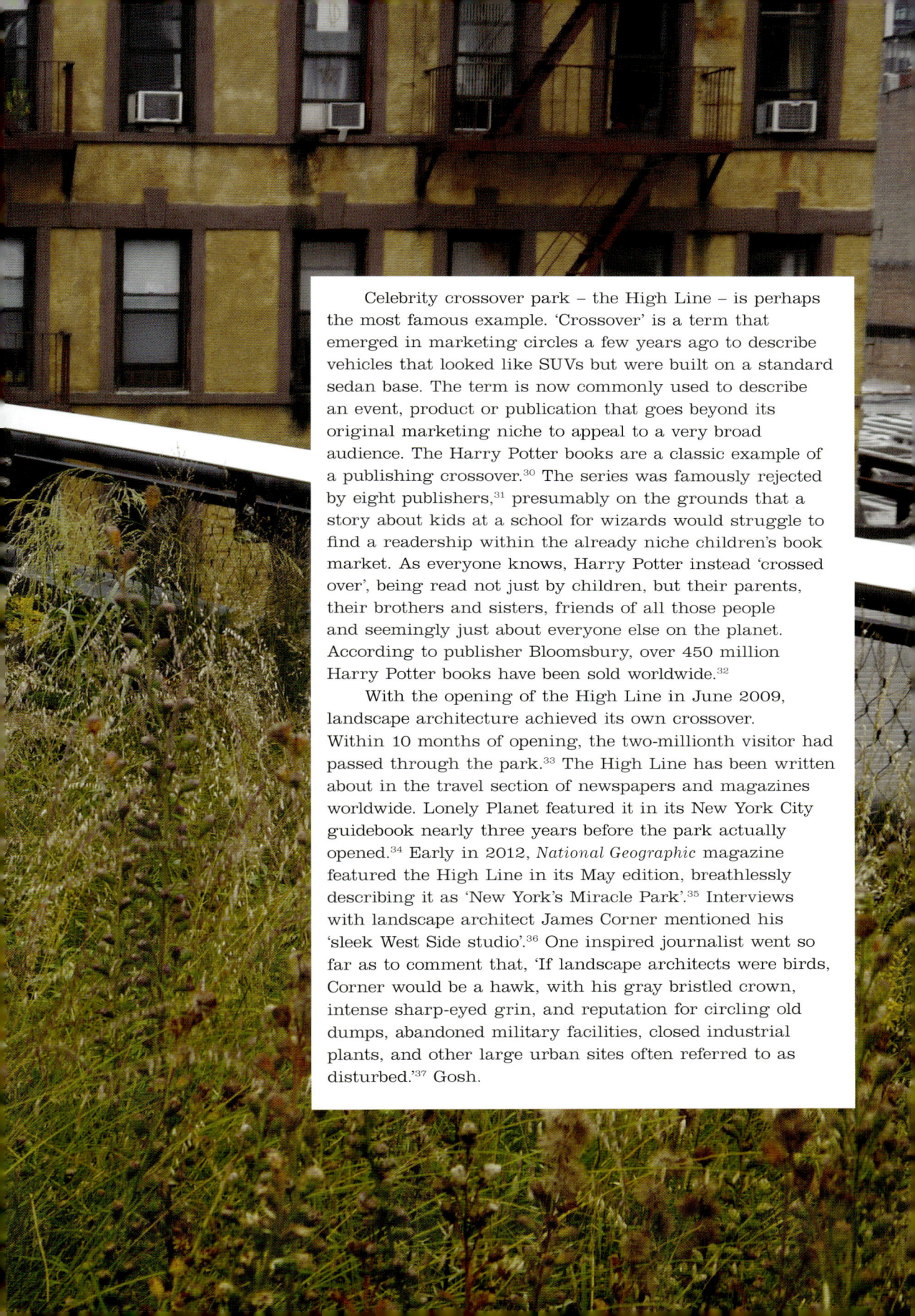

Celebrity crossover park – the High Line – is perhaps the most famous example. 'Crossover' is a term that emerged in marketing circles a few years ago to describe vehicles that looked like SUVs but were built on a standard sedan base. The term is now commonly used to describe an event, product or publication that goes beyond its original marketing niche to appeal to a very broad audience. The Harry Potter books are a classic example of a publishing crossover.[30] The series was famously rejected by eight publishers,[31] presumably on the grounds that a story about kids at a school for wizards would struggle to find a readership within the already niche children's book market. As everyone knows, Harry Potter instead 'crossed over', being read not just by children, but their parents, their brothers and sisters, friends of all those people and seemingly just about everyone else on the planet. According to publisher Bloomsbury, over 450 million Harry Potter books have been sold worldwide.[32]

With the opening of the High Line in June 2009, landscape architecture achieved its own crossover. Within 10 months of opening, the two-millionth visitor had passed through the park.[33] The High Line has been written about in the travel section of newspapers and magazines worldwide. Lonely Planet featured it in its New York City guidebook nearly three years before the park actually opened.[34] Early in 2012, *National Geographic* magazine featured the High Line in its May edition, breathlessly describing it as 'New York's Miracle Park'.[35] Interviews with landscape architect James Corner mentioned his 'sleek West Side studio'.[36] One inspired journalist went so far as to comment that, 'If landscape architects were birds, Corner would be a hawk, with his gray bristled crown, intense sharp-eyed grin, and reputation for circling old dumps, abandoned military facilities, closed industrial plants, and other large urban sites often referred to as disturbed.'[37] Gosh.

54 future park

Rhapsody on a Train Line: the park as directed by Woody Allen.

56 future park

For those unfamiliar with the project, the High Line site atop a disused, elevated rail line that traverses the Meatpacking District and Chelsea in west Manhattan. Since the first section opened in June 2009, more than 4.4 million visitors have been welcomed, nearly half from out-of-town, and half New Yorkers. In only a few short years the High Line has become one of the most highly visited public parks per acre in the city, and one of New York City's top destinations for visitors. Envious mayors are clamouring to duplicate the tourist-attracting and revenue-generating success of the High Line in their own cities. The redevelopment of abandoned rail structures in Chicago, Philadelphia, Jersey City and St Louis has already been announced.[38] The High Line has in some ways become the next 'Bilbao', referring to singular iconic landmarks that have been seized upon and replicated across the world in the hopes of generating the same success as the original.[39] As the shockwave came full-circle back to New York, design bloggers started slavering again, this time over the moodily swirling images of the LowLine, a subterranean park and shops proposed for the former Williamsburg trolley terminal in the Lower East Side. Lacking the high wattage celebrity sponsorship of its aboveground counterpart, the LowLine's promoters instead secured an initial tranche of funding online, through crowd-sourcing finance website Kickstarter.[40] Part of the money has gone towards prototyping ways to actually keep an underground park alive, a process demonstrated in an exhibition held in a former market building on the Lower East Side, and where the sense of dank, dark abandonment was an appropriate substitute for the real deal.[41] With 15 other unused and abandoned subway stations in New York and a whopping 44 unused Tube stations in London, the raw material for scores of underground parks is right in place.[42]

New York: the atmospheric proposed LowLine Park. (RAAD Studio)

Linkages

In acknowledging the High Line's incredible success, we should not forget that an earlier precedent for elevated parks was established in Paris with the Promenade Plantée, which has been welcoming visitors to stroll its lofty paths since the early 1990s.[43] Unless one looks up, and many do not, it's possible to walk right past and miss the steps leading up to the promenade. Many others have obviously looked up though. The regulars are easy to spot – that couple is surely always there after lunch, sitting tight together while he reads the paper. That young man has also read more than one book lying completely at ease on that bench. Perhaps because it's not set up for cycling, the Promenade Plantée attracts a slow-speed fan base. Elderly couples, younger ones, those in love, nuns – how do they cope on the fast-paced boulevards below?

This page – Promenade Plantée.

Promenade Plantée, Paris: the former rail viaduct syncopates the northern side of the Avenue Daumesnil; shops and artisan studios occupy the space beneath.

The Parisian flaneur, a species thriving as strongly as ever.

Linkages **59**

Promenade Plantée.

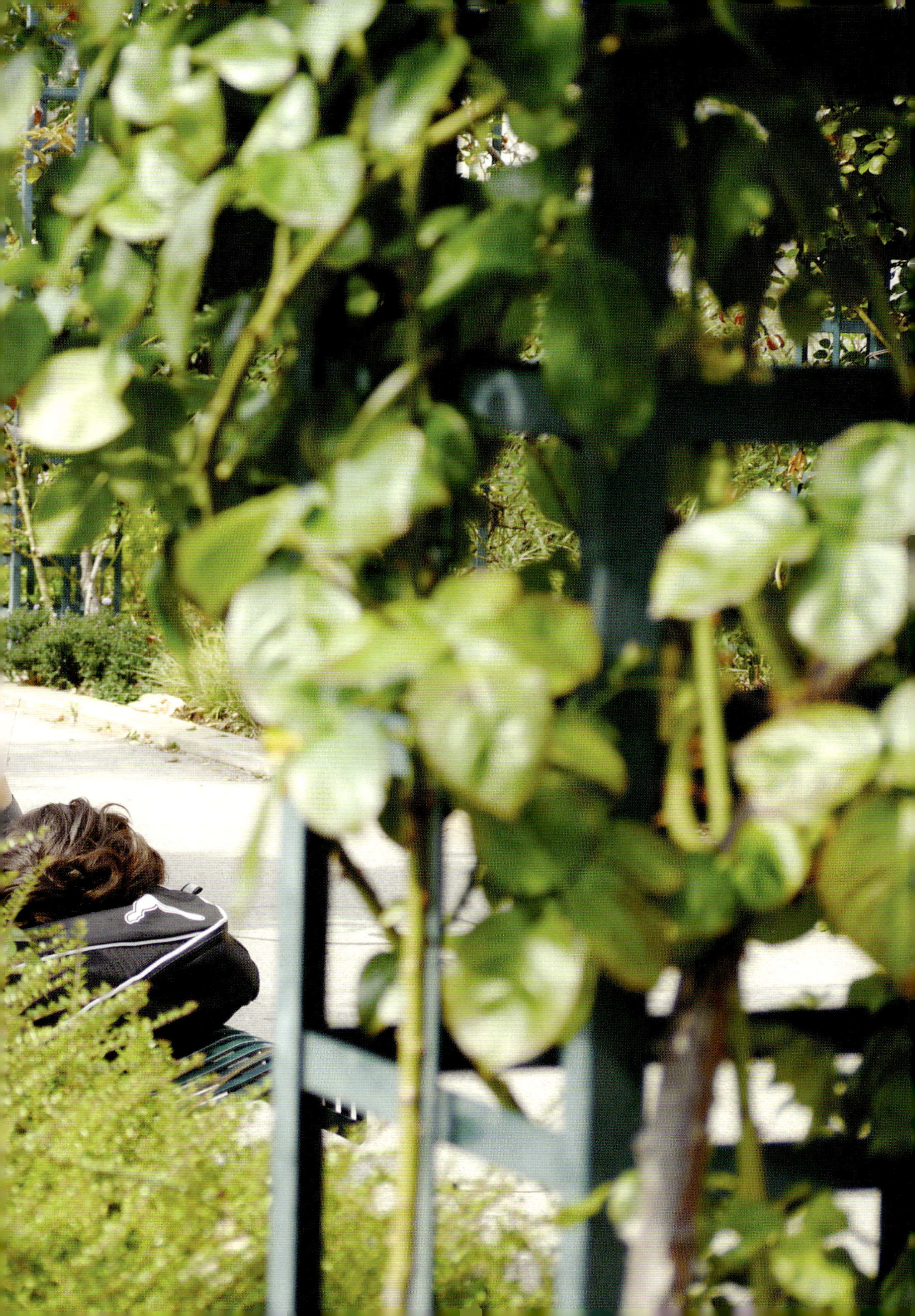

Getting from busy railway to promenade is generally a reactive process: a rail line falls into disuse or disrepair and people start to question what should be 'done about it'. In the United States, the growth of the interstate highway system in the 1960s led almost immediately to a decline in railways for both passenger and freight movement. Today over 3000 km of rail line falls out of use each year, and organisations such as the Rails to Trails Conservancy (RTC) work with numerous interested citizens, volunteer groups and local councils to advocate and enable the conversion of railway corridors for public use. Similar organisations to RTC exist outside the US – RailTrails Australia plays a similar role here in promoting the concept. The most extensive Australian rail trail is the Brisbane Valley Rail Trail which, when completed, will stretch for 64 km. Trails of less than 1 km have also been established. Victoria has the most extensive collection of rail trails in the country, many of them built on the corridors of old timber logging rail lines and incorporating remnant timber infrastructure such as bridges.

Midtown Greenway, with the Midtown skyline in the distance. (AlexiusHoratius via Wikimedia Commons)

Railway reserves are ideal for conversion to public parkland and cycle and pedestrian paths due to their original engineering with smooth curves, gentle grades and minimal cross-traffic.[44] Unfortunately for linkage proponents, the sections of rail line that are available for conversion are usually those that are no longer useful or profitable for rail companies, such as those servicing old, long-abandoned mines, or those in remote corners of cities. The rural or suburban location of many rail trails enables them to be used for a wide range of activities including walking and running, cycling, mountain biking and horse riding. While these can, and have been, converted into very attractive and well used trails, they risk becoming ends in themselves. They generally don't offer good connectivity to other activities or destinations, and visitors have to make a special trip to get to them.[45]

The ones that are most successful in attracting high levels of public patronage follow rail lines that are deeply embedded into the urban fabric of a city, such as the Midtown Greenway in Minneapolis. This 9 km shared pedestrian and cycle path follows the route of a former grade-separated rail track, attracting thousands of visitors a day.[46]

Minneapolis: the Midtown Greenway. (Micah Taylor via Wikimedia Commons)

Midtown Greenway: community gardens connect the sunken greenway with the streets and neighbourhood above. (Payton Chung via Wikimedia Commons)

Linkages   **63**

Even more exciting opportunities result when reborn rail lines become more than just an add-on layer to an existing city, and become city-shaping devices in their own right. The Atlanta BeltLine project aims to do just this. Atlanta is a city shaped by railways; at one point it was even unofficially known as 'Terminus'.[47] One of the most famous shots in the defining Southern film, *Gone With the Wind*, is the crowd scene in front of the Atlanta Rail Depot, even though it was filmed in Hollywood, on a recreated set. Atlanta is also the birthplace of Martin Luther King Jr. Many believe that race issues, along with urban growth and transport are the three conditions that have shaped Atlanta's development.[48]

The Atlanta BeltLine project was initiated as a way of addressing many difficult city-scale challenges and shaping the growth of the city for the next 25 years.[49] It is an ambitious and visionary project to utilise the 35 km of rail corridor that encircles the inner city as a mechanism to 'combine greenspace, trails, transit and new development', changing the pattern of urban sprawl, ensuring growth is 'spread equitably across the City' and providing 'urban amenities and public spaces accessible to all Atlantans'.[50]

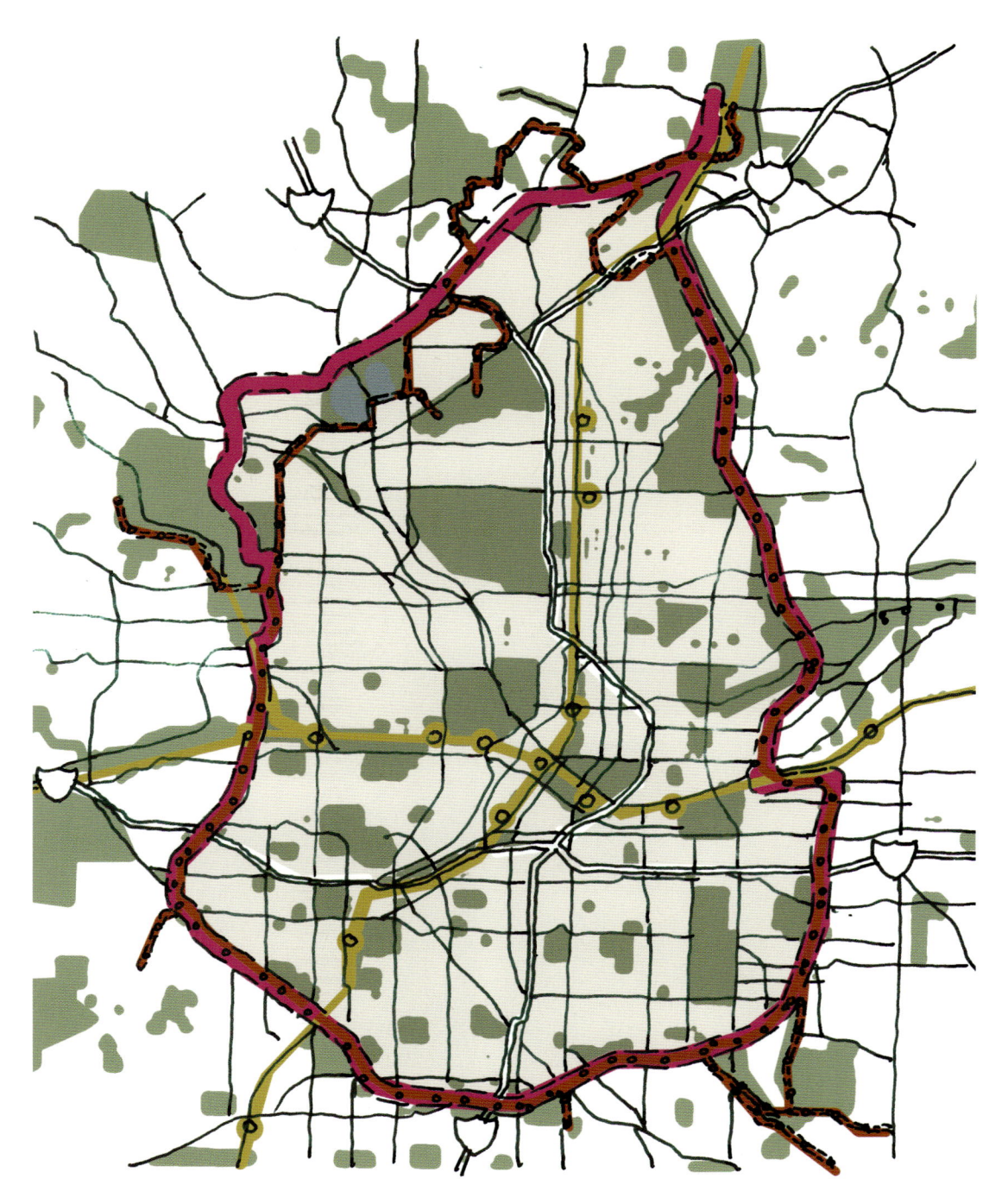

Map of Atlanta showing the extent of the BeltLine.

Linkages 65

1. & 2. Historic Fourth Ward Park, Atlanta: the water play fountain at the cooling, energetic heart of the park.
3. Water travelling through the park: creek bed.

66 future park

Connecting Historic Fourth Ward Park: amphitheatre.

One of the first new greenspaces to be developed is Historic Fourth Ward Park. Well known by many today as the location of the Martin Luther King Jr Historic Site, the historic Fourth Ward (or Old Fourth Ward) was a proud neighbourhood, home to blacks and whites, including early integrated communities. Sadly, many sought-after residential streets were destroyed by fire or demolished for planned freeway expansions. In the last half of the twentieth century, some Fourth Ward districts fared better than others. The white population moved to outer suburbs. The Boulevard area in particular was afflicted with drug and crime problems. Since the turn of the century Fourth Ward has started to evolve again. Some districts are gentrifying, led by a thriving live music culture, and white residents are moving back. Areas closest to the BeltLine are changing fastest, and Historic Fourth Ward Park is one of the major catalyst projects planned in this part of the city.

future park

Above – Water travelling through the park: lake.

Opposite –

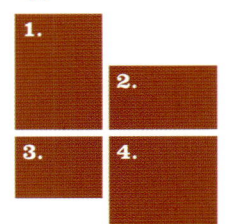

1. *Connecting Historic Fourth Ward Park: paths and steps to neighbourhood above.*
2. *Water travelling through the park: water play.*
3. *Connecting Historic Fourth Ward Park: lakefront promenade.*
4. *Water travelling through the park: dry rill.*

Historic Fourth Ward Park sprawls over undulating, sunbaked terrain. Its backbone is a watercourse that shape-shifts as it moves through the park. Coming in from the bus stop on Ralph McGill Boulevard the ground starts to slope down, and water is directed to a rock-lined creek bed. Further along, the stones line up shoulder-to-shoulder to edge a rill – big ones to the back, smaller ones to the front, swirling circles at the end. The water reappears in the lake, a big figure eight of water rimmed with emergents and crowned with a vigorously pounding fountain. Midday, mid-week, there are plenty of people. Locals walk their dogs proprietorially. Schoolkids run amok in the water play fountain, the other link in the water trail. Water crashes down and up, this is no delicately tinkling thing. After several hours they stop, line up, and walk back out into the rest of the day. Linkages and topography define this park. One experiences both viscerally at Historic Fourth Ward Park. Stairs and walls are carved in on all sides, connecting the low, flood-prone areas to the residential streets high above. Visitors follow the water down to the very lowest point, swirling around the lazy curving promenade, before ascending back into the light.

Linkages

Although hit hard by the Global Financial Crisis (GFC), projects continue to take shape, and the BeltLine becomes more tangible, leading some to question whether it might not be 'the best sustainability project in America'.[51]

Few Australian cities face the same challenges as Atlanta, but some have a similar opportunity waiting to be explored. Mackay, on the central Queensland coast, was once home to a woman, the wife of a manager of a sugarcane mill, who became so famous she had a dessert named after her. Admittedly this is an unusual way to honour outstanding achievement, but then Dame Nellie Melba was no ordinary mill manager's wife. Today Nellie Melba would not recognise the city where she once escaped the sweltering heat with musical gatherings at the School of Arts.[52] From its original core on the south bank of the Pioneer River the city has expanded in all directions, first to the south-west, then heading east towards the coast. Further suburbs developed to the south, at Bakers Creek and Ooralea, and spread across the river to North Mackay. The most recent development has been to the north, where a necklace of separate suburbs has strung itself in close proximity to the varied protected beaches.

It may have once been known as 'Sugaropolis', but few signs of the cane industry are visible today in the city of Mackay. When the Sugar Research Institute on Nebo Road closed, the property was sold for private development. A planned mixed-use precinct of housing and retail looks to be starting up again after stalling post-GFC. Allied health professionals already operate out of the old main building. The Institute used to grow cane on a block of land behind the main facility. It has been fallow for over 10 years. The rest of the cane land is being pushed further out, or out altogether, as farmers sell. Their land now grows brick houses; the rattling, small-gauge cane trains snake between fences not fields. In the main streets of Mackay city itself, there's no visible sign either of the public railway that opened 120 years ago to break the monopoly of the private cane rails.

Train travellers arriving in Mackay are instead greeted with a station, 5 km from the city centre, that displays the unique architectural style of contemporary Queensland Rail vernacular; ruthlessly cost-driven, relentlessly humanity-free, as far from the proudly aspirational and civic-minded buildings we used to build for 'the public' as it is possible to be. This new station was built in 1994 to coincide with the construction of a rail bypass that diverted heavy rail, both passenger and freight, from the city centre and out to lines running to the south and north of Mackay.

Avenues of trees line the former railway corridor into Mackay city.

The former railway corridor in Mackay: a potential linear park.

If you take a taxi from the railway station into town you'll probably go 'the back way' for some of the journey. Your driver will take you along heavenly sounding Paradise Street,[53] before turning off somewhere near the State High School on Milton Street. For a good part of your journey to town, the view will include a wide green strip of tough lawn, down which marches a batallion of trees. In some places it's wide enough to easily accommodate two rows of still-growing figs and one of eucalypts. For some of its length the lawn acts like an extremely wide green median. Roads run parallel on both sides, edged in turn by houses and the occasional block of flats. The high school sits to one side as the long green park turns a corner. Just at that point the ground rises up in a mound that obscures a skatepark. Past the skaters the avenue of trees stops, and after another couple of blocks, so too does the lawn. The entire thing covers an area far greater in size than Queen's Park, the oldest in the city, and like the High Line it was not originally a park at all, but the corridor occupied by the railway until it moved to the outskirts.

In the past decade Mackay Regional Council has invested heavily in its Bluewater Trail.[54] This multi-million dollar network is a remarkable linkage park in itself, connecting people both back to and along a vast length of the Pioneer River from the Botanic Gardens to the rivermouth. On a fairly ordinary winter weekend families cycled, kids and dogs in tow, shopping was transported, and fishing spots were crammed along the western segment of the Trail. The following Monday, the bluewater sparkled for tourists, mums and kids, more fishermen, and workers enjoying a quiet lunch beside the river on the Bluewater Quay precinct, through the city centre and beyond. In addition, Council has built an instantly popular swimming lagoon in close proximity to the trail,

The Bluewater Trail.

championed the expansion of the Mackay Botanic Gardens and commissioned a study exploring the future of Queen's Park. It has commissioned studies for revitalising the CBD, and the south-western growth corridor is expanding. In all this investment in the future of the city, it sometimes appears to the outsider that the potential of the former rail corridor has been overlooked. Yet this half-forgotten strip has the potential to become one of the most unique pieces of public parkland in Mackay, while connecting the city's other green and blue jewels. Like the BeltLine, the entire Bluewater Trail could become much more than a series of pathways, and instead become a focus for inner-city development and connectivity.

All images this spread – The Bluewater Trail.

Linkages **75**

The Bluewater Trail.

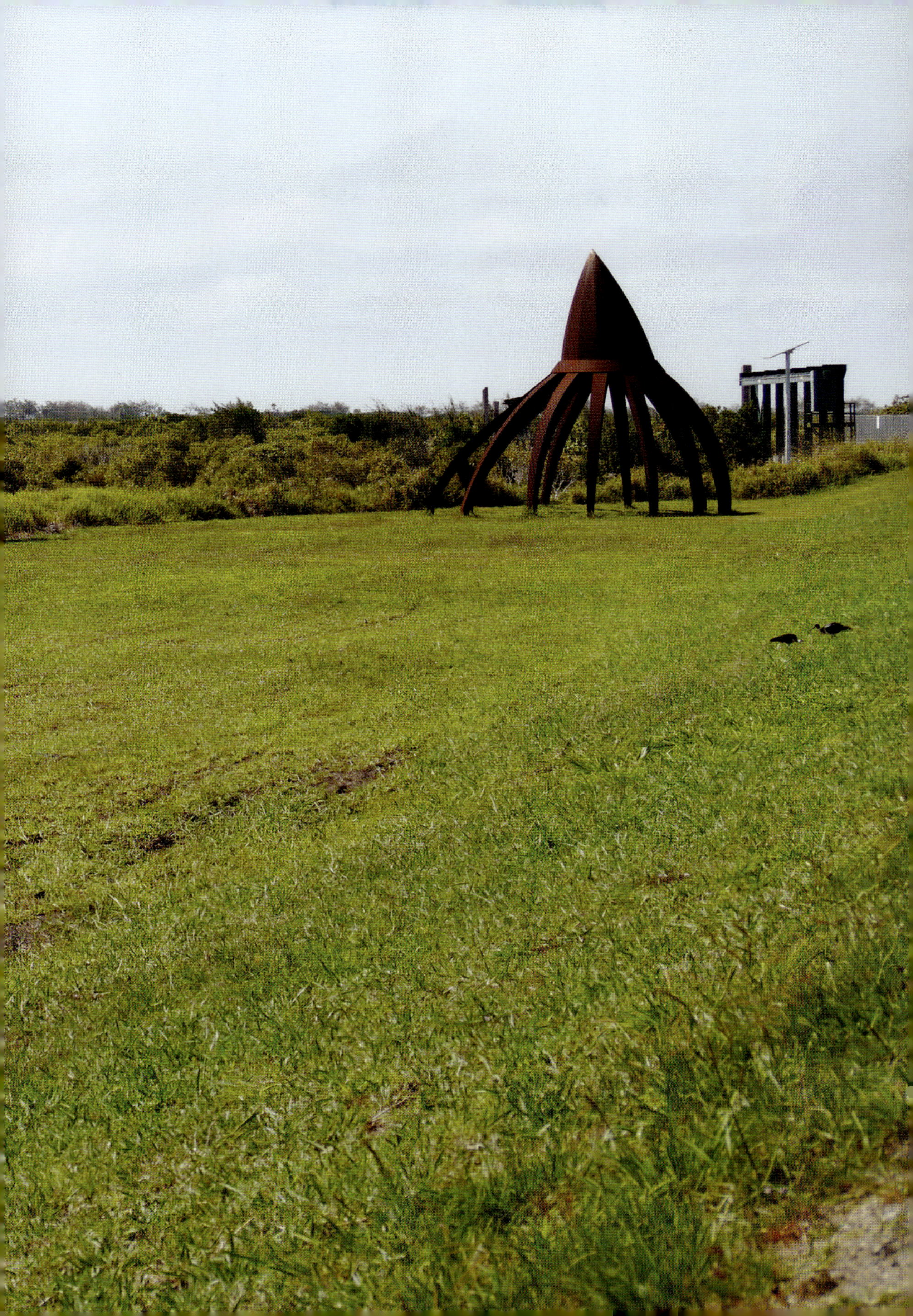

While rail lines have always been a corridor for movement of trains, passengers and freight, they undeniably form barriers to cross movement from one side of the tracks to the other. What projects like the Atlanta Beltline do, and what a Mackay 'Green Line' could do, is convert barriers into connections. This is also something that is achieved very powerfully with the development of former military and political boundaries into Linkage Parks.

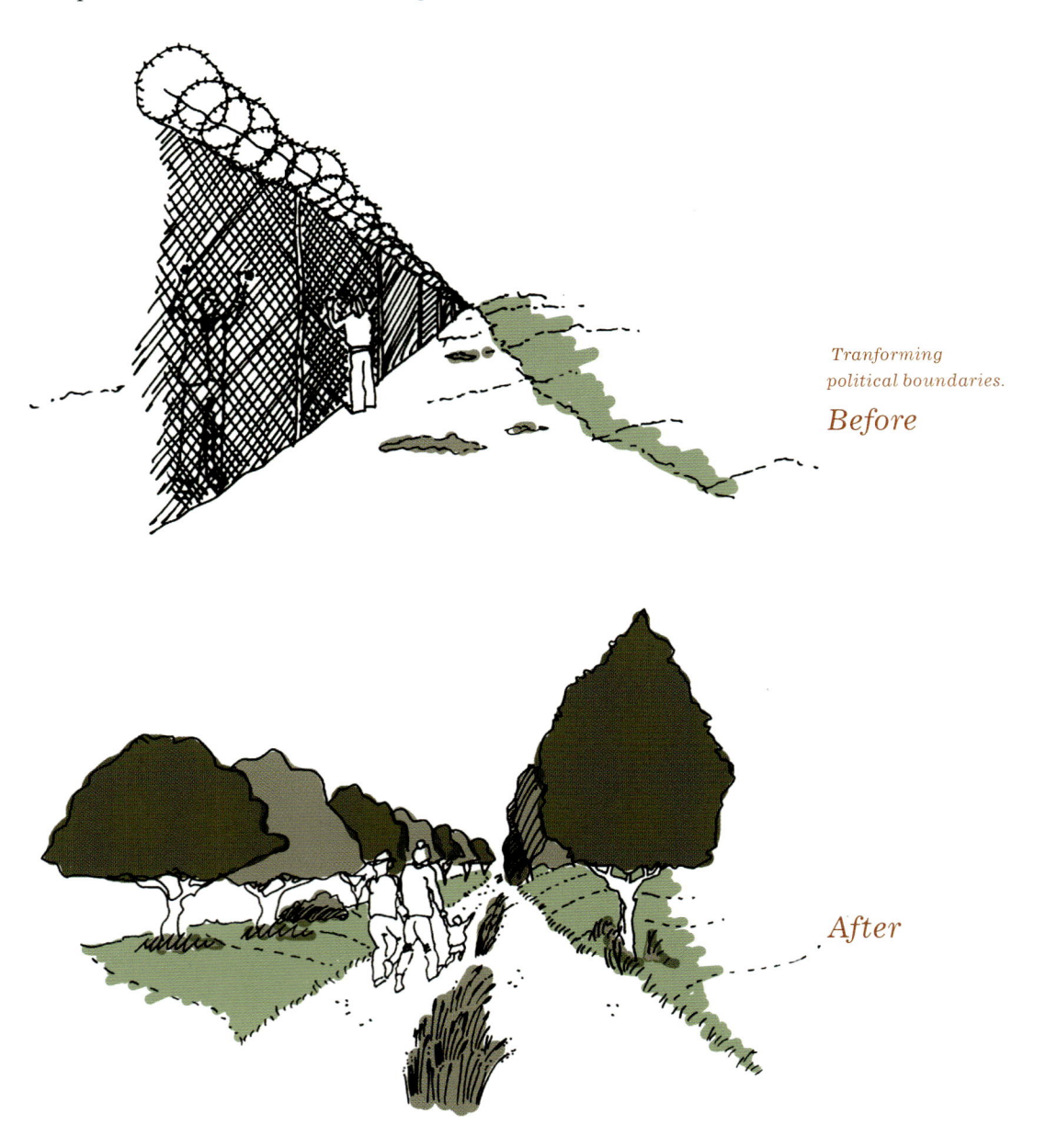

Tranforming political boundaries.

Before

After

The border line clearly delineates the extent of deforestation in Haiti compared with the Dominican Republic, its contiguous neighbour. (NASA via Wikimedia Commons)

Political boundaries are cultural landscapes with strongly differing meanings depending on which side of the boundary the viewer is from. As Professor of Geography Mark Monmonier observes, 'much of an international boundary's power stems from restrictions on cross-border movement and disparities in civil administration and socio-economic well-being'.[55] Sometimes the disparity in cultural landscape is quaintly amusing, such as the schizophrenic Wallangarra Railway Station, on the Queensland–New South Wales border. Built to facilitate a change in rail gauge between the states, the long, pink station is graced by a sloping skillion verandah roof over the New South Wales platform, while the sun is kept off the Queensland platform by a gently vaulted roof. Other times, the cultural change is mirrored by a distinct change in physical landscape too: the landscape along the Haiti–Dominican Republic border contrasts so greatly it is visible from space.

1. *Sustainable Border Fence: proposal for US–Mexico border with solar panels installed. (Ronald Rael Architect)*
2. *Sustainable Border Fence: proposal for US–Mexico border with burrito stand imagined as an opportunity for exchange. (Ronald Rael Architect)*
3. *US–Mexico border: Tijuana, Mexico is on the right of the image, and the US Border Patrol's San Diego Sector is on the left. (Sgt. 1st Class Gordon Hyde via Wikimedia Commons)*

Existing 'working' borders might inadvertently result in idiosyncratic landscapes, but are rarely the site of deliberate landscape interventions. The 'Sustainable Border Fence', by San Francisco architects Rael San Fratello,[56] is one proposition that rethinks these contested landscapes. The project explores the use of solar collectors and trapping of stormwater to the benefit of adjacent communities, the creation of cycle and pedestrian paths, and the installation of a burrito stand into the fence itself to allow for social and commercial exchange. The proposals are offered as an alternative, humanising way of spending the projected US$49 billion to be spent maintaining the fence over the next 25 years.[57]

A landscape approach to rethinking the US–Mexico border is doubly powerful. As landscape writer Rebecca Solnit reminds her countrymen, 'those portrayed as invaders are in fact maintaining [America's] garden', as Mexicans have for a century been brought to the United States to 'do the work citizens don't want – namely, to toil in...the gardens of the wealthy, [and] the agricultural fields'.[58]

Dutch landscape architect Joyce van den Berg coined the term 'trauma landscape'[59] following her study of the Berlin Sperrgebeit, or 'no-go zone' – the land occupied by the former Berlin Wall and its adjacent defended realm. Studying the no-go zone as a university project, van den Berg was initially surprised to find that it had never been comprehensively mapped. Published maps from the Cold War period were deliberately inaccurate and misleading, and she finally completed the task with the aid of a former Stasi officer who had access to maps made specially for the military.

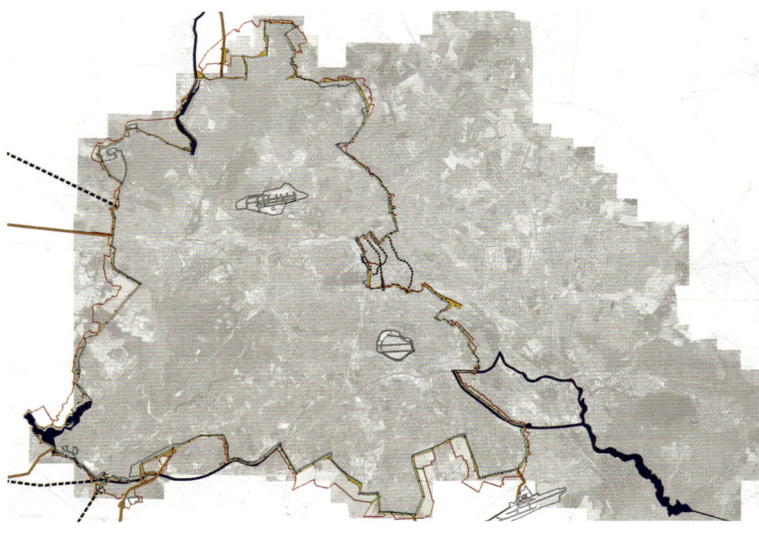

All images this spread – Berlin Sperrgebeit.
1. The map completed with the help of previously classified documents. (Joyce van den Berg, Studio Berg)
2. Aerial view of the Berlin Wall in 1989, showing the extensive no-go-zone. (CMSgt. Don Sutherland via Wikimedia Commons)
3. Visualising a new future. (Joyce van den Berg, Studio Berg)
4. One of the last remaining watchtowers, at Hennigsdorf in north-west Berlin. (Thorbjoen via Wikimedia Commons)

Van den Berg's design proposal outlined a gentle and positive transformation of the space. At the heart was a two-lane bikeway tracing the exact lines of the east and west borders, along with extensive diverse planting. Some parts of the route are already used for cycling. Others have been sold and redeveloped. To date, and despite pieces of the actual wall being preserved in museums and galleries all over the world, no German government agency is charged with considering a consolidated approach to the zone.

Linkages

Similarly, despite the potential to create a quite remarkable transnational parkland network, there is currently no deliberation on how a park-like approach might enable access to, and raise awareness of the Roman Limes, which form a cross shape marking the boundary of the empire from 'Scotland to the Black Sea and the communist Iron Curtain from the North Cape to Greece'.[60] In Utrecht, the northernmost extent of the empire is largely invisible on the surface of the city, but by night is revealed as eerily evocative lines of light glow through cracks in the pavement. In this way, landscape architects OKRA manifest the ghosts of the past, but do not overwhelm us with them. We're used to seeing bold, coloured light as part of a contemporary night-time streetscape, and could think nothing more of it. Once the light lines' meaning is known though, the distance between us and our fellow travellers of two millennia ago is suddenly not all that great.

The post-conflict transformation of political boundaries into Linkage Parks retains a physical reference to the cultural artefacts of the boundary as well as offering the possibility of a mediating neutral zone as a meeting ground for new beginnings. Embraced by the citizens of Ljubljana, Slovenia, is The Path of Remembrance and Comradeship. It marks the location of a World War II barbed wire fence surrounding the town that was constructed by the Italian army in 1942 to suppress anti-fascist resistance by separating the city from countryside. The fence was nearly 30 km long, with its own 80 metre-wide no-go zone, and included over 200 fortifications. It remained in place for 1170 days until liberation, when it was immediately demolished.[61] The first official commemorative walk around the fence line occurred in 1957, and was organised by a returned servicemen's group. The same year saw The Path declared a protected monument, with the proviso that a memorial walk be held each year. Formal transformation of The Path into a circular, linking parkland was completed in 1985.

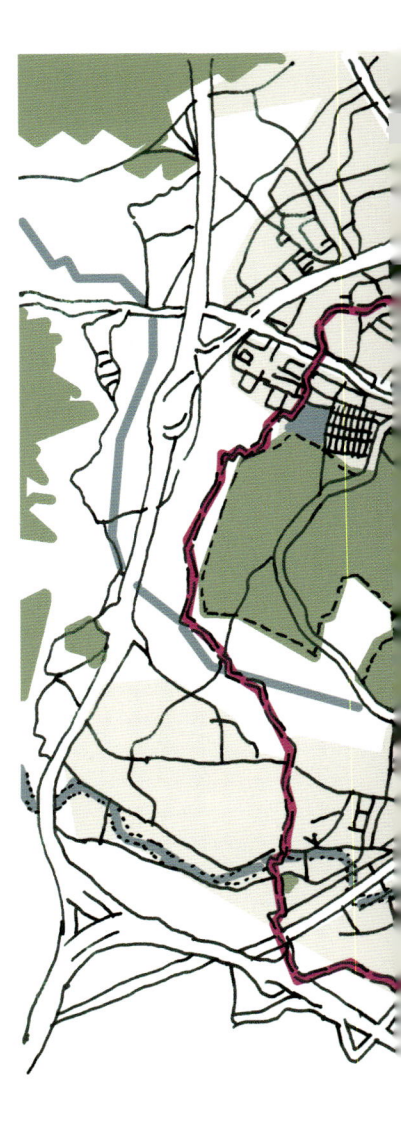

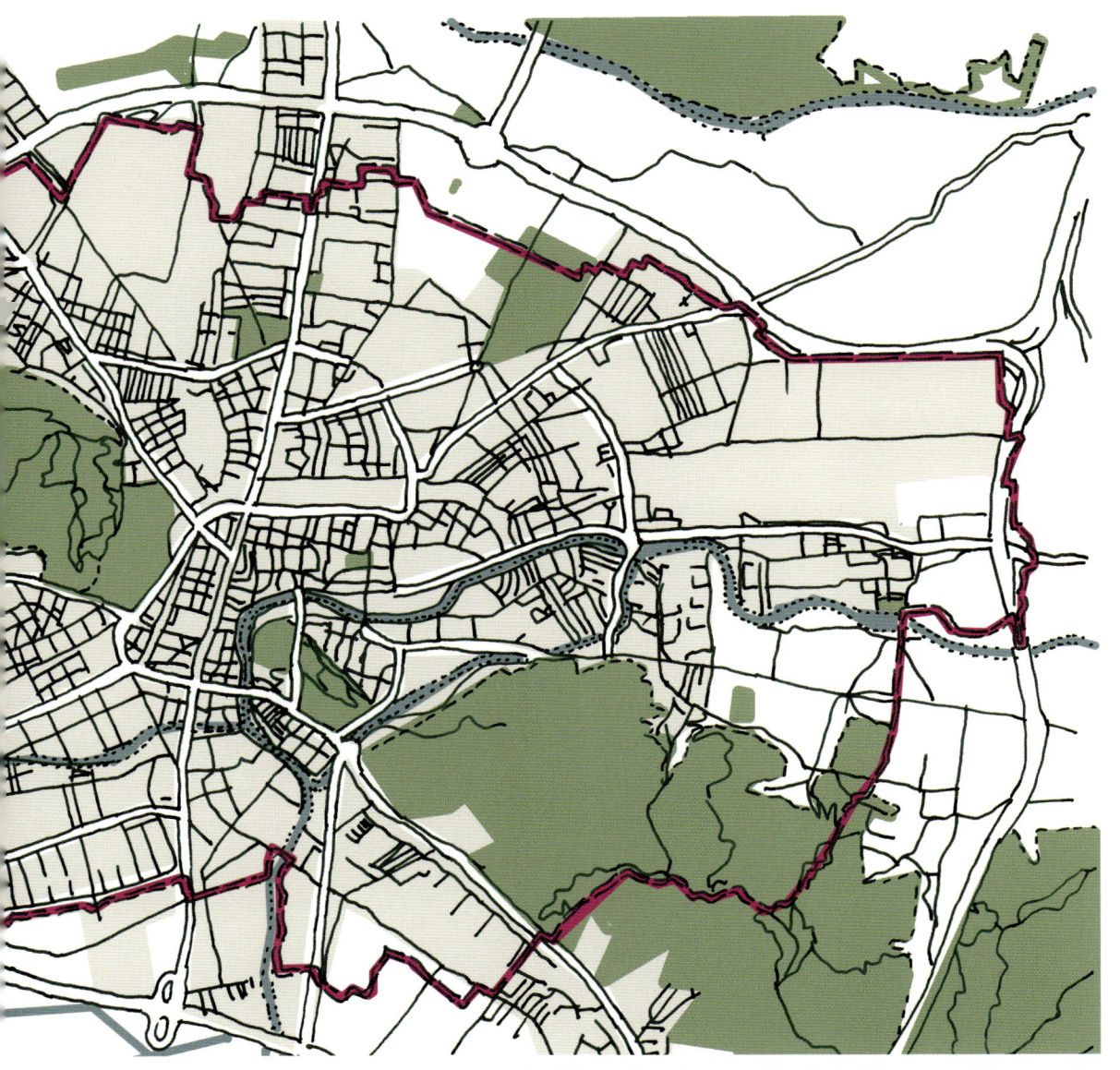

Ljubljana, Slovenia: map of the Path of Memory and Comradeship.

Linkages **85**

The New Dutch Waterline (Nieuwe Hollandse Waterlinie) traces the line of a much older military fortification, a system of water-based defences initiated by the Dutch in the sixteenth century. With most of the country lying below sea level, the Dutch used their superior ability in manipulating water to build their defensive line. The Waterline was both incredibly sophisticated and virtually invisible. The backbone of the system was a series of dykes, behind which the national army, residents and valuable resources could remain, while the land in front was flooded, along with any invaders. Cities and towns beside and along the Waterline were fortified, and the line constantly upgraded through to WWII, providing a north–south barrier nearly 100 km in length. The Waterline, with its enclosing path-topped dykes, canals and flood basins, now forms the backbone of a park and recreation network, and national approach to development intimately meshed with the landscape and townscape of the Netherlands.

Map showing the extent of the New Holland WaterLine.

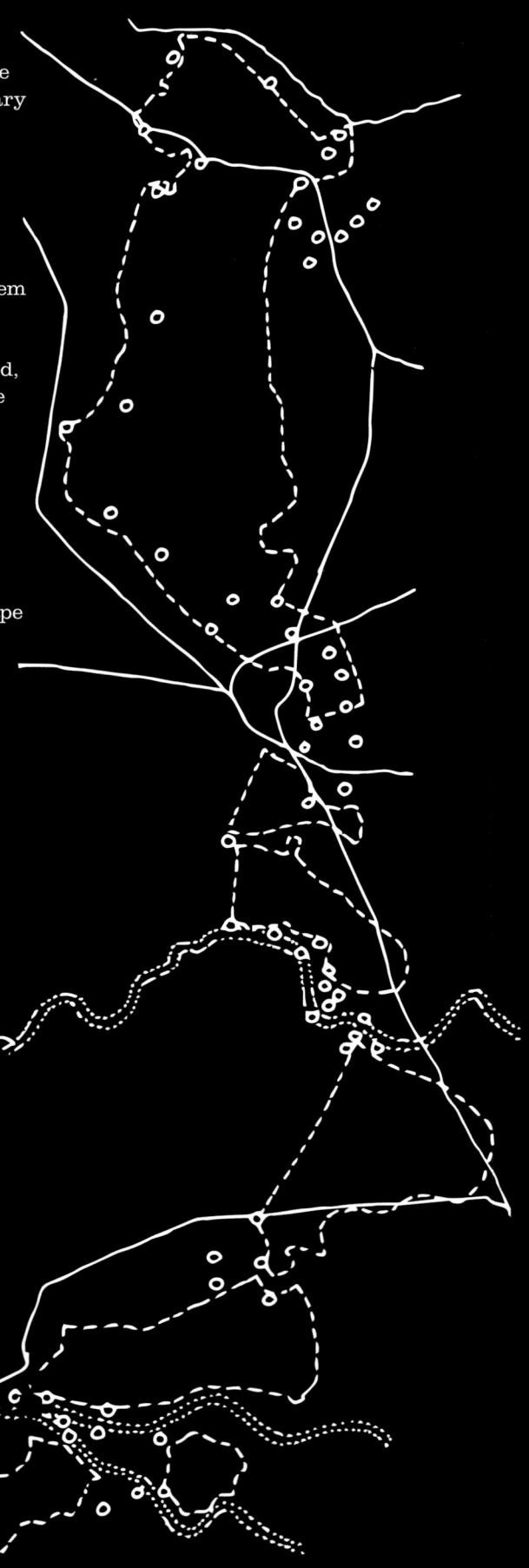

New Holland WaterLine: section explaining the three parts of the defence system. (OKRA)

Plan showing the WaterLine crossing the country, and showing other cultural and tourist features as part of developing a 'recronomic' strategy. (OKRA)

Linkages **87**

It is enshrined as one of the 20 'National Dutch Landscapes',[62] and is listed as a UNESCO heritage site. Most significantly for our discussion, the New Dutch Waterline moves beyond the realm of a single river, road, or even city to embrace a nationwide linkage.

This dyke has been reconstructed and then sliced through, to show the scale and strong form of the fortification. Visitors can now cross through the formerly impenetrable defensive line. (Ben ter Mull)

Linkages 89

New Holland WaterLine: the defensive system hidden in the landscape. (OKRA)

Waterton–Glacier International Peace Park, on the Canada–USA border: panorama from the Red Rock Falls Trail. (drumguy8800 via Wikimedia Commons)

Linkage Parks cross over, through, and between things.

At an even broader scale are the so-called 'Peace Parks': the nearly 200 Transboundary Protected Areas that straddle political boundaries to delineate areas of important environmental or ecological significance. Proponents believe the Peace Park approach provides an alternative method for bringing conflicting parties together: focusing on the particular environmental issues that are valued by both sides, it is easier to depoliticise discussions and instead focus on common ground. The tragedy in Darfur is used to illustrate how focusing on issues of environmental security would allow deforestation to be addressed, soil fertility to be restored, food production to occur, greater economic independence to be achieved and, ultimately, a greater chance at political stability.[63]

The Peace Park approach results in different types of parks, and five typologies are now formally understood. Along the US–Mexico border, discussed earlier, several initiatives already exist to recognise and protect the fragile desert ecosystem. The resulting places vary in the extent to which they welcome human visitors.[64] Conversely, the first Peace Park exists at the other end of the United States, the Waterton–Glacier International Peace Park at its border with Canada, and is a place we would more readily understand as somewhere we might visit and spend time.

So what are the conditions necessary for the creation of Linkage Parks? While the pre-parkland conditions may have been caused by a range of factors, all implemented projects have been realised through an overarching governmental directive. This makes sense: Linkage Parks cross over, through, and between things. They require not just the identification of potential tracts of land, but often the strategic acquisition and reconfiguration of the land necessary for the project. They require the cooperation, engagement and active participation of an extraordinary range of stakeholders, from private landowners to large companies, developers, transport agencies, utilities and services agencies, cultural, heritage, environmental and finance agencies, and all the levels of approvals and regulations that each one of these brings with them. The vision and commitment of a governmental champion is necessary to harness the collective energy of such a diverse group over an extended period of time. This was certainly the case in the creation of the Emscher Landscape Park in Germany.

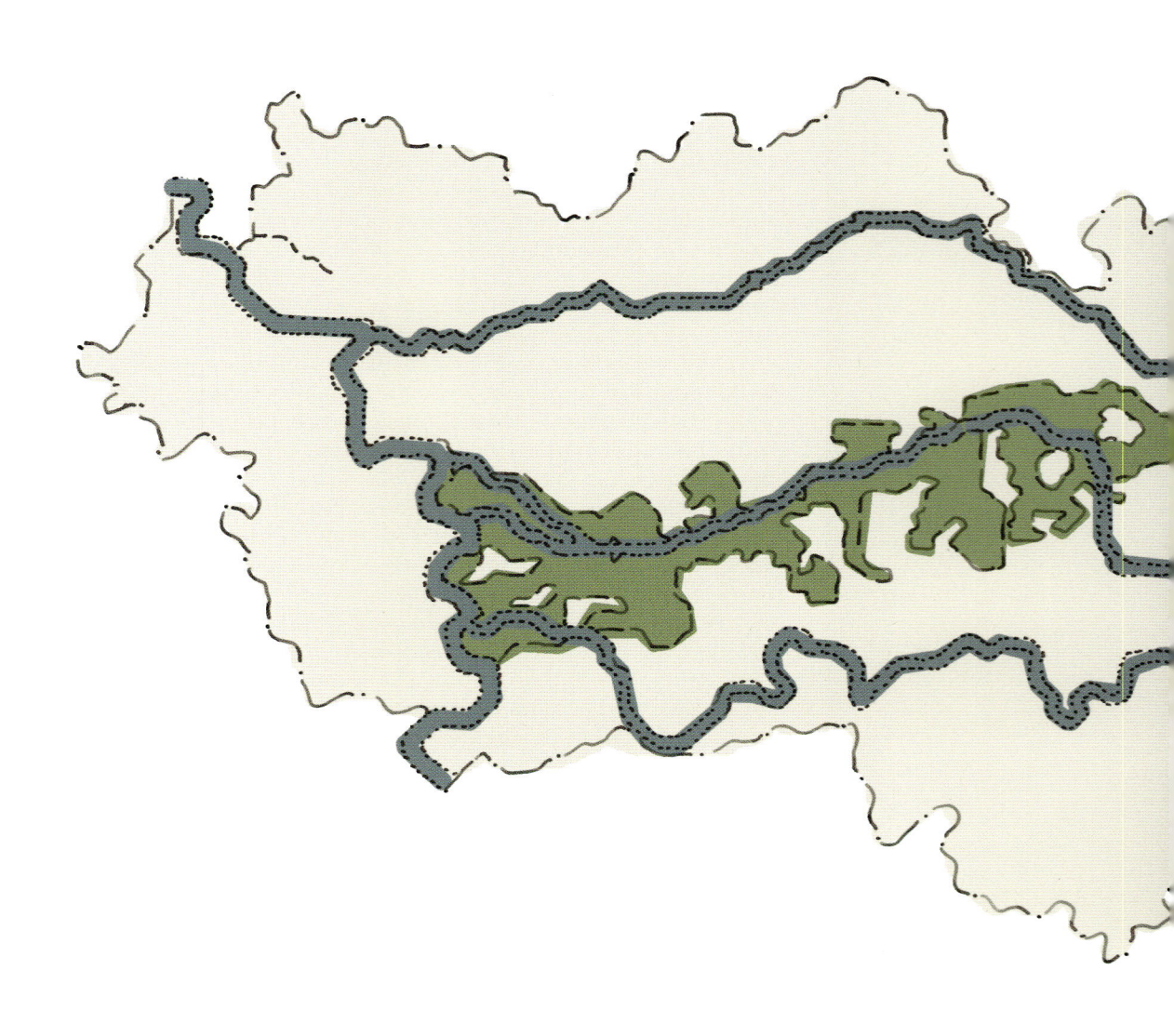

Map showing extent of the Emscher Landschaftspark across the Rhine–Westphalia region.

The Ruhr region lies in Germany's central far west. The Emscher River runs east to west through the region, between the Lippe and the Ruhr, and all three drain into the Rhine. The Emscher valley region, once known as 'the backyard of the Ruhr', was the heartland of German industrialisation. Fuelled by extensive coal deposits, the collieries and steelworks of the region were critical to wartime armament production, and then to the so-called 'economic miracle'[65] of the 1950s and 1960s. As settlements and people followed industry and employment eastwards, the Emscher region became the most densely populated area in the Ruhr valley, with the highest concentration of road and transport infrastructure.[66] In the 1970s Germany started to become less competitive in the global coal market. By the late 1980s it was all over: mines, smelters, refineries, coking plants and blast furnaces all closed their doors and were silent. With no freight to carry, trains stopped running. The employment rate was more than 15 per cent, and a sense of hopelessness enveloped the population.[67]

The communities and economics of the Emscher region were not the only things that had changed. Nearly a century of extractive and heavy industry had created a landscape forever altered: slag heaps and tailings formed huge mountains, toxic run-off and leachate contaminated the ground, massive industrial structures dwarfed houses and the Emscher River carried a 'cloudy broth' of untreated sewage and wastewater for over 80 km between its concrete banks.[68]

What was next for the Emscher Valley? Realising the scale of the environmental and economic impacts the State Government elected to take a regional approach. In 1989 it established the International Building Exhibition Emscher Park (known as the IBA) with a 10-year mandate to 'achieve the ecological, economic, and urban revitalization of the Ruhr Valley and the Emscher River through the creation of collaborative partnerships with local authorities, private industry, professional associations, environmental groups, and citizens'.[69] Over the duration of the IBA 120 individual projects were realised, with 17 cities electing to participate.

Linkages   **93**

Map showing major IBA projects throughout the Emscher Landschaftspark.

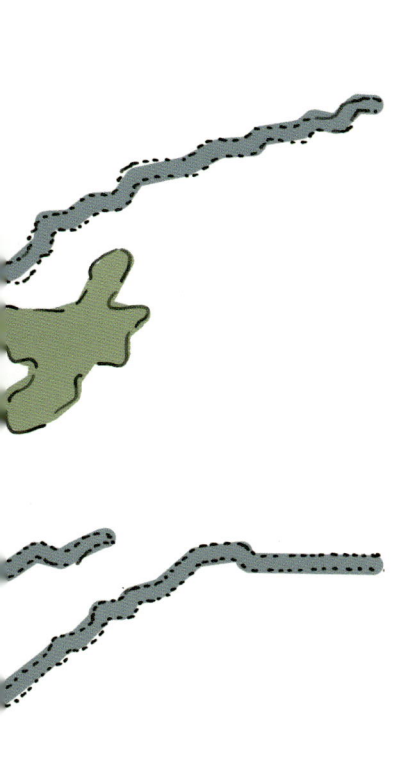

The IBA audaciously based its strategy for the region around the creation of a 'Landschaftspark' – a landscape park centred on a rehabilitated Emscher River. Thus as the Emscher region was born and shaped by its subterranean landscape of coal, so too could the landscape now become a shared regional asset. The Landschaftspark concept transformed the 'mosaic of original, intact countryside, former industrial sites and farmland into a continuous park structure'.[70] This was done in three moves. First, the entire open space system was conceived as a 'large-meshed fabric', extending from Duisburg in the west, through the entire river valley to Dortmund and beyond.[71] Second, seven partially existing north–south greenways were strengthened and woven through the fabric of the overall park. Third, a series of individual projects has embedded individual sites further into the parkland fabric and connected them via an extensive network of paths and bikeways.[72]

Most of these individual projects were based in some way around the remnant industrial infrastructure. In its second radical move the IBA's development philosophy proposed that everything from the predominantly industrial past was worth preserving.[73] The reuse of the industrial landscape has given Emscher some of its most memorable and well-visited highlights. The best known is undoubtedly Landschaftspark Duisburg-Nord. Peter Latz led the competition-winning team that turned a former Thyssen blast furnace into a tourist attraction, as well as developing a long-term master plan for the entire 200 ha site.

In 'official' photographs of Duisburg-Nord the sun is shining, and the rusty metal glows against the blue sky. On grey, rainy days the place is otherworldly. Strangely, the absence of blue erases all sense of background, and the enormous blast furnace feels like it could be a million miles from anywhere. The 10-minute walk from the tram stop feels like crossing into another world: one minute you're at a typical, suburban street, with street signs, and footpaths and front fences, then you are walking along a gravelly track, with big trees and low plants crowding around. You know it must be here somewhere, but you can't see it yet … and then you do! Looming out of the cold grey sky, it's the blast furnace.

Linkages   **95**

In the cold and drizzle it's amazing just how many other people are there too. Near the entry kids are getting a history lecture, every table near the hot dog van is taken, people queue patiently to let earlier groups come down the blast furnace staircase, every climbing spot in the outdoor arena is taken, and three boys in blue play their way around the entire perimeter.

All images this spread – Landschaftspark Duisburg-Nord.

Linkages **97**

1. & 2. Landschaftspark Duisburg-Nord: the light installation by Jonathan Parks. (Tobias Arnst via Wikimedia Commons)
3. & 4. Landschaftspark Duisburg-Nord.

Linkages

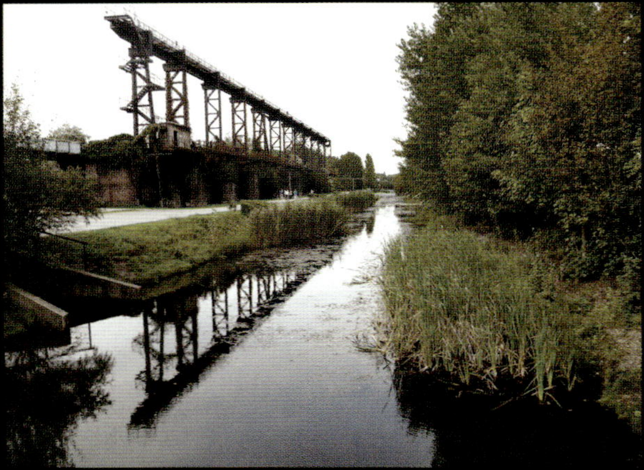
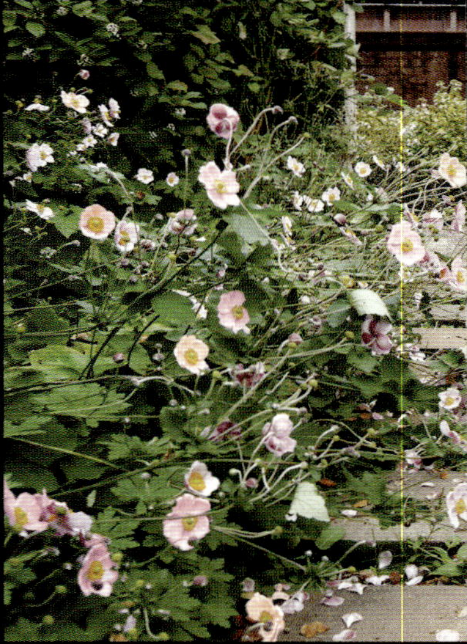
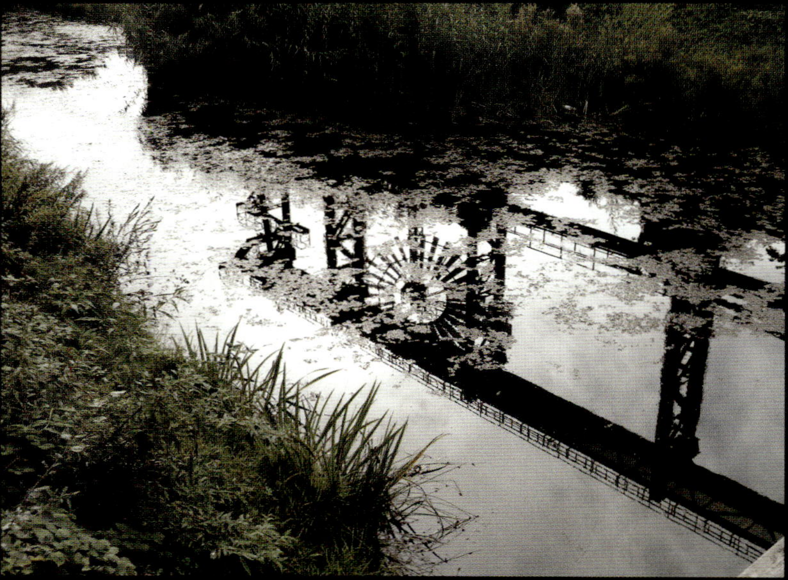
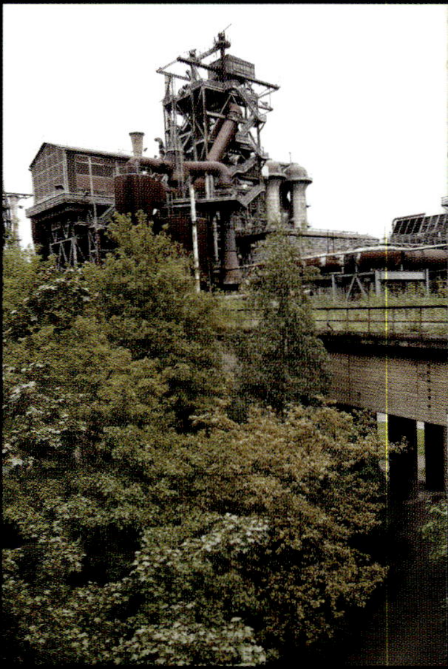

*All images this spread –
Landschaftspark Duisburg-Nord*

Landschaftspark Duisburg-Nord.

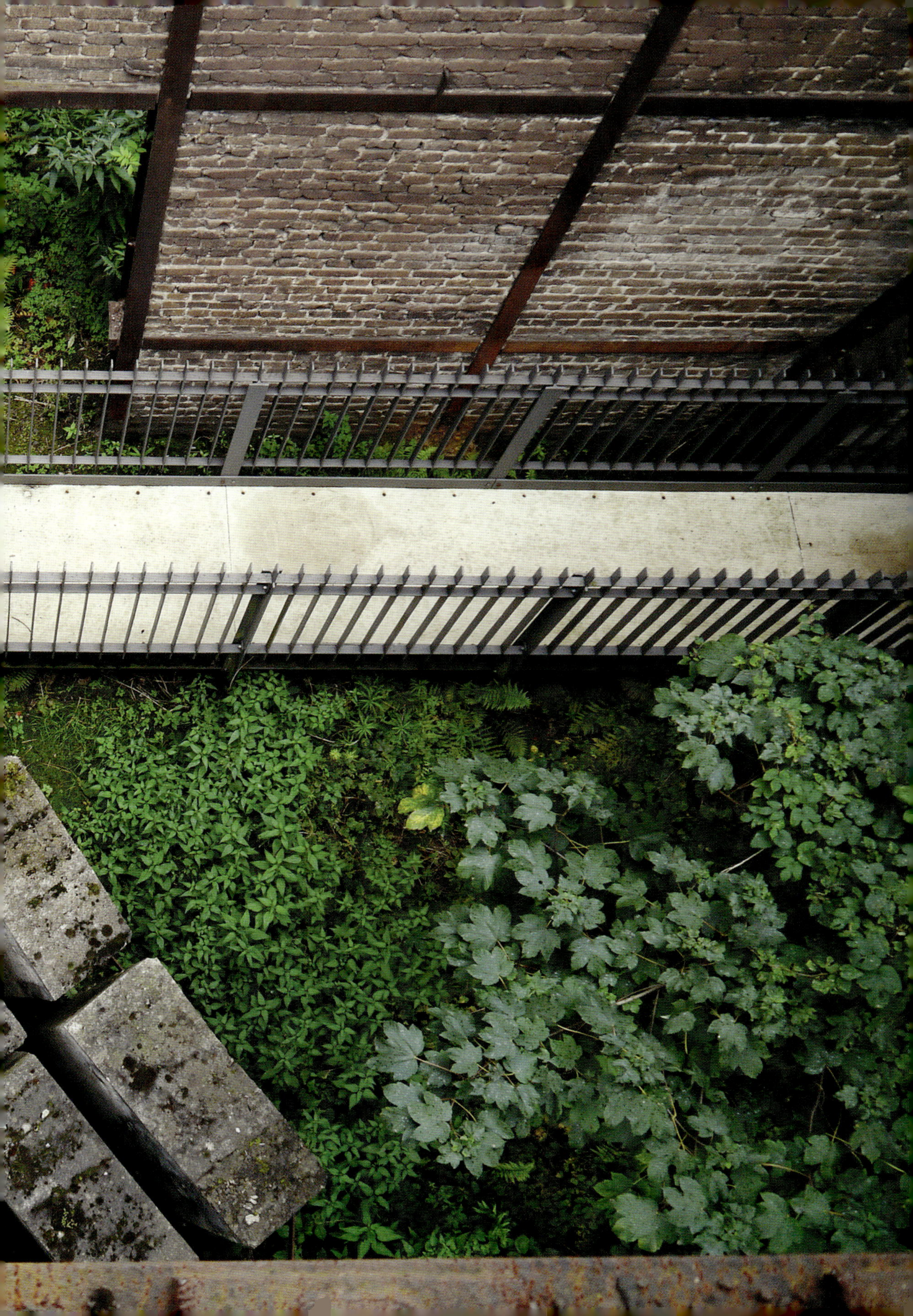

Zollverein World Heritage Site, Essen.

A few days later there are just as many people at Zollverein, to the east of Duisburg in Essen. Taking the tram to Zollverein is an even more surreal experience. You alight at a perfectly normal tram stop, across the street from a row of handsome houses. You cross the street, walk to the end of the houses and turn left. Somehow hidden earlier by the proscenium of houses is Zollverein, once known as 'the most beautiful colliery in the world', a UNESCO World Heritage Site, and today the cultural and artistic centrepiece of both the Emscher Landschaftspark and the Ruhr region. The 55 m high former pit head stands sentinel over the place. OMA, the office of Dutch architect Rem Koolhaas, completed a master plan for the site in 2002. The landscape master plan was the work of Agence Ter.[74]

Individual projects such as this have been undertaken throughout the Emscher valley, and the preservation of industrial-era artefacts has enabled the region to retain and build on its unique identity.[75] When the IBA's mandated term ended in 1999, responsibility for carrying the Emscher Landschaftspark forward shifted to a new management team,[76] and a new master plan has since been created and endorsed. In 2010 the Ruhr region was the European Capital of Culture, hosting some 10.5 million visitors at 5500 events,[77] many of them in the landmarks and landscapes of the Emscher Landschaftspark.

As we have discussed, Linkage Parks are only possible with overarching government commitment. Creation of the Emscher Landschaftspark has required not just the commitment of the German government during the IBA, but the ongoing commitment to an inter-municipal planning culture that involves the federal level, 20 regional cities and towns, two rural districts, three administrative districts and two new cross-regional institutions. Another reason given for the success of Emscher Park is that all stakeholders took the question of what to do next very seriously. A report by CABE, the UK's landmark Commission for Architecture and the Built Environment, identified the level of intellectual debate at the start and throughout the IBA process as one of the most critical lessons learnt.[78] The use of the IBA as a political tool is also important. The 10-year timeframe gave confidence to politicians, investors and the public: it was adequate to enable significant progress and completion of many projects, while also having a known and fixed end point. The IBA leadership also harnessed the power of the media and marketing which was essential in reversing the perception of the Emscher as a blighted area.

All images this spread –
Zollverein World Heritage Site, Essen.

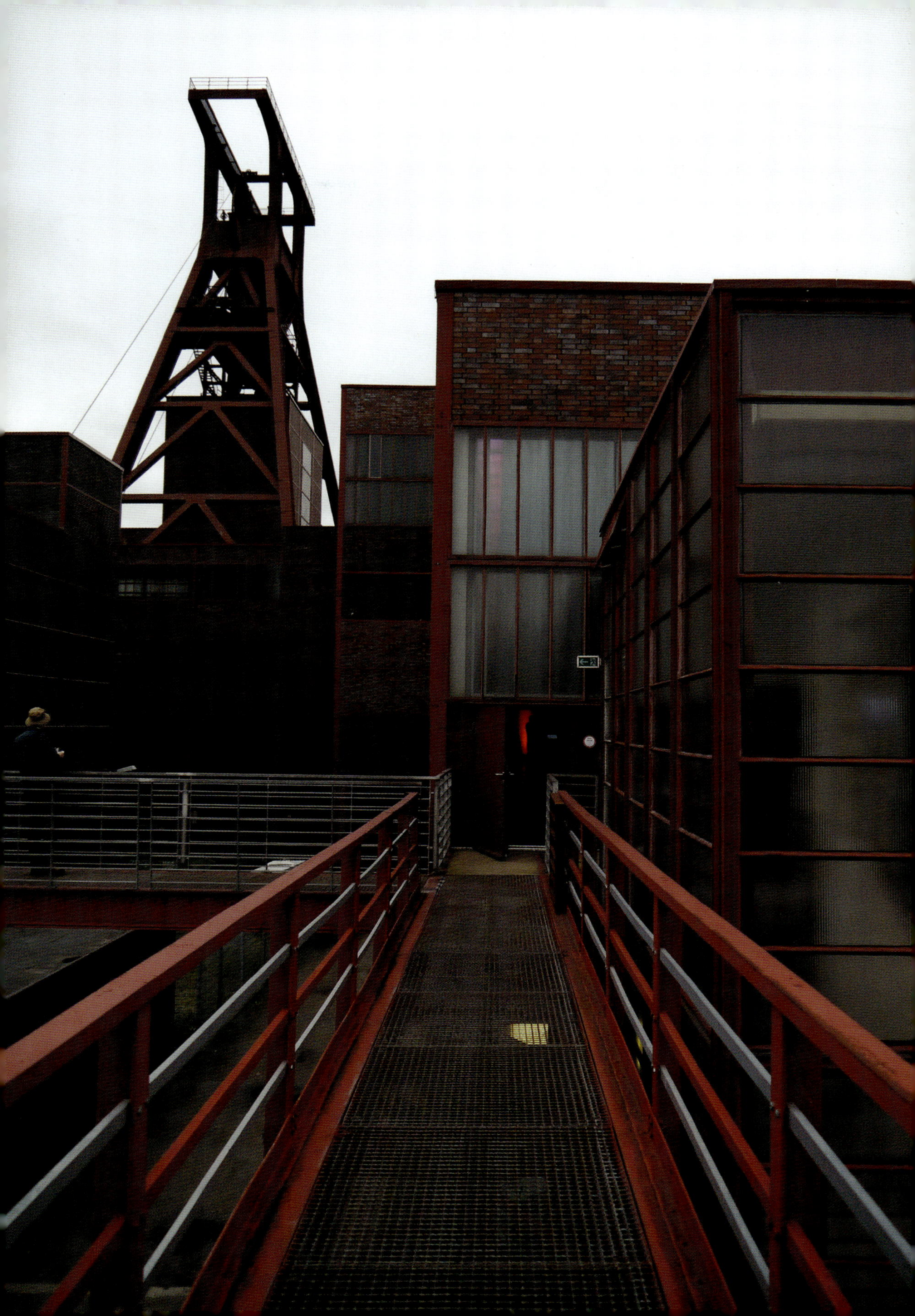

Zollverein World Heritage Site, Essen.

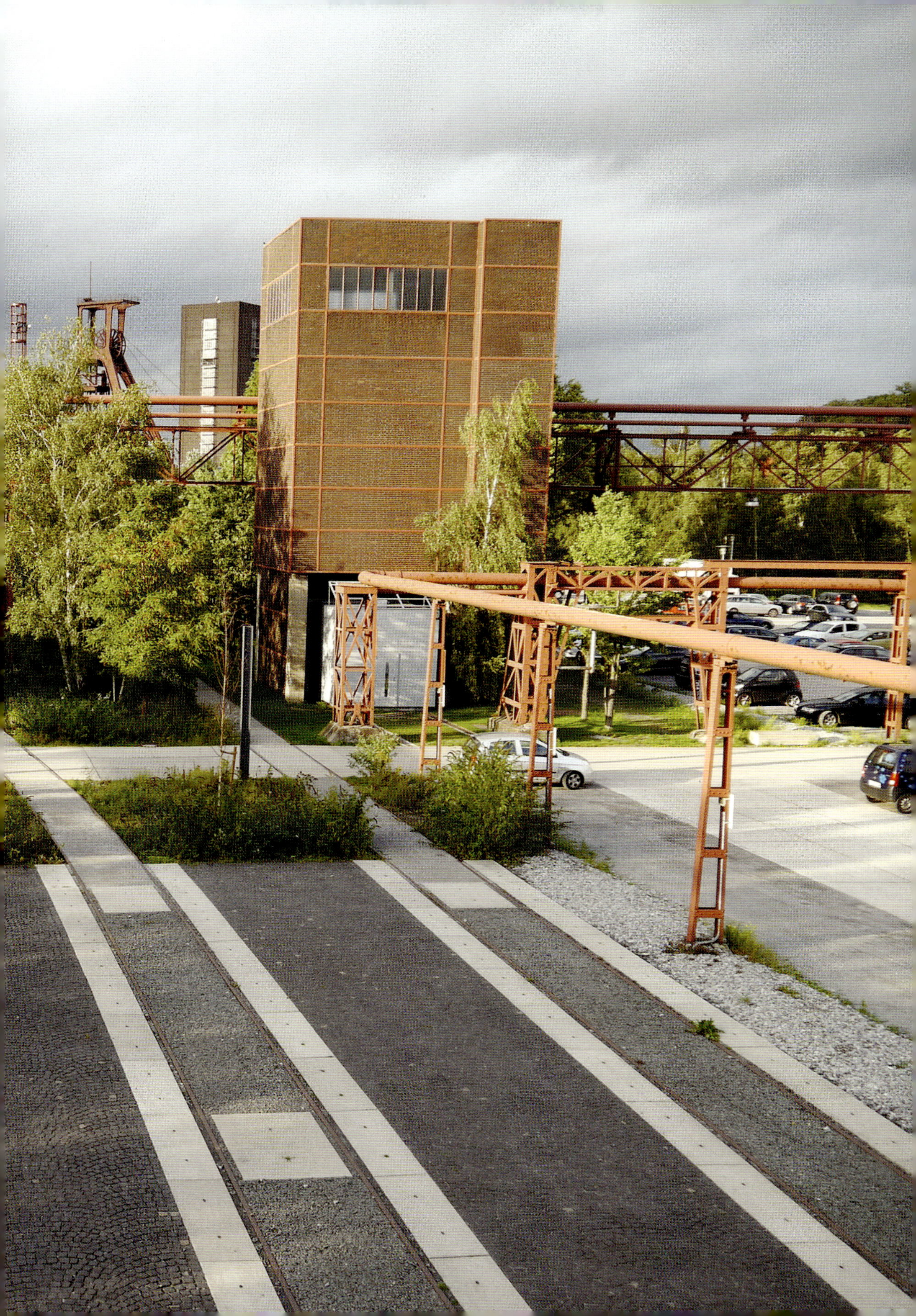

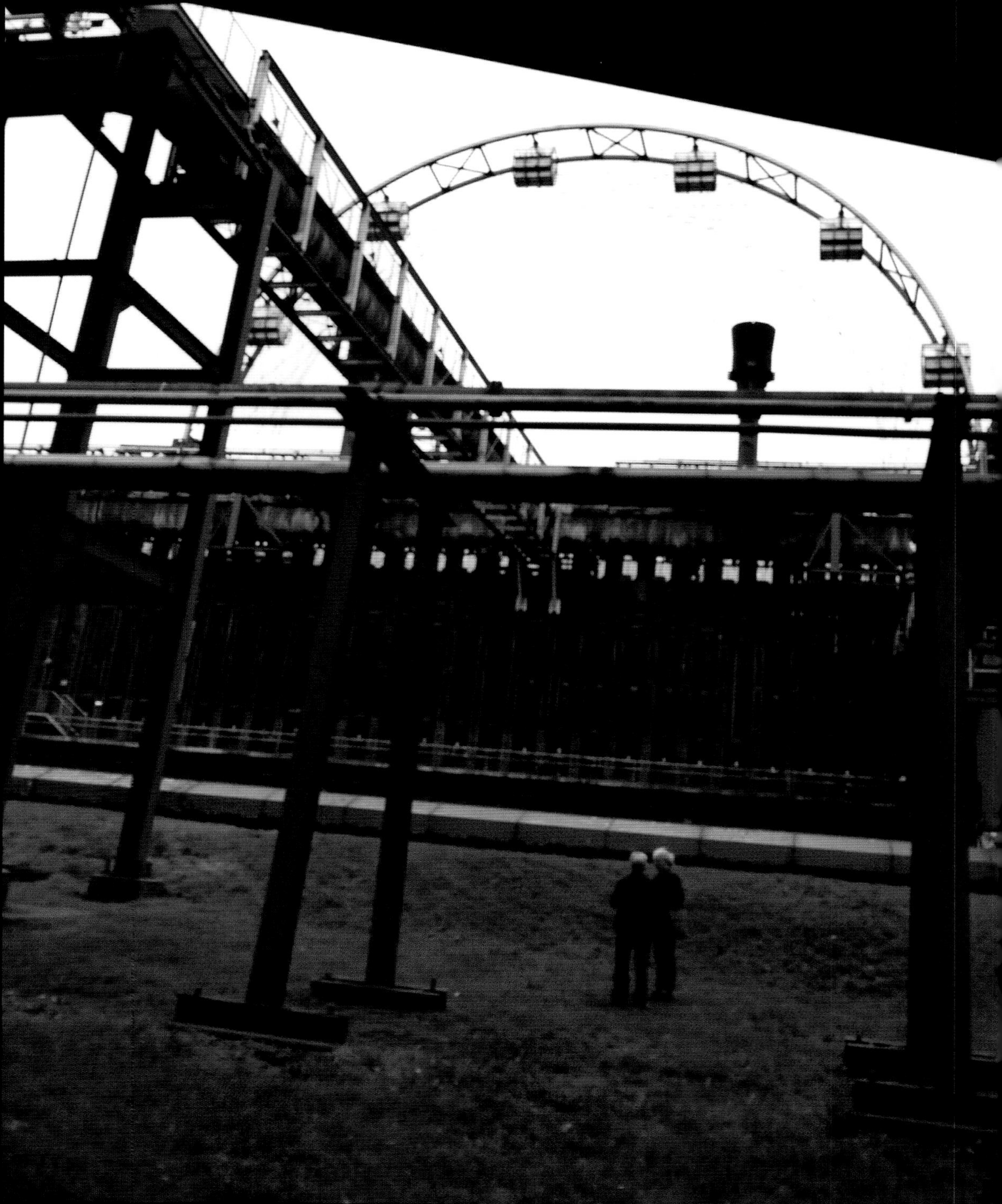

The perception of blight can be as damaging as the reality. While perceptions drive investor confidence, fear and government reactions in many thriving liberal democracies, it is especially hard to change perceptions once a city or country has started to decline. Planning, environmental, recreation and parks departments are often among the first to be disbanded by local and state governments under financial strain, even though the services they provide and the communities they serve may be facing an even greater need than when times were good. In some places though, parks and landscapes have been embraced as opportunities to address both the perceptions and realities of blighted cities.

All images this spread – Zollverein World Heritage Site, Essen.

Linkages 111

02
Obsolescences

Obsolescences

In 1785, nearly 150 years before pork chops and sides of beef started rolling down the High Line like supermodels down a catwalk, New York became the capital of the United States.

Congress sat in lower Manhattan on the 11th of January, and one of its first initiatives was to approve detailed surveying to clearly establish the boundary of the young state. The same year, a baby boy was born in Germany. He grew up privileged, and developed a gift for eccentricity, including a love of 'oriental dress' and a preference for transporting himself in 'a coach drawn by four tame white stags'.[79] He spent money freely in pursuit of his passions. When his wife, Lucie, ended their marriage to demonstrate her unwillingness to continue supporting him, he travelled to England in a failed attempt to find a new cashed-up bride. Returning to Germany he moved house, and took up again with Lucie, with whom he was eventually buried in a pyramid in the middle of a lake.
As one does

Cottbus, Lower Lausitz, Germany: Branitzer Park, the landscape park created by Hermann Ludwig Heinrich Fürst von Pückler-Muskau, after whom the 2000–2010 IBA was named. (Axel Donath via Wikimedia Commons)

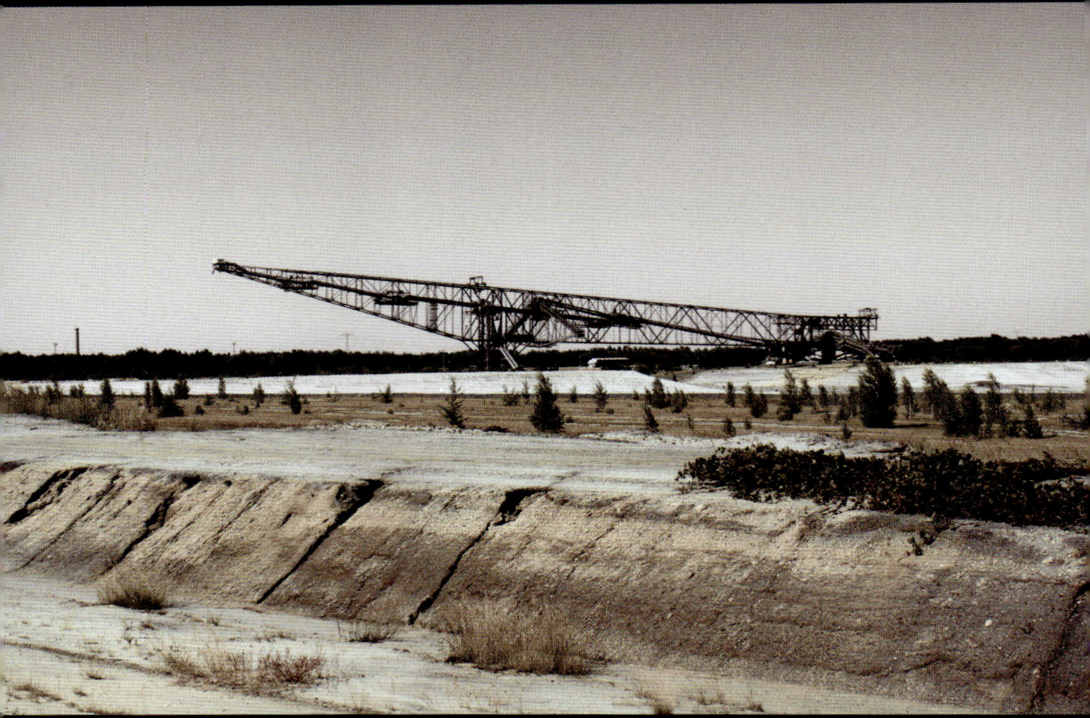

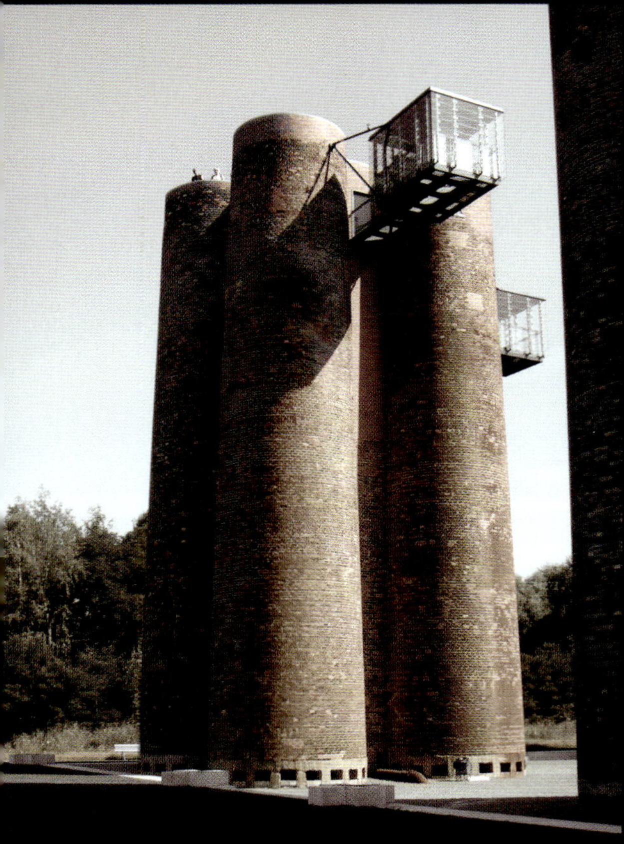

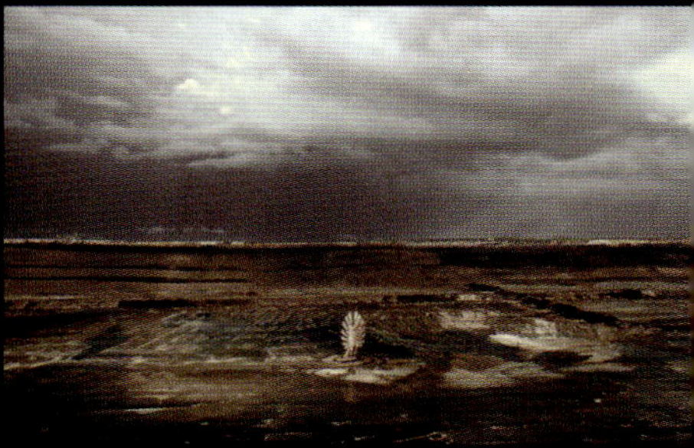

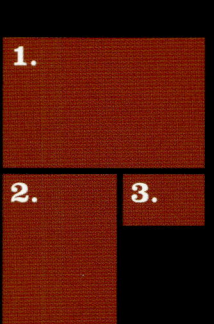

1. Lichterfeld, Lausitz: the F60 Overburden Conveyor Bridge is half a kilometre long, yet is dominated by the open-cut mining landscape. (LutzBruno via Wikimedia Commons)
2. Lauchhammer, Lausitz: the Bioturme (bio towers). (OnkelJohn via Wikimedia Commons)
3. Welzow, Lower Lausitz: the sculpture Phoenix, installed within the open-cut mining landscape. (Siegfried Laumen via Wikimedia Commons)

The man's name was Hermann Ludwig Heinrich Fürst von Pückler-Muskau, and as well as Lucie, his other enduring passion was for parks and gardens. He created a series of projects throughout the Lower Lausitz region of eastern Germany, including the remodelling of the family estate that nearly bankrupted him, and into which he incorporated elements of the local mining landscapes. He died on the eve of German unification, the commencement of a new era in European history, and nearly 150 years later, on the dawn of a new century, his passion and eccentricity were honoured in a new history-making German endeavour.

Once humankind overcame the keenly anticipated, but ultimately anti-climactic possibility that the world was about to end, many things happened in the year 2000. Among them was the start of the Internationale Bauausstellung (IBA) Fürst-Pückler-Land in Germany's Lausitz region. Naming the project Fürst-Pückler-Land (Prince Puckler Country) acknowledged the park-making eccentric, and his connection to the landscape of the area. The IBA process was chosen in the hopes of emulating the success of the IBA Emscher Landschaftspark[80] in revitalising the Ruhr region of western Germany. Many of the projects initiated under IBA Emscher have achieved worldwide renown, and the bold approach and commitment by all involved acknowledged that non-traditional solutions would not work. Enlisting weird Prince Pückler to the cause reinforced that 'out of the box' thinking was also expected for Lausitz, a region with potentially even more challenges to overcome than the ruined steel and coal landscape of the Emscher Valley.

Like Emscher and the wider Ruhr region, the lower Lausitz had also been an established industrial powerhouse. While the Ruhr traded with the world, the Lausitz supplied an internal market. During the Cold War East Germany relied on its own resources, generating power from the means available, abundant brown coal and lignite. In the Lausitz, 200 million tonnes were mined, and 25 000 locals displaced as their homes were sacrificed to increase production. After reunification the mines stopped nearly overnight, unemployment rose to 25 per cent and nearly a quarter of the population left the region.[81] The IBA was instituted to helped define a new future for Lausitz. Over a 10-year period, 30 major projects were developed. Some, as at Emscher, centred on the built mining legacy, like the 500-metre-long F60 spoil conveyor. Dubbed the 'Lying Eiffel Tower', the F60 was initially headed for demolition, but has since been visited by over half a million people. Mining also shaped the landscape of the lower Lausitz. Lignite occurs close to the surface, and is open-cast mined by more or less digging it straight out of the ground. Enormous craters result. These are gradually being transformed into 14 000 ha of 'the largest artificial lake landscape in Europe… the Lausation Lake Land'.[82]

Obsolescences   117

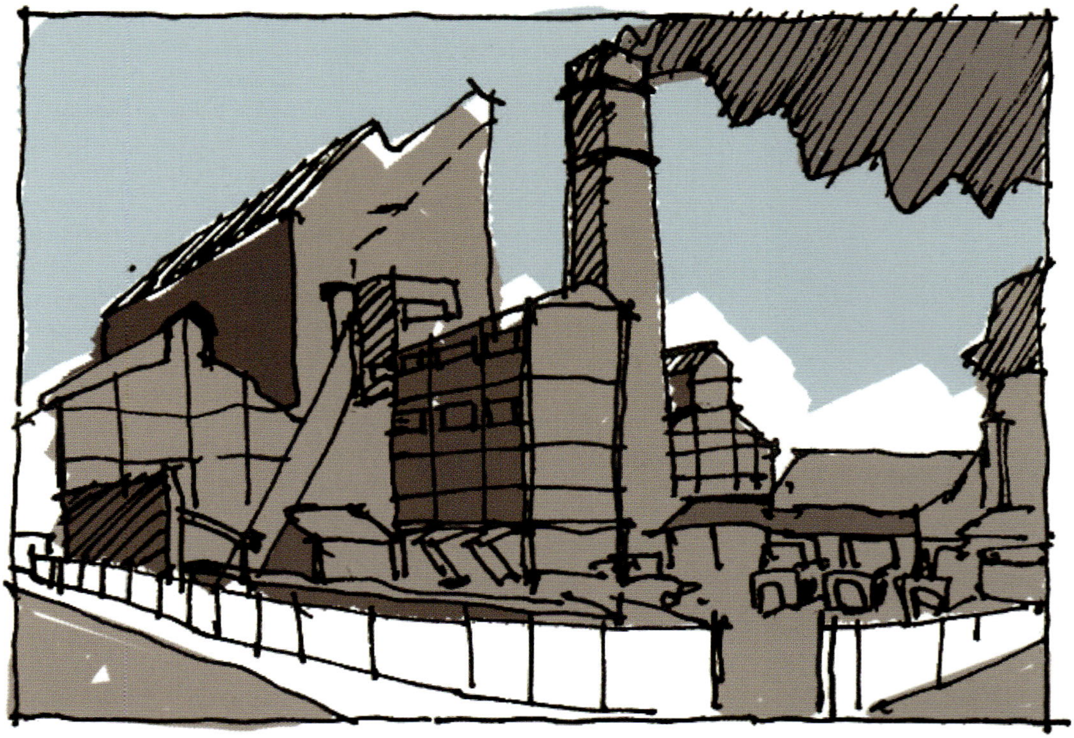

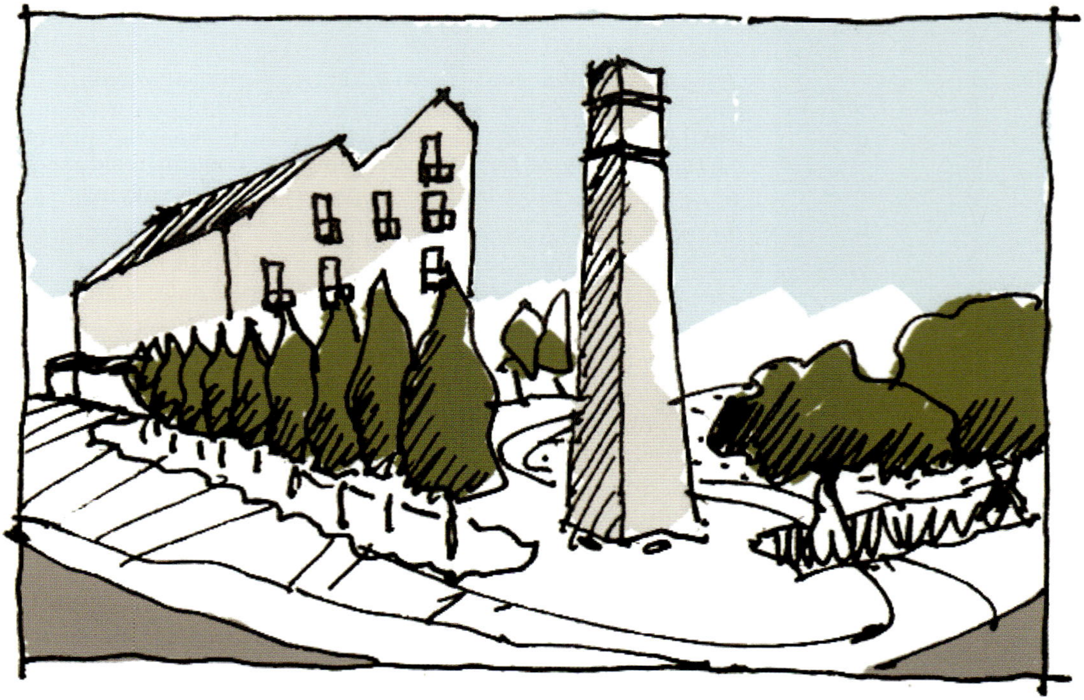

How brownfields become parks.

At the broadest and simplest level, both the IBA Emscher Landschaftspark and IBA Fürst-Pückler-Land are enormous brownfield projects. Brownfield projects transform sites from industrial uses into new, different uses, which can vary from new building development to parkland and recreation spaces. As the majority of former industrial sites contain residual contamination, most brownfield projects involve varying degrees of environmental remediation and restoration.
There are examples of brownfield projects in cities across the world, and brownfields have provided one of the richest sources of new public parkland over the past 30 years.[83]

Brownfields exist because a previous land use has become obsolete. Vacant or abandoned buildings and land are the global hallmarks of urban obsolescence, a phenomenon widely referred to as 'shrinking cities'. If vacancy and abandonment are the common thread, nearly all other aspects of urban obsolescence and shrinking cities differ. The pattern of shrinkage varies across nations and individual cities, and there are many causes. Along with post-industrial change, cities may also shrink because of suburbanisation, financial crisis, the predominance of ageing or low-fertility populations, the dissolution of socialist systems, war and natural or manmade disasters. Many cities and regions have shrunk because of a combination of several of these factors.

Obsolescences **119**

Hakodate, on Hokkaido Island in Japan, is shrinking from a combination of deindustrialisation, suburbanisation, low birth rate and an ageing population.[84] It has also been affected by a shift in regional centres and natural disasters. One of three Japanese ports opened to foreign trade under the Kanagawa Treaty in 1854, Hakodate grew to become an industrial centre for shipping, fishing and shipbuilding, as well as a strategic transport route. The old city grew up along the waterfront, on an hourglass-shaped peninsula extending into the bay. The sunset view back across the water and city from Mount Hakodate was once regarded as one of the three most attractive night-time panoramas in the world. Today the lights glow brightest out towards the horizon where new suburbs have established, leaving the downtown streets in increasing darkness. The picturesque historic centre consistently ranks Hakodate as one of Japan's best loved cities, yet even as old waterfront industrial buildings are reclaimed for restaurants and other tourism uses, more and more homes are left unoccupied and uncared for. Since 1980 the city's population has decreased by 15 per cent. In the seven historic districts it has shrunk by 60 per cent. Projections suggest that by 2030 every third person living on Hokkaido Island will be older than 65.[85]

Venice, poised between Europe and the Mediterranean Sea, has lost half its population in the last 40 years. So great has been the flight to the mainland that, like Hakodate, the night-time view along the Grand Canal reveals far more darkened windows than illuminated ones. Venice is shrinking from a combination of deindustrialisation, natural disasters and an ageing population, with one-third of all Venetians aged over 65. Despite brief success in the 1960s oil boom, the development of the Porto Marghera industrial precinct disconnected this part of the Veneto from a broader regional economy, created a legacy of land and water contamination, and disrupted or disregarded complex and long-established interactions between the islands of the Venice lagoon, two-thirds of which are now vacant. A major flood in 1966 precipitated concerted efforts to save Venice's above-water built environment, and even though the fragility of the city has driven many residents to seek greater security on the mainland, it has also contributed to an unrelenting growth in tourist visitation. Seven million people visited Venice in 1996; today 20 million come each year, most of them for a day only.

1. *Beneath the blue sky, crumbling walls and shuttered windows belie the tourist version of Venice. (Joshua Hinwood)*
2. *The abandoned island of Madonna del Monte, in the Venice lagoon. (Chris 73 via Wikimedia Commons)*
3. *Tourists throng the Rialto Bridge during Carnivale. (Herbert Sponner via Wikimedia Commons)*

For special events like Carnivale, up to 100 000 people cram into what some fear is becoming a theme park rather than a city. For visitors disembarking at the train station, squeezing in a great extruded mass through the gaps and cracks between buildings, braving Piazza San Marco and jostling for the final table at Harry's Bar, it must be almost inconceivable to think, among all that thronging humanity, that Venice is a shrinking city. Yet with more residences each year converting to tourist accommodation, and more shops selling Venetian masks than bread and milk, it is not hard to believe those who predict that Venice will be a ghost town by 2030.[86]

Dresden, the beautiful Baroque city decimated by Allied bombing in World War II, was again a victim of politics following the fall of the Berlin Wall in 1989. In the decade that followed, the city shrank by 60 000 people, 12 per cent of its population. Dresden was one of many East German cities that underwent severe 'system shock' in the early post-socialist years. Expectations of economic growth and opportunity were high, but the opposite happened. The resulting high unemployment rates saw swift and substantial out-migration to the former West Germany, accompanied by decreasing birth rates. The urban policy focus, however, remained on growth, and suburban housing expansion increased to the point where post-unification housing construction and out-migration both peaked in the same period in the mid to late 1990s. Since then Dresden has seen population increases in some parts of the city, including the restored and rehabilitated inner suburbs, at the same time that other areas continue to shrink. Compared with other eastern cities Dresden is performing well. Compared with strong cities in western Germany it continues to suffer, with strategic flexibility and adaptability to change considered the critical focus for the future.[87]

Manchester, Liverpool, Sheffield, Newcastle and Leeds were among the cities in the United Kingdom that suffered population losses with the decline in their manufacturing bases. In 1999 the UK Government released *Towards an Urban Renaissance*, in response to declining town and city centres, and 1.3 million vacant commercial and residential buildings. The document was significant in directing policy towards inner-city regeneration, reuse of existing industrial building stock, and a virtual ban on 'out-of-town' greenfield development.[88]

In Australia, natural disasters, such as flooding or prolonged drought, were key contributors to population decline in regional Australia in the years 2010–2011.[89] Some mining areas also shrank. This continues a long-term trend in Australia that has seen continued population decline in 'the bush', coupled with continued migration to capital cities and the east and west coasts.[90] While more than 80 per cent of all Australians now live within 100 km of the coast,[91] a coastal location is no guarantee of success or opportunity, neither is remaining in the country necessarily an indicator of vulnerability.[92] For those cities and towns that have suffered from population loss, declines in the agricultural, extractive and manufacturing industries have precipitated the shrinkage, and it is worse in single industry towns.[93]

The Trundle Hotel. The main street of this New South Wales town is one of the widest in Australia, a remnant of times when the town was the centre of a thriving and expanding agricultural region. In 2012, Trundle participated in a television program, Country Town Rescue, *and offered farm houses for rent at $1 per week in an attempt to entice people to resettle in the country. (Mattinbgn via Wikimedia Commons)*

While Australians are a nation of city-dwellers, they are more accurately a nation of suburb-dwellers. The quest for 'the Australian Dream', private home ownership, is one of the key drivers behind Australia's incredibly high internal mobility rate. Whether from the country to the city, from capital to regional city, or inner to outer city, more than 40 per cent of the population had moved to a different permanent address between the 2001 and 2006 national census,[94] and the majority of population growth in Melbourne, Sydney and Perth occurred in the outer ring of suburbs. The 2011 *State of Australian Cities Report* observed (and possibly opined) that 'greenfield developments remain the predominant way to accommodate population increases within Australia's cities'.[95]

Urban obsolescence and shrinking cities are not contemporary phenomena; settlements have grown and shrunk since the first groups of humans decided to experiment with living more closely together. As capital of a world-changing Empire, Rome had a population of one million people.[96] When the Empire fell, so did Rome, losing power, prospects and people to scores of competing cities and regions. Not until the early 1960s did Rome's population levels match those at the height of the Empire. From Late Antiquity until the Early Modern period, Asian and European history is full of examples of cities decimated by not just Empire collapse, but disease, war and natural disasters like fire, drought, earthquake and flood. Jared Diamond, in his best-selling book *Collapse*, puts forward an argument that war and drought were fundamental contributors to the decline of ancient Mayan civilisation, and to the complete abandonment of cities that once housed populations in the millions.[97]

Obsolescences **123**

Craco, a much smaller monastery town in southern Italy, survived from 1060 to 1963 – a millennium – when its remaining 1800 residents were relocated to a new town, Craco Peschiera. The new town has also declined, with only 800 inhabitants at the turn of this century. Nine centuries of poor agricultural conditions, disease, earthquakes, landslides and war all contributed to massive out-migration, and the inexorable shrinking of Craco, which remains in ruins today. Former residents and their descendents gathered in 2008 to visit the town, and a growing diaspora continues to meet annually in New York.[98]

In the latter part of the nineteenth century, some cities and towns in Europe, Asia, Latin America and the United States thrived and grew as industrialisation changed the way products were manufactured, and railways changed the way they were transported. Others declined and shrank. Late nineteenth century and contemporary urban obsolescence and shrinkage in Europe has predominantly been the result of industrial change, post-socialist change and low birth rates. In the United States for the same period, urban shrinkage has largely been driven by increasing suburbanisation.[99]

Throughout the world, and across time, mining has been an industry especially prone to volatility, with consequent dramatic impacts on cities and towns. The IBA Fürst-Pückler-Land project is responding to the impacts of post-socialist change on a lignite mining region, which included a dramatic increase in unemployment, out-migration and urban shrinkage. In Australia, gold fever brought tens of thousands of people from China, the United States, the United Kingdom and elsewhere. Charters Towers, in north Queensland, grew from a founding party of four to a population of 25 000 in under 30 years.[100] At its 1899 peak Charters Towers was colloquially known as 'The World'; so great were its multifarious attractions that anything a person could want was available without ever having to leave. The city famously possessed 65 hotels, as well as banks, a gold exchange, churches, schools, thriving sports and cultural activities, public parks and streets full of handsome buildings outwardly displaying civic pride and optimism. Yet barely 13 000 people live in the entire Charters Towers Regional Council district today.[101]

Mining regions are where they are because of geology. Long after economic and political forces affect mining, the underlying geology can be read in the seams and fault lines of the impacted cities and towns above. The patterns of urban shrinkage vary across the world. Germany is shrinking in the east, and generally manifests an east–west divide. The United Kingdom is divided north-to-south, with most shrinking occurring in the north. It is generally understood that London is the only large British city that is not in some way shrinking. France is shrinking in its centre, and urban shrinkage in the United States is concentrated in the central north region known as the 'Rust Belt'. There are also different patterns of shrinkage within cities themselves. Rust Belt city Cleveland, for example, has areas of high shrinkage next to areas of high growth; what researchers call an intertwined pattern.

Some European cities like Glasgow, and many American ones, show a 'donut' pattern, which happens when the city centre is hollowed out as people move to outer suburbs. The one commonality to all cities and regions experiencing obsolescence and shrinkage is a political and planning preference for growth and aversion to planning for shrinkage.[102] Western cultures are pro-growth; acknowledging or planning for shrinkage is seen as giving up, or accepting failure. The folly of an unmoderated growth preference taken to its (il)logical conclusion is evidenced in rising numbers of so-called 'ghost estates'.

Over the past decade new suburban housing developments have been built with great enthusiasm in countries as diverse as Ireland, Spain and China. In each of those countries, thousands of new and partially built homes now stand empty and abandoned in cities and regions that have now shrunk before they ever grew, the result of the GFC. Ireland's 'ghost estates' were a focus for national frustration even before two-year-old Liam Keogh followed his pet dog through a gap in a fence and drowned in a pool of water on the unfinished Glenatore housing development in Athlone.[103] There are an estimated 2800 such sites across the country[104] containing up to 400 000 housing properties.[105] Glenatore was approved during the so-called 'Celtic Tiger' boom, and planned to contain 66 terrace houses and apartments. A 2011 national house survey revealed that only five were occupied. For the same period, the number of homeless in Ireland rose to 5000, with 100 000 households on waiting lists for social housing.[106]

A similar story can be found in Spain, where courts granted nearly 530 000 foreclosures between 2008 and September 2011, and where banks have been asked to 'set aside' additional funds to cover 175 billion euros (AUD$224 billion) in toxic real estate assets. In addition to ghost housing estates, Spain also has ghost buildings, unfinished and abandoned, and entire ghost satellite cities. Sesena, south of Madrid, was planned as a city of 30 000 people, with over 13 000 apartments, street and road infrastructure, parks and playgrounds and ample shops. Fewer than 40 per cent of the homes were built, scant numbers of those are occupied.[107]

Sesena, Toledo: the Residencial Francisco Hernando housing development. (simplifica via Wikimedia Commons)

Obsolescences

Kangbashi: Inner Mongolia Vast, empty plaza, with ongoing construction in the distance. (Uday Phalgun via Flickr)

Even more dramatic are the widely circulated images from China showing examples of new buildings, suburbs and entire cities standing either half-built or completely finished but never occupied. The most infamous is Kangbashi, built as the new urban centre for one million workers of Ordos, a coal mining community in Inner Mongolia.[108] Visiting the city in 2010, a reporter for *Time* engagingly described how 'an occasional pedestrian, appearing like a hallucination, can be seen trudging down a sidewalk, like a lone survivor of some horror-movie apocalypse'.[109]

Shrinking cities have been the subject of focused study for barely more than a decade, with Germany and the United States leading the charge. This is despite the clear-eyed observation of local residents dealing with the reality of industrial change in their lives and cities, and social geographers who observed the growing impact of contemporary 'agribusiness' on small and medium-sized country towns in rural America. Writing in 1966, renowned scholar of the urban landscape John Brinkerhoff Jackson observed, 'It will undoubtedly take us time to get used to [declining] country towns downtowns, growth of retail and commercial hubs outside the city centre, and rise in poor, low-skilled and unemployed population and other indications of a population decline; we think of America as forever booming and expanding. It is true we are no longer disturbed by the abandoned one room school or the crossroads General Merchandise; but how will we take the abandoned, more or less modern, high school with monster gymnasium?'[110] Perhaps this merely indicates that each generation, coming to its own realisation about a situation, tends to believe it is the first time the situation itself has existed – cities where today's adults and their parents lived are declining, the 'high school with monster gymnasium' where today's voters once played for the championship sits abandoned, so we must be facing a serious problem.

Perhaps it merely reinforces the culturally blinkered attitude to urban growth as success, and anything else as failure.

Even though the examples described earlier demonstrate the myriad causes, manifestations and persistence of urban obsolescence, there has now been considerable effort given to actually defining the topic. A group of international scholars working in the field met in 2004 and agreed to define a shrinking city as:

> 'a densely populated urban area with a minimum population of 10,000 residents that has faced population losses in large parts for more than two years and is undergoing economic transformations with some symptoms of a structural crisis'.[111]

Numbers also help in understanding the magnitude of the phenomenon.
- In the second half of the twentieth century, 370 cities with populations greater than 100 000 shrank by at least 10 per cent.
- More than a quarter of large cities around the globe shrank during the 1990s.[112]
- One in six cities worldwide was shrinking substantially before the Global Financial Crisis in 2008.[113]
- In the United States, of the nation's 20 largest cities in the 1950s, 16 have since shrunk. Of those, the cities of Buffalo, Cleveland, Detroit, Pittsburgh and St Louis have lost more than 50 per cent of their resident population.

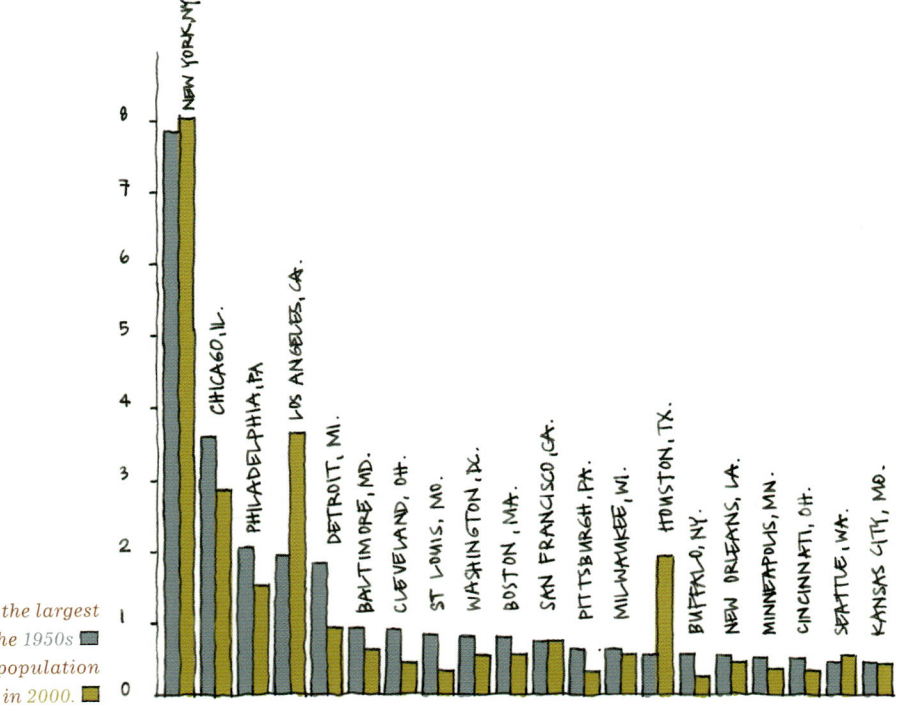

Population in the largest US cities in the 1950s compared with the population in 2000.

Obsolescences **127**

American shrinking cities are strongly represented in the Rust Belt, the steel and car-making region of the North and Midwest. So many photographs have been taken of Detroit that some now regard the relentless drive to find and capture the latest burnt-out house, or the afternoon sun shining through empty factory windows, as sensationalist, exploitative and willfully misrepresentative – a kind of 'ruin porn'.[114]

Among American scholars there are nuances of approach that may at first seem like nit-picking over insignificant details, but that actually ensure the broadest understanding of how urban obsolescence and shrinkage occurs in the United States, and also what options are available for communities living with shrinkage to consider.

One research effort is focused on what participants poignantly call the 'Forgotten Cities'. They are characteristically old, small and poor, and the 150 cities in the United States that meet the criteria are home to 7.4 million people.[115] They are found in the North-eastern, Midwestern and Mid-Atlantic states, and include well-known places such as Flint, Michigan, the birthplace of General Motors, and much-defended hometown of film-maker Michael Moore; Gary, Indiana, hometown of Michael Jackson and his family, and, as all aficionados of fine musical comedy will know, the subject of a song written for the 1957 hit *The Music Man*; and Albany, capital of the state of New York, and the longest continuously chartered city in the United States.

Other groups use the term 'Legacy Cities' to describe places that have been losing both jobs and population over a sustained period of several decades. Legacy Cities are found not just in the North-east and Midwest, but are scattered across the country, including such places as Birmingham in Alabama, and New Orleans in Louisiana. They vary in size, and include large cities like Detroit, medium cities such as Youngstown, Ohio, and small towns like East St Louis, Illinois. Using this broader definition means that around 45 million people are living in these shrinking cities – twice the population of Australia.[116] For this reason alone it is important to understand the challenges of urban obsolescence and shrinkage, and to acknowledge and build on the work happening 'on the ground' to position shrinking cities for new and different futures.

Most agree that most shrinking cities have gone through a similar historical trajectory. They have had a sustained period of growth, with strong industry and infrastructure, the creation of civic institutions and an increase in population. This has been followed by an equally sustained period of decline, eventually leaving cities and communities to confront a new reality.[117] Among many challenging issues, one of the new realities facing most shrinking cities is an abundance of vacant and abandoned land. Much of the creative work being undertaken by shrinking city residents, students, researchers and economists focuses on this land.

Among many challenging issues, one of the new realities facing most shrinking cities is an abundance of vacant and abandoned land.

Abandoned house in Delray, Detroit. (Notorious4life via Wikimedia Commons)

The abandoned Packard Automobile Plant in Detroit. (Albert Duce via Wikimedia Commons)

Across the Rust Belt and beyond, people passionate about their hometowns, and students and researchers passionate about cities, have realised that when combined with existing community assets, vacant land is one of the greatest opportunities shrinking cities possess.[118] They are testing and implementing innovative proposals for the treatment, reconfiguration and management of vacant urban land. Whether the number is 150 cities or more, it is an exciting prospect to imagine the possibility of overturning the negative impact of tens of thousands of hectares of abandoned and vacant land, by its transformation into green and park-like places that positively affect health and wellbeing, property values, job creation, environmental resilience and sustainability and contribute to a better future for up to 45 million people.

Vacant land can be developed for private or public use. The most common scenario involves an existing resident taking over the use and maintenance of an adjoining vacant house lot.

Before

After

Gradually taking over neighbouring vacant property.

The process can happen formally, with a vacant lot passing into city ownership and being offered for sale, or informally, with a resident starting by mowing or caring for a next-door block and gradually establishing landscape elements like planting, garden furniture or a shed. Philadelphia's Office of Housing and Community Development runs a Small Vacant Lot Program[119] which allows residents and not-for-profit groups to apply for ownership of local vacant lots that can be used for driveways, gardens, expanded yards or other green initiatives. The City of Saginaw polled its citizens about addressing the issues associated with decline when formulating a new master plan. From a list of five strategies over 58 per cent of respondents gave their number one ranking to 'Offer adjacent vacant lots to existing homeowners at a reduced rate'.[120]

When design firm Interboro studied how this process was occurring in parts of Detroit they found many homeowners who had expanded their properties to include the adjacent lot. In one example, two sisters lived in rented accommodation until falling property prices after the 1967 riot enabled them to buy houses on the same street.

Two lots separated the sisters, but as these were gradually abandoned and then demolished the sisters were able to also buy this land and consolidate their properties. They ended up owning two modest houses on a 1/4 acre lot (one-tenth of a hectare), the same size parcel as a typical suburban Detroit house lot. Interboro suggested that this process did indeed represent a new form of suburbanisation; in previously densely built and densely populated parts of the inner city, residents were actively recreating their neighbourhoods in a low density, suburban style, with a single house on a large plot of land.[121]

This 'New Suburbanism' is important not just because it demonstrates a hands-on and ground-up response to individual property vacancies, but because it illustrates one solution to how shrinking cities might adapt at a citywide scale. New Suburbanism fundamentally changes the scale and character of neighbourhoods for future purchasers and residents. The city stays the same size, but deliberately accommodates far fewer people. 'De-densification' is one of two city-scale theories for how city officials, planners and residents can plan for shrinkage.

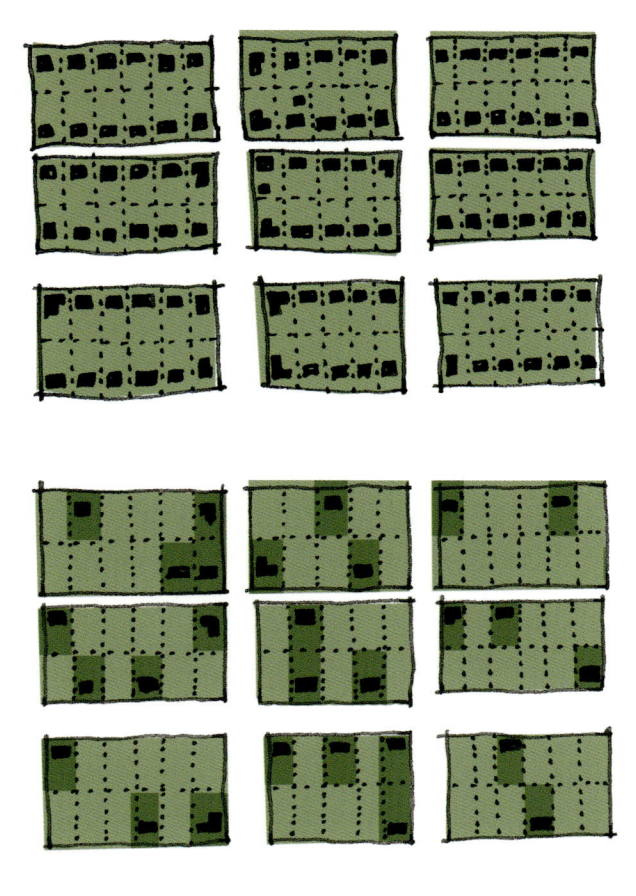

De-densification.

Obsolescences   **131**

The other theory creates 'urban islands'.[122] Under the urban island model, still viable and thriving parts of the city are retained and protected, while vulnerable and abandoned areas are eliminated. Any remaining residents are relocated, remaining buildings are demolished, and the entire area reverts to nature. Both models require strong structural and legislative support at the local government level: for urban islands, government support is needed to define and enforce the plan; for de-densification, support is required to enable it, through easier mechanisms for transferring unencumbered property ownership to new private buyers. Urban islands are generally thought to be a tougher sell politically: few people want to be told that their neighbourhood is beyond saving and the best solution for everyone is to bulldoze it out of existence. It is only when decline has become so protracted, and abandonment and vacancy left to continue virtually unchecked, that it becomes a more palatable solution. That appears to be the situation in Saginaw, Michigan.

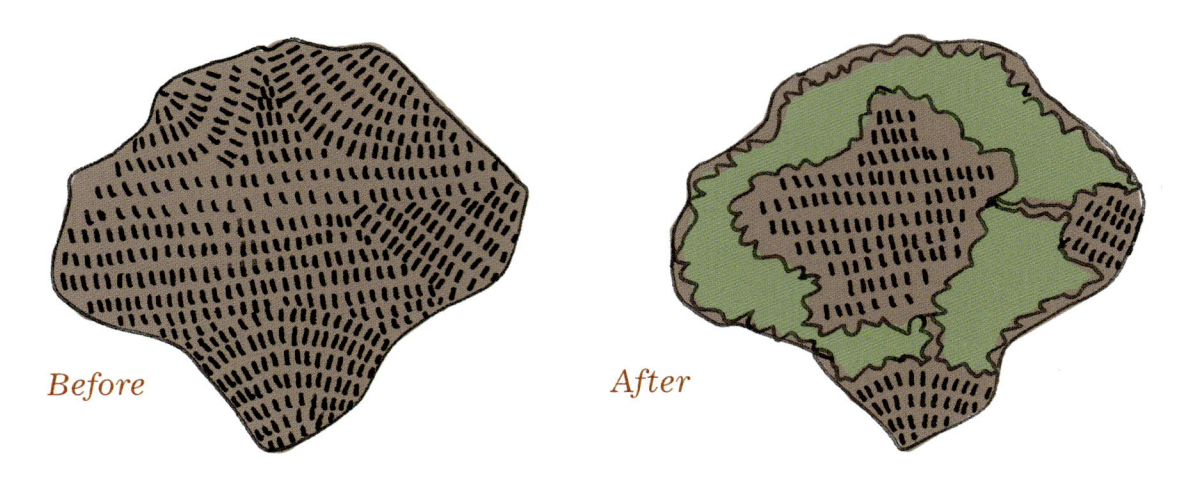

Before *After*

Urban Islands.

	In April 1968 Simon and Garfunkel released *America*, a paean to leaving home to search for bright lights and success. In the song a couple travel to New York from the Midwest, hitch-hiking from Saginaw, catching a bus in Pittsburgh, and describing the people they see along the way. When the song was released, America, the country, was still deeply involved in the Vietnam War, and recovering from the assassination of President John F. Kennedy. Less than three weeks later Martin Luther King Jr would be killed, and after two months Robert Kennedy would be dead too. New York was in decline; only a few years later it would be on the edge of bankruptcy. Many listened to the song and could hear an implicit questioning of the direction the country had taken.

Saginaw was a prosperous city. Located less than 150 km from Detroit, its initial fortune came from timber, not cars. At the beginning of the twentieth century car-related manufacturing increased, and General Motors established a presence in the city. Saginaw contributed substantially to wartime munitions supply, and manufacturing continued to surge in peacetime. Many fine buildings remain from both boomtimes.[123]

Saginaw: the late nineteenth-century Caskey House, part of the Central City Expansion Historic District.
(Brenna Moloney)

Saginaw: in the midst of great challenges, some businesses are thriving in the old town, on the west side of the river.
(Brenna Moloney)

Obsolescences   **133**

Saginaw: the mid-century Alden B. Dow House. (Brenna Moloney)

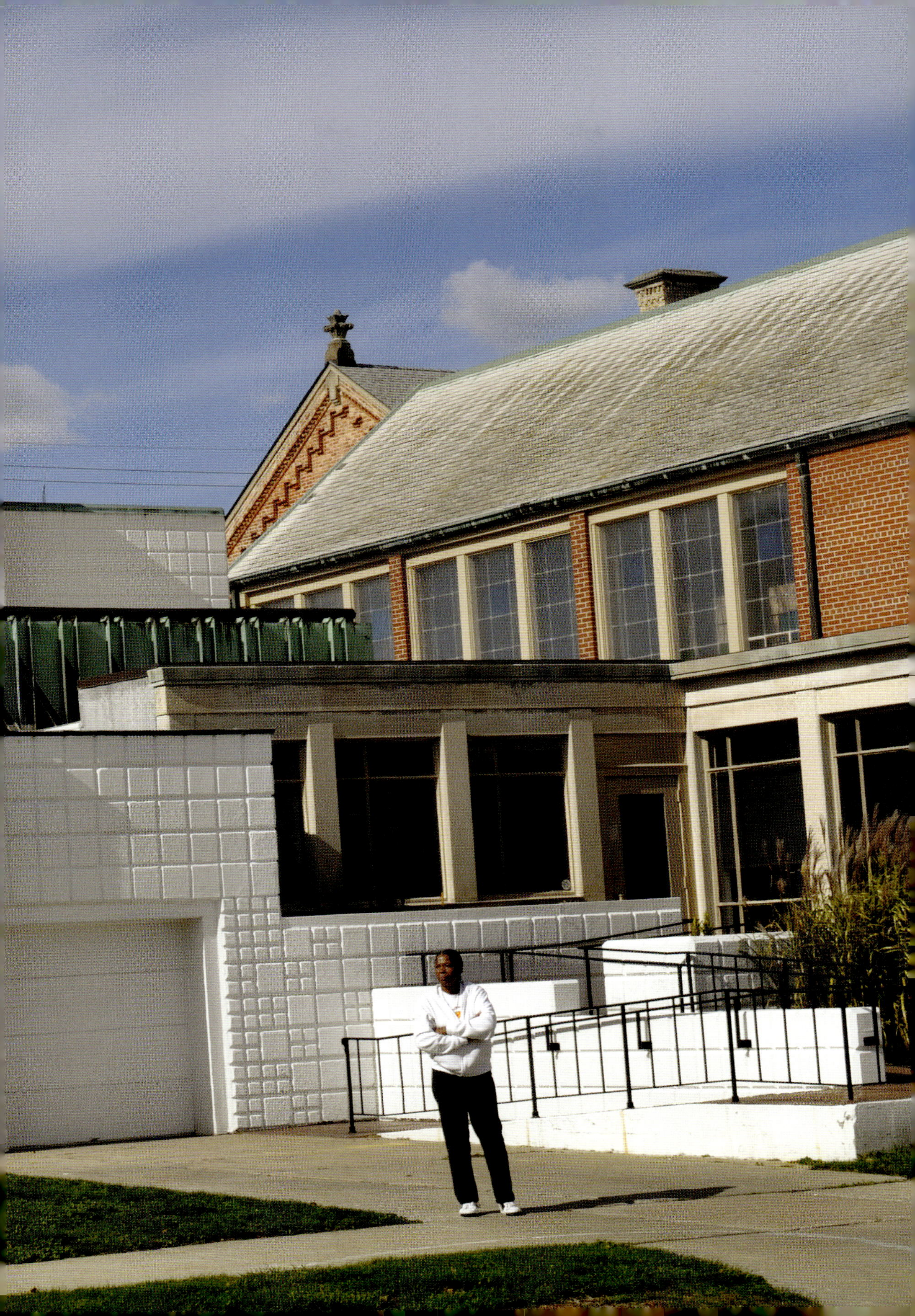

From the time of the Great Depression, many African Americans moved north to cities like Saginaw in search of better work opportunities. For many years legally enforced segregation limited them to the east side of town. When segregation ended the population in the formerly all-white western part of the city became more balanced, but the east remained mainly a black district. The decline of manufacturing industries hit these communities hardest. Saginaw's population dropped rapidly from a peak of 98 265 people in 1960 to 51 508 in 2010.[124] In 2009 houses in the highest value part of town were selling for barely US$66 000.[125]

Abandonment and vacancy rates today remain highest on the east side of Saginaw. In 2009 the local council decided that 140 ha towards the north-east of the city would be declared a 'Green Zone', and together with the local land bank authority it applied for federal funding to move the remaining 1000 residents to new housing and demolish all but a few public and community buildings.[126] Under proposed new zoning designations the Green Zone would be classified as 'Green Reserve Opportunity Area', and 'envisioned to be converted to attractive low maintenance natural areas intended to beautify and enhance key areas in the City through parkways, landscaped roadway buffers, gateways, landscaped open areas, and open meadows'.[127]

A row of houses in the Central Saginaw Historic District. (Brenna Moloney)

Flint and Pere Marquette Union Station, East Saginaw, on the fringe of the Green Zone. (Brenna Moloney)

Saginaw: former carwash near the train station. (Brenna Moloney)

With the Green Zone in place, the area to which the council would have to provide services would be reduced. There would be fewer call-outs by the police and fire departments to abandoned buildings, less need to provide lighting and sewerage services, or road maintenance. Reducing the provision of services and infrastructure in the Green Zone, the argument goes, would make more available for the rest of the city.[128] As well as demonstrating how the urban island process might unfold, the Green Zone is also based on the premise of transferring formerly private land into public ownership and use. A similar strategy also underpins most of the recent research and exploration of vacant and abandoned land in shrinking cities. Options and questions for the strategic reuse of vacant land cluster around four general approaches: the creation of green infrastructure, right-sizing municipal infrastructure, creating productive landscapes and land banking.

Green infrastructure is the term given to 'the network of natural landscape assets which underpin the economic, socio-cultural and environmental functionality of our cities and towns – i.e. the green spaces and water systems which intersperse, connect and provide vital life support for humans and other species within our urban environments'.[129] What is nice about this definition is that it starts from a position of essential, demonstrable benefit – landscape elements are not just in the 'nice to have, but…' category. It also suggests that green infrastructure operates at a range of scales, needing to work systemwide across entire cities, but then also in individual and particular locations.

Site stabilisation.
Before

In towns and cities looking for solutions to excess vacant land, green infrastructure provides many opportunities and benefits. The first benefit such an approach can provide is site stabilisation.

Site stabilisation.
After

Obsolescences **139**

Evidence from many places shows that two things thrive on vacant and abandoned lots: weeds and rubbish. Both perpetuate the impression that a site is uncared for, which can ultimately invite more dumping, retreat by neighbours and a lowering of property values in the immediate area. For over a decade the Pennsylvania Horticultural Society (PHS) has been using its Philadelphia Green program to promote land stabilisation in a city with over 30 000 vacant lots.[130] The PHS has developed what it calls 'a basic "clean & green" approach' that uses lawns and trees as the two key building blocks for reversing the perception of defeat, increasing community cohesion and empowerment and creating a temporary public use – it turns messed-up lots into mini parks.

Philadelphia: the site of a former leather company building, now a mini park. (Smallbones via Wikimedia Commons)

There are, no doubt, many readers who might find the advocacy for lawn problematic. Landscape architects, in particular, would have found it almost impossible not to have heard the growing denunciation of the lawn by influential landscape architect Diana Balmori and others over the past decade.[131] Anti-lawn proponents attack the lawn as an 'environmental hazard', a 'socially treasured object [that] became suspect', and call for 'nothing less than the abandonment of this developed and admired form'.[132] Others observe that, unlike gardening – 'a painstaking exploration of space' – lawns only succeed through 'overcoming… local conditions'.[133] The language of the Pennsylvania Horticultural Society, in its Reclaiming Vacant Lots guide, could not be more different: 'Lawns are attractive and provide a good surface for community activities such as picnics, games, or relaxation. Lawns also help keep dust down, slow down the flow of rainwater in strong storms, and prevent soil from eroding off the site'.[134] For those living with vacant lots strewn with car bodies and old tyres, the 'environmental hazard' of lawn is no doubt a trade-off they are willing to make.

As cultural geographer David Lowenthal observed,

> **'What makes one landscape appear harmonious, another incongruous, is the entire experience of the viewer.'**[135]

The clean and green site stabilisation approach also appears to have significant social benefits. A study undertaken by the University of Pennsylvania compared vacant Philadelphia lots and improved, or 'greened', vacant lots over a 10-year timeframe. Across the four sections of the city that were examined, the study revealed that greening vacant lots was associated with significant reductions in gun crime and some decrease in vandalism. Many residents also reported reduced stress and more exercise.[136] Another study demonstrated that houses in the immediate vicinity to lots that had been 'cleaned and greened' experienced up to a 30 per cent increase in property value.[137]

Unfortunately, citizen-initiated greening is not without its challenges. A Philadelphia coffee shop owner who removed 40 tons of rubbish from a vacant next door lot, and installed seating and plants and footpaths, was later threatened with legal action by the site's owner, the Philadelphia Redevelopment Authority, and ordered to return it to its original condition. As Nate Berg reported in *The Atlantic Monthly*, cleaning up the lot was as much a good business decision as a Good Samaritan act, and the owner took the initiative after failing to elicit action from the city authorities. In doing so though, he trespassed on the property of another party, and the heavy-handed response from the PRA has almost completed undermined any chance of the two parties working together to enable the community to continue to benefit from its new mini-park.[138]

Scientific study also underpins the effectiveness of remediation, which is the second possible benefit provided by green infrastructure. Many cities and towns whose fortunes were built on mining and manufacturing bear an enduring legacy of contamination. The pollution of air, water and ground can have a lasting impact on the health of children and adults, and the cost of clean-up can be significant. On many former industrial sites the cost of site remediation is defrayed by the profitable redevelopment of the site. In the United States, federal and state funding is available to support remediation, but again, it is usually only available for sites where significant redevelopment is proposed. This traditional remediation approach poses a problem in shrinking cities where the likelihood of immediate, significant economic investment is low and the quantity of vacant, contaminated property is high. Green infrastructure provides options for addressing site contamination, and thus improving the environmental functionality of shrinking cities and towns.

Bioremediation is becoming an increasingly well known, non-traditional remediation technique. The term refers to 'any process that uses microbes, fungi, plants or their enzymes to make a contaminated site safe'.[139] Phytoremediation is a technique that uses plants to remove, transfer, stabilise and/or degrade environmental contaminants in soil, sediment and water.[140] Mycoremediation uses fungi instead of, or in symbiotic association with plants. The process works in several ways, depending on the species and type of contaminant, and the technique has different applications depending on the type of industrial contamination, and on the environmental conditions and geographic location of the affected site. In New Zealand, for example, phytoremediation is being tested as a possible solution to pollution caused by the agricultural and timber industries. In Australia its most likely application will be on land affected by mining.

Lead contamination is a problem in many former industrial cities. When testing in 2004, the Board of Health in Cleveland, Ohio, found that in large parts of the city, over 30 per cent of children tested suffered from lead poisoning.[141] In shrinking cities like Cleveland, the problem is made worse by the presence of vacant lots. At the time, Cleveland had over 1300 ha of vacant land, increasing the risk of dust carrying lead with it into the air. The strategy document adopted by the local council acknowledges that phytoremediation techniques are more commonly used for non-residential applications, such as landfills, fuel storage facilities and agricultural lands, and advises Cleveland residents to focus on planting out vacant lots with 'low-mow native turf grasses or other ground covers' to reduce the amount of airborne lead.[142]

Cleveland, Ohio: the American Steel and Wire Co. c. 1897–1924, a declared US Superfund site. (Photographer Unknown via Wikimedia Commons)

Site remediation.

Before

After

Obsolescences 143

Dr Barry Noller is overseeing a Lead Pathways Study being undertaken by the Centre for Mined Land Rehabilitation at the University of Queensland.[143] The study was commissioned by Xstrata, which mines zinc, lead, silver and copper in its Mount Isa mines in western Queensland. Mount Isa attracted media attention in 2010 over concerns that many children were being exposed to excessive amounts of lead from the mine.[144] State Government testing indicated generally elevated lead levels in Mount Isa children. In February 2011 local mother Sharlene Body lodged a AUD$1 million compensation claim against Xstrata, the Mount Isa City Council and the Queensland State Government on behalf of her son, who is alleged to have registered blood lead levels more than three times the World Health's Organization's recommended minimum. As part of its efforts to better inform the community, the local council posted information on its website and published a simple brochure. Parents were advised to cover any areas of bare earth in yards with lawn or planting, or as a last resort, concrete, to help minimise dust, and therefore airborne lead particles. It seemed to me to be a good opportunity to explore phytoremediation options.

Australian studies have shown the success of native species such as *Lomandra longifolia* and *Poa labillardieri* in trace metal accumulation of soil-borne lead.[145] My landscape imagination ran away, visualising the backyards, public parks and street edges of Mount Isa planted with robust native plants that not only suited the climate and increased amenity, but were working to reduce contamination and improve the health of residents. Quickly, Dr Noller relegated such thoughts to the realm of uneducated fancy. There are no known 'hyperaccumulator' plants for lead. It is not a contaminant that can be treated with phytoremediation, and is best treated by adding apatite calcium phosphate to modify the soil.[146]

Phytoremediation of a former service station in Ronnde, Denmark using Salix.
(Lcl via Wikimedia)

Research in the United States continues searching for plants that may be useful in treating lead-contaminated soil. One study achieved success in using *Brassica juncea* (Indian mustard, or mustard greens) to decrease lead concentrations in field tests in New Jersey and Massachusetts.[147] At the time of writing, the results of research led by Dr Samantha Langley-Turnbaugh into the use of *Spinacea oleracea* (spinach) to phytoextract lead were still awaiting publication.[148] Dr Langley-Turnbaugh has previously written about the potential of *Brassica juncea* and *Helianthus annuus* (sunflowers) to absorb lead in their roots and translocate it to shoots.[149] Those who scoffed at proposals to use oysters to clean New York's polluted waterways[150] will no doubt find much amusement in the idea of Popeye's favourite food ridding the land of contamination. Yet if the right species are available, phytoremediation is a valuable technique in shrinking cities. It is cost-effective, stabilises vacant land, and because it takes time to work, it fits in a system where quick turnaround of land for development is not an issue. Bioremediation remains no less logical, and far more cost-effective an approach than the one we currently use – scraping the affected soil from the site and transporting it miles away to be buried.

Remediation techniques reach their fullest potential when part of a broader ecosystem restoration process. Ecosystem restoration is the third benefit of green infrastructure, with positive, measurable effects including air cooling and filtration, improved soil health, erosion and stormwater control and functioning wildlife habitats. Like healthy natural ecosystems, restored urban ecosystems work best when they are diverse and well connected. With their abundance of vacant land, shrinking cities have enormous potential to create citywide, green, and park-like networks that stabilise vacant sites, help remediate contamination and restore ecosystems services. Air cooling and filtration is best achieved with significant tree cover. Countless studies have enumerated the benefits of increasing the number of trees in our cities and towns, and the results of these studies have then formed the basis for citywide policies in many parts of the world.[151]

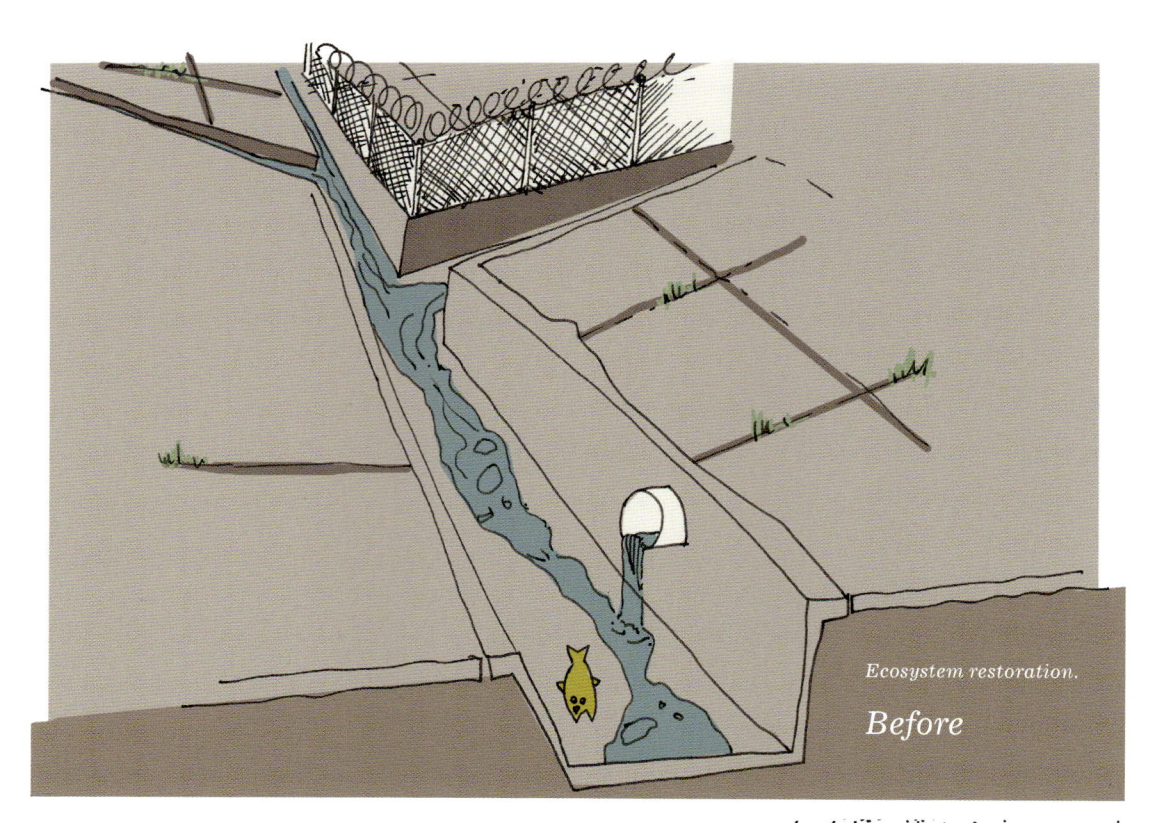

Ecosystem restoration.

Before

After

146 future park

Portland: raingarden in a residential street. Stormwater run-off enters through the broken kerb.

Soil structure is also improved by planting trees and other vegetation. Improved soil structure increases fertility, decreases erosion and improves water infiltration. Planting indigenous or endemic plant species helps crowd out weed species and provides habitat for local fauna. It also assists with slowing stormwater run-off. Using ecosystem restoration to manage urban stormwater and improve waterway health is a growing area of focus for city councils everywhere. A range of manmade or 'engineered' solutions can be used, including simple turf-lined swales, rain gardens, bioretention areas, constructed wetlands and 'daylighted' streams. These are implemented to supplement or replace existing traditional stormwater systems of underground pipes, kerb-and-channel and culverts.

Globally, Portland is revered as the epicentre of contemporary urban stormwater management, but it is certainly not alone in its uptake of water sensitive urban design ('WSUD').[152] Shrinking cities have a potential advantage. Large quantities of vacant land provide enormous flexibility and opportunity to create a genuine water sensitive green network, free of the many space and ownership constraints that accompany such projects in growing cities. Shrinking cities also have quantities of existing infrastructure, such as very wide road reserves, and expansive paved car parks, that are now surplus to requirement. Under a citywide WSUD scheme, roadside swales or bioretention systems could replace unused asphalt, and formerly impervious surfaces could be reclaimed.

Obsolescences **147**

The example presented in *Re-Imagining: A More Sustainable Cleveland* graphically demonstrates the potential of green infrastructure. In a series of simple, clear maps, the report shows that impervious surfaces cover most of the city, tree canopy is sparse, and nearly all creeks and streams were buried so that new development could occur.

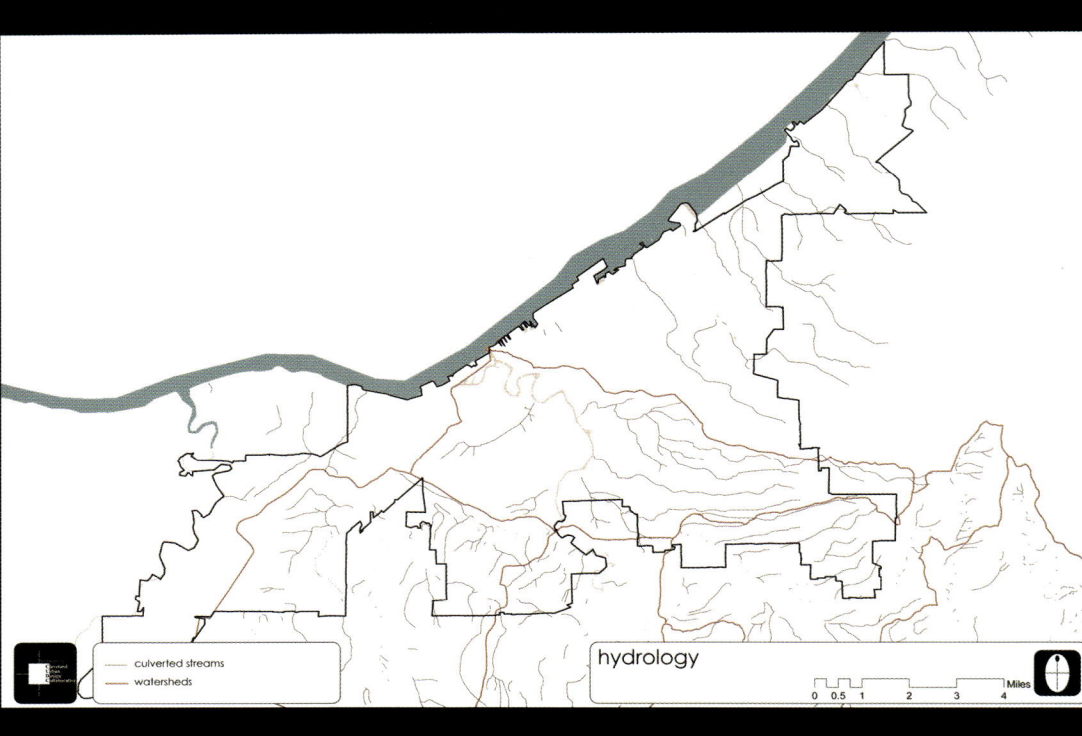

culverted streams
watersheds

hydrology

0 0.5 1 2 3 4 Miles

Three watersheds were then examined, and the current green infrastructure functions – air pollution removal, carbon storage and sequestration, and stormwater control – were modelled. The authors reviewed the total amount of vacant land in each study area that could be transformed to provide additional ecological services. The projected potential green infrastructure functions were then calculated, both by volume and financial value to the city.[153] Cleveland has since begun working with the Environmental Protection Agency on two WSUD schemes using vacant and brownfield sites. One is the size of a single lot, and will reduce local flooding in a residential neighbourhood. The other is a US$3 billion, 25-year plan where the city will build green infrastructure and WSUD on vacant lots, reducing stormwater run-off and combined sewer overflow into Lake Erie, and create additional community parkland.[154] By also providing parks and green space, WSUD gives something extra back to the community, something that traditional 'grey' infrastructure does not – as Tom Barrett, the Mayor of Milwaukee put it, 'You can't have a picnic... in a deep tunnel.'[155]

vacancy (parcel neocando)

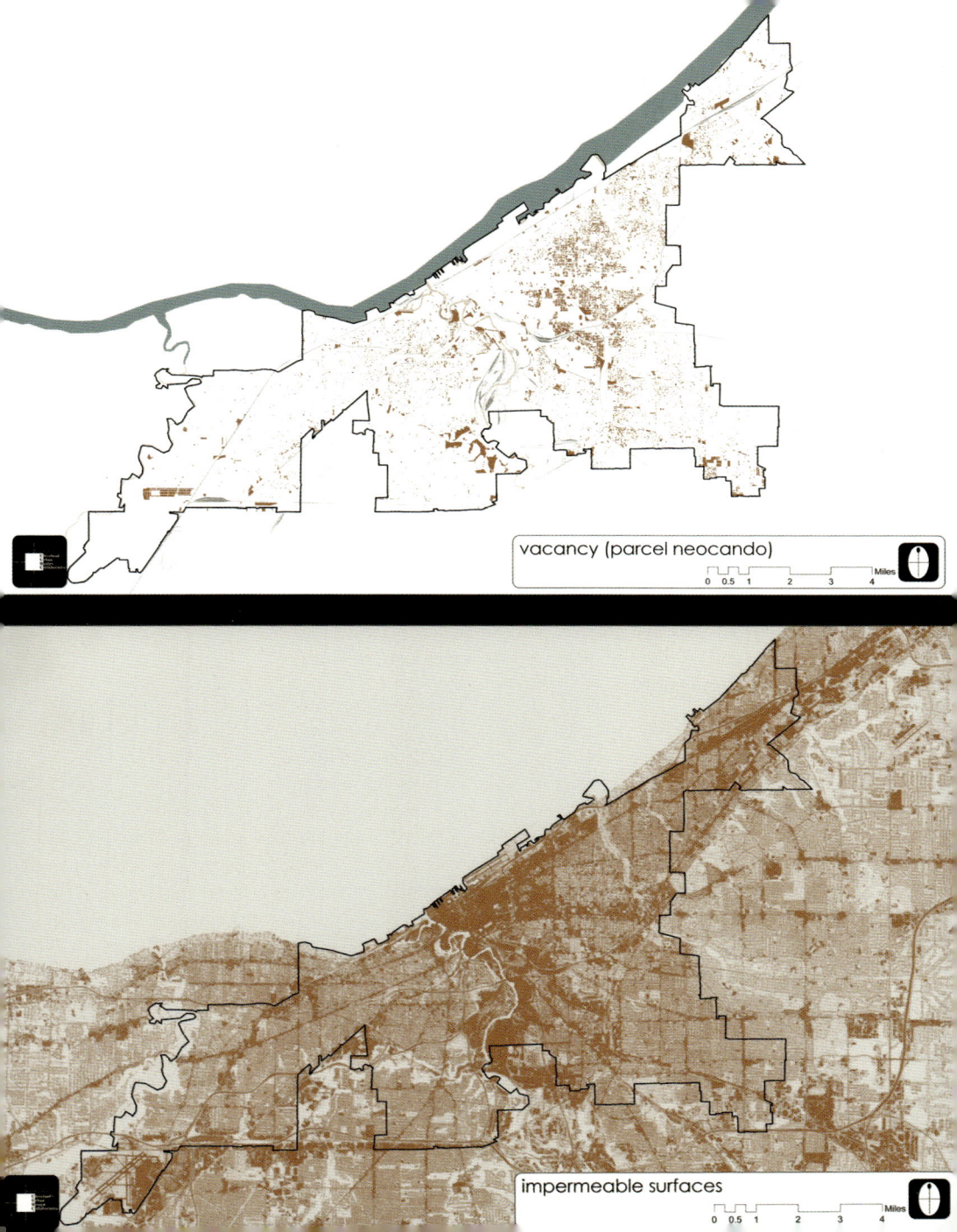

impermeable surfaces

A recent American report concluded that incorporating green infrastructure practices into urban stormwater management could 'reduce energy costs, diminish the impacts of flooding, improve public health, and reduce overall infrastructure costs'.[156] In Philadelphia, the city council considered two options for addressing its combined sewer overflow problem. The WSUD plan was chosen over a traditional 'pipes and pits' solution because it saved money and provided public health benefits. By working within the constraints of low budget and small quantities of vacant land, the city has chosen to implement a system that it estimates will prevent 1–2 deaths per year, prevent up to 250 lost work or school days annually, and reduce up to 140 deaths from excessive heat over the next 40 years.[157]

There is one thing that links all the different types of green infrastructure; they are all productive. If we consider our original definition of green infrastructure – 'the green spaces and water systems which intersperse, connect and provide vital life support for humans and other species within our urban environments' – it seems logical for shrinking cities to explore the many ways in which their vacant land can be used to make hot places cooler, poisoned places safer, waterways cleaner and communities healthier and more resilient. Beyond green infrastructure, vacant land can be put to even greater productive use through urban agriculture and decentralised energy generation.

There is one thing that links all the different types of green infrastructure; they are all productive.

Productive landscapes.

Before

Productive landscapes.

After

Urban agriculture is a concept it's been hard to avoid in recent times. If it's not been Brooklyn hipsters harvesting honey from rooftop beehives, it's Vietnamese immigrants swapping leafy greens in the community garden of a Melbourne housing complex. *National Geographic* magazine produced a photo essay on urban farming. Pioneering Berkeley chef Alice Waters, one of the early proponents of local, seasonal eating, started local schoolchildren looking after pint-sized vegie patches, so they would learn where the food they eat actually comes from. In a twist that had many outsiders thinking 'only in America', parents at some of the schools where children's gardens were created, successfully banned the next stage of the process – eating the food.[158]

In some cities urban agriculture is on the agenda because of concerns over 'food miles', the distance food travels to reach our tables. In other towns the concern is rising levels of childhood obesity and diabetes, due to a lack of exercise and diet high in processed foods. Still other cities are affected by food deserts, where neighbourhoods are served by several fast food restaurants, but lack a grocery store. And finally, many advocate urban agriculture as a response to contemporary agribusiness, genetic engineering, and the dominance of the food industry by multinational corporations.

1.
2.
3.
4.

1. Chicago: City Farm on the site of former highrise public housing. *(Linda via Wikimedia)*
2. Ghent, Belgium: community garden in the neighbourhood of Rabot-Blaisantvest. The garden is built in raised plots constructed over the concrete slab of a former factory. The slab was retained to cap contaminants. *(Lamiot via Wikimedia Commons)*
3. San Francisco: Hayes Valley Farm, a community-built farm on San Francisco's former Central freeway. After the Loma Prieta earthquake of 1989 damaged the on-ramp and off-ramp, the lot between Oak Street, Fell Street, Octavia and Laguna was vacant for 21 years before the City authorised the site for interim use. The farm is now a permaculture demonstration site. All the soil has been upcycled from the urban waste stream. The farm has used 764.5 cubic metres of horse manure, 1529 cubic metres of woodchips, and 45 359 kg of cardboard to cover over an acre of its 0.89 ha lot. *(Zoey Kroll via Wikimedia Commons)*
4. Cleveland: the 128th Street Community Garden. *(Jeff Schuler)*

Obsolescences

Philadephia: Glenwood Green Acres community garden. (Tony via Wikimedia Commons)

Shrinking cities are also pursuing urban agriculture, both in response to the concerns listed above, and as an economic opportunity. Community gardens are thriving in many shrinking cities and towns. As an indication, a Google search for 'community gardens Cleveland' delivers 20.5 million results. Searching for 'community gardens Philadelphia, St Louis, Buffalo, Detroit, or Kansas City' also produced greater than 20 million hits. This is by no means any sort of scientific study – it only shows how often particular combinations of words appear together in cyberspace. But it does tend to suggest that more people are talking, writing and sharing information about community gardens in those six cities than in, say, Saginaw (1.67 million hits), Flint (2.1 million), or Youngstown (just over 250 000 hits).

Cleveland's community garden scene is well established, with more than 150 gardens. Many of the gardens have their own equally thriving web pages and blogs, where members plan events, share information and provide links to other like-minded organisations.[159] Cleveland's council supports community gardens, as do local non-profit and community groups, and urban research groups from local universities.

Some believe the current community garden renaissance began in the 1970s, when school gardening programs were being phased out and several plots were offered to community groups. Around the same time the 'Summer Sprout' program began, initially as a way of encouraging community gardening to provide better nutrition for lower-income families. Under Summer Sprout, local residents could access an Ohio State University Extension Program, and receive training, support and even basic gardening supplies.[160] The city council also elected to use available federal Community Development Block Grant (CDBG) funding to promote and support community gardening.[161]

Philadelphia also has community gardens dating from the 1970s, although the movement may well have started from the founding of the Vacant Lot Cultivation Association in 1897. As well as its 'Clean & Green' program, the Pennsylvania Horticultural Society runs 'Garden Tenders' training, for local residents interested in starting or joining a community garden, and acknowledges exemplars as 'Keystone Gardens'. Community gardens exist throughout the city, in both gentrifying neighbourhoods (like Warrington Garden) and declining, shrinking ones (like the Montgomery Mini-Farm), with a 2008 study revealing that over US$ 4.9 million worth of summer vegetables had been produced by community gardeners in the previous year.

Together with her landscape students, Ann Whiston Spirn spent a lot of time observing and working closely with local community gardeners. In one project Spirn had students spend a weekend with a gardener so they weren't tempted to start designing in a vacuum. Even with this approach, and other meetings with the community, Spirn quotes numerous instances where student proposals (including her own) could have ended in failure. Spirn was also curious about the high incidence of vacant land, abandoned property and stormwater problems – flooded basements, burst pipes, sinkholes – in the Mill Creek neighbourhood. She discovered that Mill Creek was named after an actual creek, long since tamed in a concrete culvert. Frustrated with local council plans for the neighbourhood, she started the Mill Creek Project, bringing together primary school students, her own landscape students, parents, teachers and a local community garden group to develop 'a new curriculum organized around "The Urban Watershed" [and combining] learning, community development, and water resource management'.[162] Spirn looked to weave stories of green infrastructure and urban agriculture into the weft of Philadelphia's vacant land, and her time in the city coincided with other strategic initiatives.

As in Cleveland, a local university program, Penn State's *Urban Gardening*, and community driven support, PHS *Philadelphia Green*, were born during the period of deindustrialisation in the 1970s, to support community involvement in food production on vacant land. Despite Philadelphia Green becoming somewhat of a poster child for urban community garden programs, the number of productive gardens in the city has actually declined from 501 in 1996 to 226 in 2008.[163] This occurred for several reasons, including the ageing of the key gardeners themselves, and the near-complete removal of the city's community garden support mechanisms. In 1996 the USA Congress stopped funding for USDA community gardens, the university's Philadelphia Extension office stopped supporting community gardening, and the Pennsylvania Horticultural Society moved its philanthropic funding focus away from community gardening.[164] City planning policy changes followed, also reducing the ability of residents to grow food on small, vacant lots. In 2008, community gardens grew more produce than was sold at all the city's farmers' markets and urban farms combined, and much of that produce was then given away to people in need. The Philadelphia experience suggests that, with 'financial, material and technical support', productive gardens can provide not just food, but social and community benefits.[165]

Kansas City is another shrinking city where 'financial, material and technical support' for community gardening may be threatened. Community Block Development Grant funding has supported the non-profit Kansas City Community Gardens (KCCG) organisation for nearly 30 years. In 2012 council representatives voted on a recommendation to reduce KCCG's funding to zero. Later in the year KCCG received 'a grant of US$147 830 from the Health Care Foundation of Greater Kansas City (HCF) to help expand the agency's Schoolyard Gardens Program. It is 'currently assisting over 990 low-income families, 178 community groups and 105 schools to produce food from gardens'.[166] At the same time, KCCG is one of three organisations, alongside Cultivate Kansas City and Lincoln University's Cooperative Extension, that is jointly running 'Get Growing Kansas City'. With funding provided by the Health Care Foundation of Greater Kansas City, this is a two-year campaign to provide mini-grants enabling new community gardens to start, and existing ones to produce more food, particularly in areas of high need.[167] Along with Lincoln University, the University of Missouri also runs an extension program, in this case the 'Master Gardener' scheme, providing horticultural training for those who then volunteer to share the knowledge in their communities. Master Gardeners are involved in several productive community gardens in Kansas City.[168]

In January 2012, Kansas City's council adopted Resolution 120046 in support of improved food access for residents. Among the strategies and policy changes that council staff have been tasked to carry out is this one: 'Identify and adopt land use policies and zoning regulations that encourage citizens to produce as much food as possible at home, in community gardens and urban farms, as well as educate and empower citizens to responsibly grow and distribute food to Kansas City, Missouri, residents, institutions, and businesses'.[169] For a city with 5000 vacant hectares,[170] changing policy could unlock the productive potential of some of this land.

Urban agriculture is a key strategy to improve access to fresh fruit and vegetables for residents of the so-called 'Green Impact Zone' in central Kansas City. Data mapping completed in 2010 showed that nearly a quarter of all lots in the Zone are vacant or abandoned, with several blocks where more than 75 per cent of the lots are vacant, and 11 blocks with 50 to 75 per cent of lots vacant.[171]

Kansas City: the Green Impact Zone.

Obsolescences

The Zone itself is in a known food desert, relative to the greater Kansas City municipal area.[172] The Ivanhoe neighbourhood sits to the north of the Green Impact Zone, and is one of the most significantly challenged. In recent years the community formed a grassroots initiative, 'Grown in Ivanhoe', and was successful in obtaining funding from the Health Care Foundation of Greater Kansas City.[173] With this Grown in Ivanhoe will educate and support local residents to grow their own produce, and run a small growers' market through the summer months, among other pursuits. The University of Missouri Master Gardener extension program is involved, and links to Kansas City Community Gardens are dotted through the Resources page of the Grown in Ivanhoe website. Clicking one link takes viewers to the KCCG blog homepage, and its plea for supporters to fight the proposed funding reduction.

Other shrinking cities, perhaps encouraged by successes elsewhere, are starting to explore productive gardens. When the City of Saginaw sought community input into its 2011 Master Plan, 75.5 per cent of respondents thought the city should plan for community gardens, while 68.2 per cent thought it should plan for urban farming.[174] Targetting a consolidated area like the Saginaw Green Zone, or Kansas City Green Impact Zone potentially increases the chances of vacant land being put to productive use in a connected, multifunctional way. By working at a scale larger than the individual lot it may also enable market gardening to become an option.

While community gardeners produce food for their own consumption, market gardens are the next step up, cultivating produce for sale. Philadelphia's 'City Harvest' program is exploring citywide food production and distribution on a larger scale. City Harvest is a linked network of community gardeners, urban farmers, seedling nurseries, distributors of compost and mulch, volunteers who cook and food kitchens who feed an increasing constituency of needy people. Here, the use of vacant land is not the primary driver, but is one of the outcomes of the program.

A similar situation exists with 'Cultivate Kansas City', a non-profit organisation that aims to grow 'food, farms and community'. While its primary focus is on 'the urban farmer as a catalyst for growth and change', one of the four items in Cultivate Kansas City's Vision speaks of creating a city where 'unused spaces are turned to food producing farms and gardens'.[175] The model is an entrepreneurial one – Cultivate Kansas City operates a farm, a training farm and a greenmarket, sells at farmers' markets, provides educational information (including a soon-to-be-released 'How to Start an Urban Farm Guide' for Kansas City), runs an annual farms and gardens tour and advocates for supportive policy change.

Cleveland's Blue Pike Farm is an urban community supported agriculture (CSA) venture that has been selling fresh seasonal fruit, vegetables, honey and eggs to local subscribers since 2006. Owner Carl J. Skalak Jr built Blue Pike in a rundown inner city industrial area, on the site of a former factory. Fit, tanned and funny, Skalak was once videotaped for a blog while wearing a t-shirt emblazoned with 'Club 200 Jazzercise'. He proudly claims that Blue Pike's vegetables are so fresh they don't even realise they've been picked yet.[176] In 2010 the city announced a jointly sponsored, three-year, US$1.1 million Urban Agricultural Incubator Project that would convert 2.4 ha of vacant land into an urban farm where volunteering residents could receive training, and raise produce for sale to local schools, restaurants and farmers' markets.[177] The Incubator Project is located in one of the many 'food deserts' that have been mapped in the city. Just down the road, local residents Damian Forshe and David Hester are working with non-profit community development group Burten Bell Carr, and former-star-basketballer-turned-urban-agriculture-guru Will Allen, to create the Urban Agriculture Innovation Zone on 10.5 ha of mostly vacant land. Allen runs 'Growing Power', an urban farm/training/retail centre in downtown Milwaukee, and it is hoped that a Cleveland version will anchor the Innovation Zone.[178]

Growing Power's goal, 'to grow food, to grow minds, and to grow community' is similar to that of Cultivate Kansas City. Will Allen was the son of a sharecropper who became a pro-basketball player. He retired to Milwaukee, his wife's hometown, and location of her family's farm. Bored after trying a corporate career, he took over the farm and bought a rundown garden centre where he could sell his produce. The centre stood on the last remaining site zoned for agriculture in the city – his commitment to urban agriculture began as he realised he could grow and sell food he had produced himself, and do so within an area deprived of fresh produce. Today Growing Power has farms in Wisconsin and Illinois, and satellite training sites in five other states. It distributes food through a farmers' cooperative, runs educational and training programs and is active in policy debate around urban agriculture. It is involved in outreach projects as diverse as the Growers of Peace Community Garden in Milwaukee, which is helping the community produce fresh produce on a site contaminated with high lead levels. In 2010 Will Allen was invited to help Michelle Obama launch the 'Let's Move' program, targeting childhood obesity, and the same year was included in *Time* magazine's list of '100 Most Influential People in the World'.[179]

Growing Power's main facility in Milwaukee is powered by solar energy to help offset its energy consumption. Along with urban agriculture, decentralised energy generation is the second form of productive landscape possible on vacant and abandoned land in shrinking cities.

Decentralised energy production.
Before

After

In the same way that cities globally are pursuing urban agriculture to provide food security, so too are they exploring decentralised energy generation as a way of ensuring long-term energy security. In Denmark, nearly 55 per cent of the country's total power comes from decentralised sources. The global average is just over 10 per cent, and in Australia, decentralised sources provide barely 5 per cent of the nation's power. Electricity generation produces 36 per cent of Australia's greenhouse gas emissions. In the five years to 2015, over AUD$45 billion will be spent on Australia's electricity infrastructure. Traditional centralised electricity systems are planned and designed to meet peak demand needs, such as summer heatwaves. Building peak demand systems is expensive, and costs are passed on to consumers. Advocates believe that if peak energy demand could be flattened by decentralising supply, power supply would become greener, and potentially cheaper.[180]

There are many technologies available for decentralised energy production. Most contemporary discussions centre on geothermal energy, wind turbines, solar power and biofuel production. Decentralised energy was briefly considered in *Reimagining A More Sustainable Cleveland*. Basic guidelines for using the four alternative methods were outlined, but the report recommended much more detailed study be given to individual sites or proposals in light of the city's very dispersed vacant land distribution.[181]

More interest is being generated by the prospect of decentralised energy forming part of a new, green, innovation-based economy in American shrinking cities. At an event in early 2012, Bruce Katz, Founding Director of the Brookings Institution Metropolitan Policy Program, outlined Buffalo's potential in this arena: 'Despite being the 50th largest metro, you are the 37th largest clean economy jobs center in the United States – with 14,500 clean jobs in 2010. Your top sectors are waste-to energy, hydropower, geothermal, fuel cells, and renewable energy. On intensity clean jobs – the share that clean jobs comprise of total metro employment – you also perform better than the U.S. and the top 100 metro average with 2.7 percent of your total jobs in the clean economy – compared to 2.0 percent for the U.S. and 1.9 percent for the top 100 metros.'[182] Katz urged the city to build on a twin platform of 'clean jobs' and an innovative manufacturing legacy.

Writer Catherine Tumber also encourages shrinking cities, in particular America's small, former industrial cities, to consider the opportunities provided by the post-carbon economy. Writing in *Small, Gritty and Green* she outlines how previous centres of specialised manufacturing are making gearboxes for wind turbines, riverfront towns are rediscovering small-scale hydro power and hydrokinetics and agricultural regions are exploring biofuel and biomass.

Tumber believes smaller cities have the 'land in abundance' to generate low carbon electricity, and that 'Youngstown and other smaller industrial cities' brightest economic prospects belong with renewables. Renewable energy, after all, is permanent… and requires stable places to steward its harvesting'.[183] It remains to be seen how many shrinking cities share that view, and then lobby for state and federal-level policy in support.

So far, all of the above discussion has focused on what shrinking cities can *do* with their vacant and abandoned land. The ultimate result for many places could be a citywide green network, that stabilises sites, provides visual amenity, is available for community use, remediates contamination, restores ecosystem services, and is sustainably productive. The missing piece of the puzzle is how shrinking cities can *manage* that land for the long term. Many of the cities and states utilise land banks, land trusts, or a hybrid of both. As described by the Virginia Tech Shrinking Cities Studio, 'Land banks are an important public policy tool for shrinking cities. They are allowed to acquire, assemble, temporarily manage, and dispose of vacant land for the purpose of stabilizing neighborhoods and encouraging the re-use or redevelopment of the property.'[184] In the United States, Ohio's Cuyahoga County Land Bank seeks out, acquires and manages vacant property until strategic redevelopment can occur. The land bank demolishes derelict buildings and supports a range of vacant land reuses, including beautification, acquisition by private homeowners and urban agriculture.[185] In Michigan the Genesee County Land Bank operates in a similar way. It runs 10 programs: Planning and Outreach, Brownfield Redevelopment, Development, Adopt-a-Lot, Clean and Green, Demolition, Housing Renovation, Sales, Side Lot Transfer and Foreclosure Prevention. All are aimed at encouraging the 're-use of more than 4,000 residential, commercial and industrial properties that it has acquired through the tax foreclosure process'.[186] The Kalamazoo County Land Bank (KCLB) was also formed 'to create vibrant communities through the elimination of blighted properties, creation of affordable housing opportunities, and the stabilization of property values'. Residents can buy a vacant Land Bank lot next to their own property for US$20. KCLB encourages residents to make use of Land Bank land for community garden or park use. The Land Bank also builds or renovates homes in six inner-city suburbs, and sells them at low cost. In 2010 the Kalamazoo County Land Bank was awarded US$15 million in federal funding, and to date has bought 65 properties and 100 vacant lots. According to its Priorities and Policies, the use of Land Bank land for 'Green Space' is last on a list of nine.[187] Number 1 on the list is 'Return of the property to productive tax-paying status'.

This reflects what many see as a flaw in neighbourhood transformation initiatives, and consequently the land banking system, despite the evidence that 'green space' *is and can be* a highly productive urban land use, albeit a non-taxpaying one. University of Pennsylvania researchers believe that their findings in Philadelphia contradict the widely held assumption that community gardens are merely a short-term land use – little more than temporary stabilisation projects that make vacant lots look nice until a 'real' development use comes along. Their 2008 Harvest Report found that while many gardens were no longer used, many also persisted. These included:

> 'most of the larger gardens in the city, whose larger number of plots accommodate the succession of gardeners more easily than the smaller gardens. One large garden we visited, the Wissinoming garden at North Hills Cemetery on the edge of Frankford, has been continuously cultivated since World War Two, when it was established as a Victory Garden. Many others, including most of the largest gardens in the city, have been active for twenty-five, thirty, or more years. Small squatter gardens are indeed temporary land uses. But we submit that the false view of community gardens in general as 'temporary land uses' is an inadequate excuse for city government not to develop a clear land policy that integrates community gardens into zoning, city and neighbourhood planning, and community development.'[188]

Land banks in American shrinking cities focus on short-term stabilisation before commercial redevelopment. They use federal and state funding to purchase properties and vacant land through a tax foreclosure process. When they work well land banks unlock land and properties owned by remote, speculating investors, who have bought at low rates and then 'sit' on their purchases until the market improves. They make no investment in either the property or the city where it is located, exacerbating decline and decay. Because there is a commercial focus there can also be a tendency for land banks to favour lot amalgamation as a way of maximising the return-on-investment. On the ground, problems with this model occur when existing community uses are ignored. This has been documented in Philadelphia, where several productive community gardens were bulldozed by land banks looking to consolidate land, which in some cases was then left to sit vacant when no development occurred.

According to Michael Messner, the very economic system on which land banking is based needs a radical rethink. Messner is the founder of Red Fields to Green Fields (RFGF), a research initiative analysing the effects of 'acquiring financially distressed properties (real estate "in the red") in major US cities, and converting them into green space: public parks and adjacent land "banked" for future sustainable development'.

Messner strongly believes that recent policies, such as the US Government purchase of $1.5 billion worth of mortgages, protects bad assets instead of trying to eliminate them. He proposes instead that the federal government should remove its capital from real estate, and that a $200 billion land bank be created 'to help finance the acquisition of excess commercial properties and convert them into parks and raw land held for future development'. This would enable the Federal Reserve to purchase Land Backed Securities, rather than the current Mortgage Backed Securities, as well as stabilising property values and creating market liquidity. The Red Fields to Green Fields project is exploring what would be needed in 12 cities to eliminate 'underperforming and underutilized property, [and] put people to work creating parks on some of the land and land bank the remainder until the economy recovers', an economy which Messner strongly believes will be 'new, Internet-based, [and] asset-light'.

The focus on assets is telling. The RFGF proposal is based on the belief that the quantity of assets does not matter, it's the utilisation of those assets that creates wealth. Messner offers the experience of the US railroad industry to illustrate: in the last 60 years 55 per cent of rail track has been eliminated in America, yet rail tonnage handled has increased more than five times, and the railroads have never been more efficient nor profitable. What this telling doesn't account for, of course, are the many things that have also been lost in the pursuit of better asset utilisation – the loss of rail service and closure of local stations has contributed to the shrinking of cities, towns and regions worldwide. While the 'belt' of abandoned rail lines circling inner Atlanta is undeniably an asset for the city today, anyone who has read the writings of John Stilgoe, among others, would pause to consider 'for whom' did the use of those rail lines once create wealth, and for whom does their closure?

Many Red Fields to Green Fields investigations focus on vacant brownfields as 'catalyst' sites. The Cleveland study cites river and lakefront parkland opportunities such as the Towpath Trail Extension and the Cleveland Rowing Foundation extension, and considers the impact of a US$1 billion investment.[189] This is a considerably different scale of investment from the US$4280 estimated for a 'thin parcel connection' in Cleveland's *Vacant Land Re-Use Pattern Book*,[190] but each also assumes a very different economic starting point.

The use of catalyst projects to develop vacant land and stimulate economic development is a much-debated strategy.

Economists like Edward Glaeser point to the failure of the so-called 'urban renewal' projects in the 1970s to deliver any actual benefit or improved opportunies to citizens most in need. Detroit's People Mover is one of his favourite examples. Built in the 1987 for more than US$2000 million, the monorail gave politicians great photo opportunities to demonstrate their success in attracting investment to the city. Unfortunately, it also requires around US$8.5 million in subsidies each year to continue operating, costs that could easily have been used to deliver more effective public transport solutions on the city's less-congested streets. Glaeser calls this the 'Edifice Error': 'the tendency to think that a city can build itself out of a decline'.[191]

Glaeser asserts that the cities that survive do so because they retain the key characteristic that has always allowed cities to survive and thrive – diversity.

Detroit: the People Mover entering Bricktown Station above an empty street and footpath. (Mikerussell via The English language Wikipedia)

Obsolescences **165**

New York: President Jimmy Carter touring the Bronx, 1977. (Photographer Unknown via Wikimedia Commons)

New York in the 1970s was bankrupt, corrupt and crime-ridden. It survived, and thrived, by embracing diversity; no longer reliant solely on its previously world-leading position in the garment trade, New York embraced financial systems. Pittsburgh survived the nearly overnight end of its industrial economy because it had embraced medicine and higher education, not just because it built parks. Manchester also embraced education and built on its unique music scene. Detroit has suffered because it put all its eggs in the one basket. While the motor industry started as a result of diversity, with small innovators in close proximity, it quickly became a victim of its own success. Mechanisation provided well-paying jobs for thousands of unskilled workers, but as the city shifted focus to serve the big cash cow that was the 'Big Three', it created an environment without diversity and the inbuilt resilience that would be needed to face a car-less future.

Joseph Schilling, one of the leading shrinking cities scholars, suggests an alternative to both the traditional and RFGF land bank models. He has advocated that land banks should incorporate features of land trusts, 'local, regional, statewide, or national organizations that protect lands with natural, ecological, recreational, scenic, historic, or productive value… managing lands for community uses in perpetuity'.[192] For many years he has promoted the idea of a 'Living Laboratory' process focusing on Buffalo, and based on the German IBA model as used in the Emscher Valley, Dessau and Lower Lausitz.

Creativity (and motivation) is high when the situation is 'do-or-die'...

In Australia, growing attention is being paid to post-mining futures in resource-dependent regions. Central Queensland University runs a sustainable regional development program focused on the coal-rich Bowen Basin area. Its studies have included developing a preferred future for Clermont, in close association with council, community groups, commerce and industry. Clermont was established as a gold town, and is now facing the closure of one coal mine and the opening of another. The community faces a complex and interconnected range of future challenges and opportunities that include planning for the medium-term challenges that will accompany the growth and operation of the new mine, and the long-term challenges of its eventual closure.[193] The Institute for Sustainable Regional Development is also exploring the option of clean technology as a viable, long-term regional development option for the Bowen Basin post-carbon. Similarly, the Office of Urban Transformations at RMIT University convened a 2012 symposium, research project and international design competition to 'propose, and demonstrate, a range of design strategies considered through a range of time frames... for transiting cities, such as Latrobe City in South East Victoria that is shifting to a low carbon future'.[194]

As they have throughout history, some cities and towns will continue to shrink. Vacant land will continue to be a defining feature of those cities and towns. While the economic rationalist might try to write these cities off as the 'collateral damage' of globalisation and megaregional growth, the sheer numbers of people involved demand that we understand and respond. In the United States alone between 7.4 and 45 million people live in declining cities. It is simply impossible that they all remain there because they lack the ability to move to somewhere better. Millions of people in Saginaw, Venice, Hakodate and Dessau are as passionate about their hometowns as those who live in expanding cities. They know that dealing with obsolescence requires creative approaches to a range of issues, from federal policy to financing and public engagement.

Creativity (and motivation) is high when the situation is 'do-or-die', making it easier to break down preconceived ideas and see the same piece of property, or even the same city, in a new light.

Timing is also critical: enough time must be spent in understanding the size, scale and nature of the problem to provide meaningful and specific solutions, but interventions, if they are to occur, must happen soon enough to bolster the community and demonstrate progress. We all have a role to play: not just in using vacant land to build 'green space', but in ensuring that parks, green infrastructure and productive landscape elements are recognised at the policy level as one of the key ingredients in addressing urban obsolescence and creating resilient and diverse cities.

03 Co-locations

Co-locations

We Australians like our cities neat and ordered – 'roads, rates and rubbish' isn't one of our favourite local government election clichés for nothing.

The perceived chaos of New York or Shanghai might be fine for holidays, but 'back home' the cities where we live have a place for everything and everything in its place. This preference for order is so much a part of the way we live that we don't even think about it, let alone question it. We didn't always live like this, or even think like this, but the way we've become urban dwellers has led us inexorably down the path to neatness and, eventually, to single and separate land uses in our cities.

When people live in isolation they need to be self-reliant. This is the same whether the people in question are families living on remote cattle stations the size of small European countries in western Queensland, or their counterparts on the Salisbury Plain, 5000 years ago before they got together with their mates over a few meads one Sunday afternoon and decided it might be fun to haul some gigantic stones into a circle so that the sun might shine through in a particular way at a particular time of day, at a particular time of the year. Or not. And lucky for us they did it then, too. If they'd had their garden renovation idea now it would never have got off the ground, being singularly impossible to complete within the allocated weekend afternoon timeframe mandated today by television programs as the acceptable maximum number of hours to be invested in any enterprise.

Those living in isolation were, and still are, responsible for sourcing their own food, finding enough water to drink, storing a fuel source for winter and disposing of the waste generated by the household. To enable this to happen the space around the dwelling had to be highly functional and serve multiple uses. Water was collected locally and used to irrigate edible plants for consumption by both people and animals. Domestic animals provided energy to work the land, and a range of edible or otherwise useful by-products, such as fur and leather. Trees provided building materials, food and fuel. Household waste was added to that from animals and used to improve the fertility of the soil. This approach, what we now call 'self-sufficiency' and teach to earnest, hemp-clad men and women in night courses, continued to work reasonably well even when previously independent households came together to form small groups or communities.

As more and more of us moved closer and closer together, we let go of some of these old habits. Some of them we brought with us though, with unintended consequences. Emptying the chamber-pot just outside was always a reasonable option when 'just outside' comprised an actual yard, with permeable soil, and possibly some organic matter such as plants or vegetables that might conceivably benefit from a daily dousing in urine. Emptying the chamber-pot 'just outside' when you live in a five-storey walk-up tenement building housing 80 people, with a similar building on either side, and more of the same all lined up cheek-by-jowl along a narrow cobbled street, is a very different prospect indeed, and not a strategy to land one's metropolis a place in *Monocle* magazine's Top 20 Most Liveable Cities.

The Ancient Romans may have gone about clad only in loosely knotted bedsheets but they were certainly on to something with reticulated sewerage systems. Proving ourselves capable of Gen Y behaviour centuries earlier than the Sunday papers would have us believe, we in the West instead chose to ignore the wise counsel and technical sophistication of our Roman brethren for not just a few years but several centuries, until the Industrial Revolution got our cities into such a state that we were left with no option but to sort things out. It was at this point that the concept of 'waste' as a private matter requiring public management started to emerge.

The centralised collection and treatment of a city's worth of waste was difficult to conceive and implement. Most Western cities relied on regular visits from the night-soil van until well into the twentieth century. Brisbane, Australia's third largest city, remained largely unsewered until the 1970s.[195] Changing this was one of Lord Mayor Clem Jones' most quoted legacies.[196]

Brisbane: outhouses behind Housing Commission houses in Norman Park, 1950. (Photographer Unknown via State Library of Queensland)

Co-locations

The provision of centralised power and energy was slightly easier, and with some precedent: waterwheels were a common and simple source of power generation even in small riverside communities. Perhaps because new technologies such as gas lighting could be easily retrofitted into existing streets, cities readily embraced the pleasures of night lighting. The push for reticulated drinking water gained momentum as a public health issue. In his famous study, physician John Snow traced the entire London cholera epidemic of 1854 to contaminated water wells.[197] The village well is so well caricatured as the source of idle gossip that it is easy to forget that its first purpose was as a piece of vital community infrastructure, providing a common public resource, and lessening the burden on individual families to find and maintain their own water supply. Once the provision of safe drinking water was embraced as a worthy cause, prodigious engineering effort was deployed to achieve this end – an ever-increasing skein of locks, dams, tunnels, filters, pumps and plants untangled itself across the landscape. As well as being produced, municipal water supplies had to be stored. The original water storage reservoirs were rivers, streams and lakes, with later models often nothing more than upscaled versions of the same. Water was stored in dams, specially excavated storage lakes, or constructed tanks, and often served an ornamental purpose as well.

Publicly accessible parks also came to be seen as required pieces of public infrastructure, as necessary for 'improving' the lives, minds and bodies of citizens as clean water, fresh air and sunshine. During the eighteenth and nineteenth centuries many of the desired qualities of public parks were also deemed relevant for cemeteries. Accordingly, what had previously been modest and sombre additions to church grounds were re-imagined as gardens, with meandering walks, attractively assembled collections of trees and plants, and ornamental mausoleums and grave ornamentations. Later lawn cemeteries also employed parkland design principles, in this case in pursuit of restful vistas, gently undulating terrain and places of peaceful, well ordered reflection.

Many older cemeteries now find themselves with new challenges. They have reached capacity and are no longer welcoming new 'residents'. Many of their oldest residents receive few or no visitors, descendants having long since grown up and moved on, leaving their collective eternal slumber interrupted only by the infrequent appearance of eager and persistent amateur genealogists. Despite this peaceable state, there is still a requirement for ongoing maintenance, an increasingly costly affair in the West, where a single blade of grass cannot be trimmed without requiring at least three types of fuel-guzzling machines, and where workplace health and safety laws are so stringent that a groundskeeper must wear personal protective equipment to climb into his own head and change his mind.

Cemetery and park.

Before

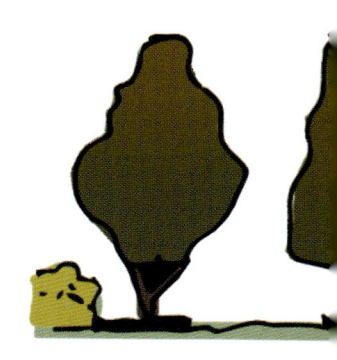

After

On the other hand, old cemeteries also offer many positives. The picturesque approach to their original layout means that many now possess significant collections of mature trees. Path layout has usually been well considered, enabling easy access to all parts of the grounds. City growth often means that formerly isolated cemeteries are now in closer proximity to residents, providing the opportunity to utilise their assets in a new way and for new generations. Some cemeteries have already started to realise their new potential, and are working in concert with local authorities to promote themselves as an alternative to traditional city parks.

Oakland Cemetery in Atlanta, Georgia provides one example of a cemetery that is very much concerned with looking after the long-term prospects of its residents by maintaining its relevance for constituents who are very much alive. Oakland is the first and only city cemetery in Atlanta, a fact illustrated by the diversity of its population. The Black section is the final resting place for many of the city's notable African-American businessmen, educators and community leaders, including Maynard Holbrook Jackson Jr who in 1973 was elected mayor of Atlanta, becoming the first African American to serve as chief executive of a major southern city. To the north-east of the Black section is the 19.4 ha Potters Field. Archaeological research in this part of the cemetery has also found evidence of a prehistoric Indian site dating from around 4500 BC. Approximately 6900 soldiers are interred in Oakland's Confederate sections, demonstrating the ongoing importance of the cemetery as an historic southern site, while a collection of golf balls placed as tributes at the base of golf legend Robert 'Bobby' Jones' headstone reflect a different kind of pilgrimage and memorial. Visitors to Oakland Cemetery should also make a point of visiting the grave of Thrasher Kyle, 1841–1907, middle child and brother to Nepoleon and Columbus, if only to delight in the sheer marvellous euphony of such a name.

Those wandering the tree-lined walks or arriving at the visitor information centre in late September will find staff readying Oakland for its annual Halloween festivities. In 2011 guided evening tours were available for three nights leading up to the end of the month. One of the local businesses providing corporate support for the event is Six Feet Under, a three-storey fish restaurant and pub located across the street from the cemetery, and doing a roaring lunchtime trade even on a typical midweek day. While we might assume that cemeteries quietly attract a small fan base of weirdos and disaffected teens for Halloween festivities, Oakland actively promotes itself to the whole community as a destination. One of the volunteers revealed that sometimes relatives of the residents complain about the lack of respect shown by such goings-on. This doughty Southern lady then explained, with iron resolve wrapped in silken manners, how maintaining the cemetery and ensuring it remains a vital and valued part of the community is the best way of showing respect to those generations who have gone before.

The community appears to be heeding the message. Along with walkers and joggers, a steady stream of cyclists use the wide and traffic-free walks to move from one part of their city to another. Less expected are the picnickers; couples, groups of friends, and families arriving with lunches to enjoy in the shade of the trees, beside a favourite garden or statue. Also glimpsed; a young man engrossed in a book, sitting beneath an enormous oak tree. Careful perusal of the

Atlanta: Oakland Cemetery.

location maps dotted across the cemetery reveals, however, that recreational use of Oakland is not such a new invention after all. It doesn't look like much today, a rectangular block of stone with a cube of the same on top, but the last remaining carriage step on the site is a reminder of the times when well-heeled ladies would travel from their homes and alight for a social stroll through the grounds. As earlier chapters have shown, Atlanta has embarked on the BeltLine, a massive city-shaping project of housing and employment renewal, transit and public parkland centred on its inner-city ring of disused railroad corridors. While BeltLine park projects are underway, Oakland Cemetery is already demonstrating how different parts of the city can be re-imagined as public parks.

All images this spread – Atlanta: Oakland Cemetery.

The last remaining carriage step

Co-locations

On the other side of the Atlantic, Abney Park Cemetery is as physically enmeshed in its community as it's possible for a place to be. The damp may have kept the picnickers away, but on a Monday morning scores of dogs take advantage of this mini-forest directly off the Stoke Newington High Street to catch up with friends, as their humans stand around having the kinds of conversations that require shoulders to be slightly hunched and hands firmly jammed into mackintosh pockets. It's a scene that might have looked familiar to Abney Park visitors a century-and-a-half ago, although the sight of grown adults deliberately stopping to collect dog poo in small bags carried on the person in anticipation of precisely that use may have given them pause for thought.

In the seventeenth century Stoke Newington was still part of London's pastoral and woodland fringe. The land on which Abney Park Cemetery now sits was owned by St Paul's Cathedral, and eventually occupied by two neighbouring estates, Fleetwood, laid out in the 1630s, and Abney House Estate, which followed in 1700. Both properties were home, at different times, to Dr Isaac Watts, recognised by authorities in the matter as the 'father of hymnology'. Although modern convention generally stipulates use of only the first two verses of his greatest hit, it is reported that Her Majesty the Queen delivered all five verses of 'O God our help in ages past' at a 2007 memorial ceremony, without referring once to her order of service. As one whose right hand is in a great deal of demand for waving at her subjects, Her Majesty would no doubt be distressed to learn that Dr Watts' right hand (or at least a carved representation thereof) lies on the ground at Abney Park today, separated by 5 m or more from its body, which surveys the cemetery from atop a handsome pillar.

At the base of Dr Watts' statue, among the overgrown shrubs and creepers is a tiny stone angel, hands joined in prayer, but headless. Metres away is the ruinous shell of the Abney Park Chapel. Sadly, Dr Watts' missing hand, the angel's head and the chapel are but the iceberg tip of countless examples of neglect that have befallen Abney Park Cemetery since its heyday as 'the most ornamental garden cemetery in the vicinity of London', and the preferred place of memorial for London's community of dissenters.

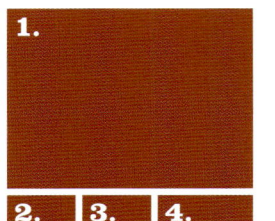

All images this spread – Abney Park Cemetery.
1. The hand of Isaac Watts.
2. The tomb of Frank Bostock, lion tamer, and the 'Animal King' of Abney Park.
3. Run-down building bordering the cemetery.
4. The dogs of Abney Park.

178 future park

Co-locations

Abney Park Cemetery: angel.

They were drawn to Abney Park because in 1840 its founders laid out the grounds to provide a series of educational walks based around an A–Z arboretum, as well as a Wesleyan training college. And although the ground was never consecrated, or designated by Act of Parliament, they also established the first non-denominational garden cemetery in Britain. Architectural design details, including the 'Egyptian Revival' entranceway, deliberately emphasised the non-denominational approach by adopting non-traditional iconographies of faith. Among the constellation of prominent nonconformists now resting in peace at Abney Park are Salvation Army founders William and Catherine Booth, and influential nineteenth century abolitionists including the Rev. James Sherman, who wrote the introduction to *Uncle Tom's Cabin*; and Dr Christopher Newman Hall, bishop, chartist and supporter of Abraham Lincoln and his anti-slavery campaign. Their cemetery neighbours, and nonconformists in a different way, were stars of the London Music Hall such as Albert Chevalier, whose wonderful 'My Old Dutch' has not, unfortunately, been performed in public by the Queen, and his father-in-law George Leybourne, aka 'Champagne Charlie'. The melody for this rousing endorsement of excessive drinking was later adopted by the pro-temperance Salvation Army and used for one of their hymns, as were many popular pub songs. A century later the singer Amy Winehouse, perhaps sensing a kindred spirit, chose Champagne Charlie's final resting place as the setting for her 'Back to Black' video. Australians might be pleased to visit the grave of Frank Bostock, the 'Animal King' of Abney Park. Famous as a lion tamer and performer, Bostock also reportedly introduced the boxing kangaroo to the stage.

Today the London Borough of Hackney owns Abney Park Cemetery. It was bought for a nominal sum following the insolvency of the commercial cemetery operator who originally bought the Park from its founding trust in the 1880s. The fortunes of Hackney and Abney Park follow a similar timeline. Both boomed and grew in the late 1800s and started declining after World War I. Both reached a low point in the late twentieth century, with the cemetery closing in the 1970s and the borough's population declining by 40 per cent to 160 000 in the early 1990s. Today it's hard to imagine an urban green space and its surrounding local authority area with more opportunities to realise and more challenges to overcome, than Abney Park Cemetery and the Borough of Hackney.

Images 1. 2. & 3. –
Abney Park Cemetery.
1. A parkland hidden in full sight.
2. New markers commemorate the early years as an arboretum.
3. The Egyptian Revival entranceway – now kept company by borough rubbish bins.
4. Stoke Newington High Street – Abney Park's front door.

While an educational intent deliberately underpinned the work of Abney Park's founders, Hackney today has a higher proportion of residents without qualifications than the rest of London and indeed Britain.

Abney Park Cemetery: the Chapel.

Despite all the hard work of the Booths and their Army, the Borough today also has a higher proportion of social housing than London taken as a whole. Although bordering the 2012 Olympic Games redevelopment area in the Lower Lea Valley, all 10 Borough wards remain in the top 10 per cent of the most deprived nationally. And although green space accounts for nearly 17 per cent of the total area of the Borough, it continues to measure poorly against national indicators for air and water quality, and the quality and distribution of parks and open space vary markedly.

The introduction to *Hackney's Sustainable Community Strategy 2008–2018* identifies recent council successes, including 'reducing infant mortality' and having 'nearly two-thirds of council homes meet the "decent" standard, compared to only a quarter five years ago'. How does a derelict yet nationally significant, heritage-listed cemetery, with citywide environmental habitat value, and virtually no funding, contribute positively to a 'sustainable community'? As well as deprivation, the Borough also has a higher proportion of residents qualified to degree level and above than London or Britain. Do they hold the key to the future of Abney Park Cemetery? Concentrations of wealth have helped other run-down parks survive, the most famous example being the Central Park Conservancy, funded largely by well-heeled neighbours, which worked in parallel with the City of New York to restore, repair and reclaim the park for all to enjoy. The distribution of wealth and education in Hackney has, however, been fairly equal across all wards. Whether this continues post-Olympics is yet to be seen. Existing public parks constitute only 23 of 255 open spaces in Hackney, with cemeteries contributing 4.4 per cent of the total open space in the Borough.[198] The Council, whether consciously or not, has embraced the philosophies of the Abney Park dissenters, actively prioritising the reduction in poverty, increase in health, education and employment, and provision of health-giving green space. Surely the spirit of Abney Park's progressive residents will ensure their final resting place plays a meaningful role in the life of the community.

As described above, Hackney is neighboured to the east by the Lower Lea Valley, site of the 2012 Olympic Games, and the largest urban regeneration area in the capital. Among the many roles it has played in the development of the city, the Lea River has been a strategic link in London's water supply chain. In the early seventeenth century the Lea was dramatically diverted into the 'New River', a series of deep channels and locks created to separate the city's drinking water supply from the toxic soup of pollutants generated by the industrial powerhouses downstream. Since 1964 the New River flow has stopped in Stoke Newington, at the East and West reservoirs, built in 1833 less than 1 km from Abney Park Cemetery.

The reservoirs were built on the site of an old brickworks, and were reinforced with stone from the demolished old London Bridge. Filter beds were planned alongside, together with a pumping station that was disguised as a baronial Scottish castle after nineteenth century NIMBYs (not-in-my-backyarders) complained about the presence of an industrial facility in the neighbourhood. Together the reservoirs constitute 17 ha of open water, and are recognised today as one of the closest open freshwater habitats to central London. Despite this, access to the precinct is limited, providing local residents little opportunity to enjoy the 'secret garden' described by then-local MP Diane Abbott in a parliamentary debate about the proposed sale of the reservoirs. Only the West Reservoir and former pump station remain in use – planning approval was granted in 1994 for it to be renovated as a climbing centre – while the reservoir operates as a leisure facility.

The attractions of the reservoir cannot be well appreciated from many of the surrounding streets. Woodberry Grove divides the two water bodies, and four-strand barbed wire atop a precast concrete fence then separates pedestrians from the East Reservoir. The New River footpath to the north of the basins provides views in, while a new platform built at the far eastern edge of this reservoir now provides panoramic views of the reservoirs and the London skyline beyond. Like nearby Abney Park Cemetery, the Stoke Newington East and West reservoirs are sites of metropolitan significance and untapped potential, providing a wide variety of recreational, educational, environmental and amenity benefits to a diverse and growing community.

London: the Stoke Newington Reservoirs. (Rob Copeland)

*Stoke Newington Reservoirs.
(Rob Copeland)*

188 future **park**

All images this spread – Stoke Newington Reservoirs.
(Rob Copeland)

A similar situation exists in New York City, where local residents have been lobbying for access to the Jerome Park Reservoir in the Bronx. This 276 million litre, 38 ha facility was built 60 years after the Stoke Newington reservoirs, and named after wealthy Brooklynite Leonard W. Jerome. Jerome was the maternal grandfather of Winston Churchill, who established his own curious connection with Stoke Newington during his time as Home Secretary, when he refused to sanction a by-law prohibiting roller-skating on the footpaths of the borough.[199] Leonard Jerome saw benefit in investing in his hobbies. He founded the American Academy of Music and the American Jockey Club, and then co-built the Jerome Park Racetrack, which for a quarter of a century hosted one of the three key races that made up the USA Triple Crown until it was demolished to make way for the new reservoir. The facility was built to store water transported to the city via the New Croton Aqueduct, the system that still delivers 10 per cent of New York's supply. Not long after, the area surrounding the reservoir was bought by the City, but not till 45 years later, in 1940, was it opened to the public as Jerome Park. Sadly for local residents this gesture was short-lived. After World War II the path around the reservoir was fenced shut, and it has remained off-limits ever since.

Jerome Park Reservoir, The Bronx: seen through the perimeter fence, the empty reservoir stretches out into the distance. (Jim Henderson via Wikimedia Commons)

As in Stoke Newington, the streets surrounding Jerome Park Reservoir offer different views into the site. Along much of Sedgewick Avenue to the west a chainlink fence atop a low stone wall affords views only of the turfed berm reservoir edge. To the south, the aptly named Reservoir Avenue provides expansive views that reveal the mighty scale of the vast, empty concrete tank. In 1996 locals fought against the site being converted into a water treatment plant. That facility is instead now being constructed in nearby Van Cortlandt Park, and rather than promoting a greater level of public accessibility, a recent report commissioned by the Department of Environmental Protection recommended that people be allowed inside the fence only for a three-day trial period to be held in 2013.

Security and safety are oft-quoted reasons for fencing urban water bodies. In 1994 the United States Environmental Protection Agency enacted Policy LT2 requiring the covering of all open drinking water reservoirs. Pressure to comply increased following September 11, with supporters of the policy claiming that open reservoirs were highly vulnerable targets, and that contaminated water supplies had the potential to quickly impact entire cities. Some groups, including the doctors, scientists and concerned resident members of Friends of Reservoirs in Portland, Oregon, have campaigned vigorously that mandatory covering is unnecessarily burdensome financially, with no scientific basis, and no proven public health benefits. Suggestions that the City was overreacting also resurfaced in mid-2011, when 29.5 megalitres of water was flushed from the Mt Tabor storage facility by the Portland Water Bureau after a young man was seen, and apparently captured on video, relieving himself into the open reservoir through a fence.

Regardless of the vocal opposition in Portland, near neighbour Seattle has pushed forward with its reservoir covering program, completing projects at the Beacon Hill, Myrtle and West Seattle Reservoirs, and planning to either cover or decommission other existing open reservoirs such as the Roosevelt Reservoir, which will cease operation once the nearby Maple Leaf Reservoir and Park opens in 2012. Maple Leaf is a poster-child for EPA LT2. The existing facility was built in 1911, as part of a wider municipal engineering program. Over the next century residential neighbourhoods gradually surrounded the reservoir, along with parkland and a well-used children's playground. Since 2009 Seattle Public utilities has been constructing a 234 megalitre capacity underground storage tank, which will then be covered and redeveloped into nearly 6.5 ha of neighbourhood park. Local interest is strong. Community members have been consulted about options for the parkland redesign, and four times as many people applied to fill the 100 available places on guided tours of the underground reservoir chambers, which took place on a cold morning in December 2011. Photos and videos posted by *The Seattle Times* and on local blogs shortly thereafter reveal the scale of the two reservoir cells, which contain over 768 concrete columns, each more than half-a-metre thick, and which have consumed the greatest part of the project's US$49 million cost.

This page
1. Seattle: built in 1911, the Roosevelt Reservoir will be decommissioned once the new underground facility at Maple Leaf Park is complete. *(Seattle Public Utilities)*
2. Seattle: the new Maple Leaf Reservoir under construction. The underground structure will be covered by a new public park. *(Seattle Public Utilities)*
3. Istanbul: Yerebatan (Basilica) Cistern – the street-level entrance building.
(賴鈺淇 via Wikimedia Commons)

This page
4. Seattle: inside the 'cathedral-like' reservoir chamber. Visitors have enjoyed experiencing this amazing space before it is filled with water. (Marcus Donner)
5. Yerebatan (Basilica) Cistern: the underground reservoir. (Moise Nicu via Wikimedia Commons)

Visitors observed the '30-second echoes'[200] and the cathedral-like qualities of the vast underground spaces. These are characteristics shared by underground water reservoirs the world over. Urban reservoirs hold the drinking water supply for entire cities or districts. Containing a city's water supply underground, simultaneously maximising storage capacity, while supporting the weight of park, plaza or building above, requires deft engineering design. Some facilities make use of trusses to span open tanks. Others rely on vaulted roof structures that come to rest on rows of columns, arrayed with relentless mathematical order. As the Seattle residents found, experiencing such spaces without their cargo of water reveals the latent beauty inherent in all good engineering design.

Hidden below the streets of central Istanbul, the Yerebatan, or Basilica Cistern, is an ancient reservoir that still operates very much like a private building, albeit an underground one.

The connection with the public realm above is not expressed, entry is paid, there is no intention whatsoever that it function as a park-like space. Conversely, in Sydney, Australia, the brick piers and vaults of a former underground reservoir are the bones around which a new public park has been elegantly draped.

Paddington Reservoir Gardens was the initiative of the local council and in 2009 it won the Australian Award for Urban Design. Before its rebirth as a park the reservoir was a deteriorating underground fuel storage tank for a service station. The design of the park celebrates all those things that had previously been considered negatives: the long-neglected structure and colonising plants are re-imagined as a romantic ruined landscape, and the unsafe, unsurveilled space below ground is now a cool, tranquil respite from the busy inner-city streets above.

Sydney: Paddington Reservoir Gardens. (Hermione9753 via Wikimedia Commons)

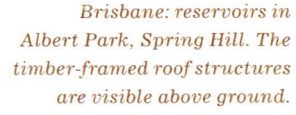

Brisbane: reservoirs in Albert Park, Spring Hill. The timber-framed roof structures are visible above ground.

Equally high potential exists in Brisbane, where three reservoirs dating from the city's establishment as a penal colony remain unused, minimally maintained and virtually unknown, despite being located next to one of only two extant convict-built structures in the city, and within a belt of public parkland more than a kilometre long located minutes from the city centre. As recently as 2009, Brisbane City Council initiated two separate adaptive reuse investigations examining the reservoir precinct; one investigating options for alternative water harvesting and storage and one looking at tourist and commercial opportunities that would involve a broader public realm master plan to connect the Wickham Terrace precinct with the central city. Neither report progressed beyond the initial concept phase.

Combining aspects of many of the examples previously described is McMillan Reservoir in Washington D.C. The open air McMillan reservoir was constructed at the dawn of the twentieth century to hold water brought to the city via the Washington Aqueduct. The aqueduct, a USA National Historic Landmark, transferred water 19 km from a dam at Great Falls to Dalecarlia, the first of the system's reservoirs, on the Maryland border. From there water was directed to the Georgetown Reservoir on the western outskirts of the capital. The pumping station at the edge of the reservoir is a Georgetown landmark, known locally as 'the castle'. Unlike its English counterpart at Stoke Newington the Georgetown structure was not decorated to reflect the architectural style of the period, but rather to reference the insignia of the US Army Corps of Engineers who were responsible for implementing all aspects of the water supply system. From Georgetown, water was directed into a dead-straight underground tunnel connecting to the McMillan Reservoir, formed by damming the Tiber, a creek which previously flowed south into the Potomac River. Previously Washington relied on a series of local springs for its water supply. A vertical pipe visible today in the middle of the reservoir is thought to mark the location of the Smith Springs, an abundant source from which water was reticulated south to the city and residential neighbourhoods.

Picturesque though it is, the still functioning reservoir attracts continued interest and attention today because of the intriguing history and contested future of its immediate neighbour, the McMillan Sand Filtration Plant. The Filtration Plant commenced operation in 1905, four years after the reservoir. Initially, no drinking water delivered to Washington via the Aqueduct was treated, the intention being that the reservoirs themselves would act as settling ponds before final distribution. The city grew too rapidly for settling alone to cope, and a series of fatal cholera outbreaks precipitated the public health decision to install a municipal water treatment plant adjacent to the McMillan Reservoir. After debating the merits of chemical versus non-chemical treatment systems, a slow sand filtration plant was commissioned.

Slow sand filtration works by passing untreated water through a modest layer of clean sand to remove any undesirables. Although the sand gets all the glory, it actually only provides a stage for the main players; the filtration is actually performed by an invisible population of millions of microscopic organisms that lives in the spaces between sand particles and digests water-borne microbes.[201]

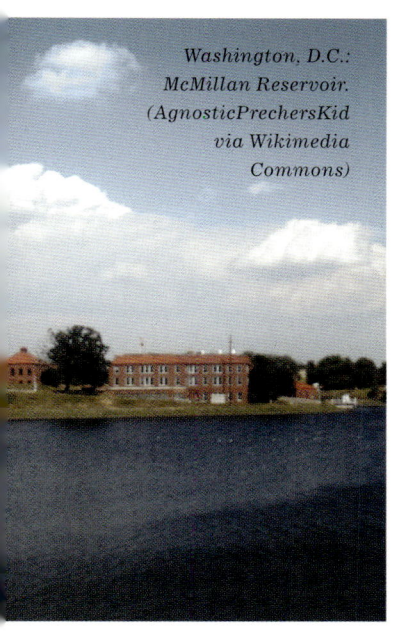

Washington, D.C.: McMillan Reservoir. (AgnosticPrechersKid via Wikimedia Commons)

Slow sand filtration is both labour- and space-intensive. The completed filtration plant at McMillan covers 10 ha. Underground are vaulted concrete cells, into which water from the adjacent reservoir would pass to be purified. Clean sand was deposited into the cells from above, and stored before use in a series of cylindrical concrete towers above ground. Also built above ground were regulator houses to enable the water flow to be controlled. In 1985 a rapid sand filtration plant was built closer to the reservoir, and a year later, after 80 years of service, the Army Corps of Engineers declared the slow filtration plant surplus to requirements, and requested its disposal. Another year later the District of Columbia purchased the sand filtration plant from the federal government for US$9.3 million, intending it to become a future development site. Since then, no development has taken place, no agreement has been reached between opposing parties as to what, if any, form such development should take, and no maintenance of the plant has occurred, resulting in ongoing deterioration of the concrete structures, including some portions where the roof has completely caved in.

Washington, D.C.: McMillan Sand Filtration Plant. The regulator houses and sand towers are visible above ground. (David Monack via Wikimedia Commons)

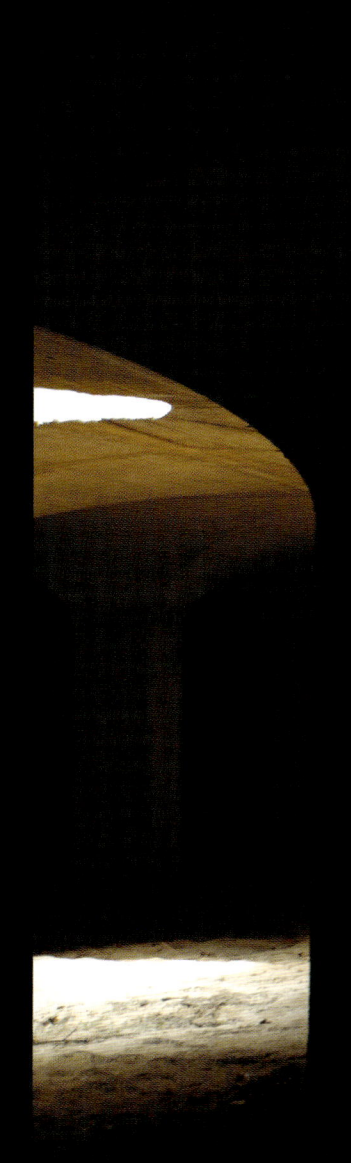

McMillan Sand Filtration Plant: the underground filtration chambers. (Ted Nigrelli)

Parkland and public space is at the heart of this decades-long stand-off, and the name of the place itself provides a starting point for examining the situation. Although initially known as the Howard University Reservoir after the campus located to its west, in 1906 both the reservoir and sand filtration plant were renamed in honour of the Republican Senator for Michigan, James McMillan, whose greatest Washington legacy was the *Senate Commission on the Improvement of the Park System of the District of Colombia*, which he chaired, and the findings of which we acknowledge today as the McMillan Plan. Before his election to the Senate McMillan had served as President of the Detroit Board of Parks Commissioners and was instrumental in the establishment of significant parkland projects in that city. With this background he was ideally placed to lead the Senate Sub-Committee overseeing the Commission charged with considering and reporting 'plans for the development and improvement of the entire park system of the District of Columbia'.[202] As for those who would actually undertake the 'considering and reporting', McMillan's Sub-Committee endorsed a Commission consisting of luminaries in their fields: planner and architect Daniel Burnham and landscape architect Frederick Law Olmsted Jr, who then invited architect Charles McKim and sculptor Augustus Saint Gaudens to join them.

The Commissioners undertook their task with zeal, aware of the opportunity to build on and strengthen the symbolism and aspiration underpinning Pierre Charles L'Enfant's original plan for Washington. In the final stages of the reporting process the editors of national magazines were urged to release their best illustrators from their daily tasks in order that they be able to complete renderings of the Commission's final proposals for the national capital. The final report delivered to the Senate was comprehensive, beginning with an overview of critical issues, an understanding of the constraints and opportunities provided by the climatic, topographic and symbolic features of the city. It proceeded through an assessment and recommendations for enhancing, strengthening and connecting all parts of the park system – ranging from The Mall, to the waterfront, the surrounding hill forts, major and minor parks, playgrounds and parkway drives – into a unified whole that at all times served the needs of not just local residents but also of visitors from the rest of the United States who, as the Commission strongly stated, had 'a right to expect, that here, at the seat of government, they shall not find merely what is considered 'good enough' in their workaday home cities… but the very best that is to be had'.[203]

In a political town famous for political term timeframes, the McMillan Plan has enjoyed longevity. It remains one of the underpinning terms of reference for all ongoing research and planning for the capital, including the 2006 *Comprehensive Plan*, and the 2011 Capital Space Plan *Ideas to Achieve the Full Potential of Washington's Parks and Open Space*. Those campaigning to save McMillan Sand Filtration Plant from development today persistently cite its inclusion in the McMillan Plan as part of an 'Emerald Necklace' of parks surrounding Washington. Although I can find no use of that term in the McMillan Report, it does state that 'the new reservoir can be made an important supplement to the park system'. It identifies the acreage at the reservoir site (67.7 acres [27.39 ha]), the total with the inclusion of the filtration plant (101.7 acres [41.15 ha]) and recommends the acquisition of additional land on the western side of the reservoir 'to provide for a drive and to afford at least a fringe of landscape under public control'.[204] Both the reservoir and sand filtration sites are also clearly visible on the maps that accompanied the Report: both Map D-287 and Map D-289 indicate that the McMillan sites are 'grounds to which the public has access but which were not primarily intended as parks'. The Report goes on to suggest ways in which the reservoir and sand filtration grounds could be advantageously linked to the Soldiers' Home grounds to the north and Howard Park to the south, creating the connectivity throughout the park system so sought by the authors.

Describing McMillan as 'grounds to which the public has access' does little to conjure the image of a sylvan paradise, but some time after his Commission duties were discharged Frederick Law Olmsted Jr commenced work on a landscape scheme for parkland at the combined reservoir and sand filtration site. When not busy running the practice he established with his brother after their famous father retired, Olmsted Jr also founded the American Society of Landscape Architects, the profession's peak representative body, taught at the Harvard Graduate School of Design in the landscape course he also helped found, and was instrumental in creating the protocols and policies underpinning the nascent National Parks movement in the United States.

For McMillan Park he conceived a broad carriage drive around the reservoir and a series of path promenades through the sand filtration plant. Soil was loaded onto the concrete roof of the plant to create a swathe of lawn. Under Olmsted's direction, McMillan was transformed into a seamless combination of municipal civic infrastructure and public park, realising many aspirations of the 'City Beautiful' movement that underpinned the McMillan Plan and becoming an early and successful prototype of co-location park.

The McMillan dilemma has become entrenched, trenchant and polarised, a bellwether for some of the most common challenges facing cities today.

Local folklore tells of people sleeping on the lawns in the heat of summer. The African-American community tells how McMillan Park provided a welcoming meeting place in one of the first integrated neighbourhoods in the city. Despite its popularity, and its enhancement by Olmsted Jr, McMillan remained under the jurisdiction of the Army Corps of Engineers. During World War II the entire perimeter was fenced, and public access has been prohibited ever since. Nearly seven decades after the war ended, and 25 years after the Army Corps of Engineers withdrew, battle lines between two different types of opposing forces are well drawn. The McMillan dilemma has become entrenched, trenchant and polarised, a bellwether for some of the most common challenges facing cities today. Sides are being taken in each of the following paradoxes:

1. The Past *v.* The Future

The site is a physical link to an important period in the city's growth and development. It dates from the time of the McMillan Plan, one of the most important documents shaping the form of the developing city. It was a landmark project resulting from the collaboration of some of the leading professionals of the day. Today the site is an important opportunity for the city to define how it will honour past glories and integrate them into the city of the future.

On the other hand, Great Leaps Forward do not happen without vision. The creators of the sand filtration site could see past what it was to what it could become. It is now the responsibility of this generation to also see beyond what the site is today, and imagine what it might become in the future.

2. Preservation *v.* Utilisation

Those for complete preservation believe the site is significant in so many ways that all pieces of the existing built fabric must be retained to properly tell its story, that keeping just the sand towers is tokenistic and opportunistic. Also that if nothing old was kept we would have no links to our heritage, and if we abandoned Olmsted projects just because they were a little worse for wear, we would have given up Central Park to the muggers and druggies in the seventies and it would be lost to us forever.

Those for utilising the site believe keeping old things for their own sake is not enough – the site had a use before, a use that helped the city grow, that paid for its upkeep and maintenance, that gave it a reason for being, and it should be used again to help the city grow and develop. Under this argument keeping the sand towers preserves the most visible part of the existing site, after all no one had access to the underground structures before. The most virulent critics of preservation believe that if all old things were kept there would be nothing new and we'd still be living in huts, and finally that there are plenty of other Olmsted projects around, and many in much better condition than this one.

3. Intent v. Opportunity

Following closely on from the above debate, some argue that McMillan was designed as integrated park and infrastructure, and question why should park use be thrown out just because the infrastructure has become redundant. Countering this is the view that this is a once in a lifetime opportunity to create a consolidated, well planned, mixed use development in the inner city, one that includes a memory of its past use.

4. Density v. Sprawl

Here, one view believes that the surrounding neighbourhood is low density and the planned development is not in keeping. The opposing view is that it makes sense to increase density and development closer in, and closer to other services – keeping this as open space forces development elsewhere, including to the city edge as sprawl.

5. Environment v. Economics

Keeping the site as parkland offsets the city's carbon footprint, improves air quality, reduces impervious surfaces and provides inner city residents with access to open space. It also prevents additional traffic congestion and pollution in the area that new development would bring.

Keeping the site as parkland doesn't add any more jobs to the city or provide any more houses. Developing the site to accommodate new workers and residents makes it more feasible to provide public transport options, which would also benefit visitors who would otherwise have to drive to the park.

6. Local v. Global

The local community will be adversely affected by construction, by increased traffic, and reduced amenity. The local community is in the best position to know what is at stake, what is to be lost and what is to be gained from changes in the local area – the High Line was saved by locals when politicians wanted to demolish it. The local community would be better served by having McMillan once again opened as useable parkland, rather than destroying the character of the area with over-development.

Opposing this is the argument that the site was developed as a city-scale initiative and is a site of city-scale importance – its future should not be dictated by local residents only. Pro-development voices believe the local community is holding the city to ransom with NIMBYism, and is already well served by a variety of green spaces.

7. Public v. Politics

The public will is being ignored, and the public is being kept in the dark about the government's real intent, and what it has really agreed with the developers. The political decision has forced the process down a one-track option – by seeking only to maximise short-term financial return the politicians have ruled out many other options that could have delivered a more well considered long-term plan.

The public is not thinking long-term or big picture, and has not educated itself in the realities of the development process, where there are many checks and balances in place. In order to deliver on its promises – minimising taxes, providing houses and jobs, improving roads and transit – governments must find solutions that best allow them to achieve these complex and often conflicting demands. Finding development partners allows public benefits to be delivered while minimising costs to the public.

8. Lead *v.* Follow

There is an opportunity to do something different here, to lead the way in adaptive reuse, to take advantage of the site features, and not roll out the same bland mixed use development with a supermarket and some housing.

9. All *v.* Nothing

This lies at the heart of the McMillan dilemma, which over a period of 25 years has hardened into a situation where neither side feels able to negotiate or compromise for fear of how its supporters will react, or of how the opposition will take advantage. Trenchant views that will brook no argument or dissention are equally empowering and alienating: as the debate enters its second generation it becomes harder for supporters to do anything other than defend their position. Strong views also make casual observers uncomfortable – is someone who chains herself to an old building to prevent its demolition a lunatic or a visionary – and run the risk of detracting attention from any other than one-dimensional discussions.

It is impossible to imagine an employer today agreeing to release a member of staff to draw pictures of parks in the national interest. The head of the Pennsylvania Railway famously agreed to relocate his proposed track and Washington Station so as to preserve the grandeur of The Mall. Despite requests under the Freedom of Information Act the current District of Columbia government refuses to fully release details of its dealings with the consortium it has appointed, without public tender, to redevelop the McMillan Sand Filtration Plant site.

A footnote
New York's Jerome Park Reservoir and its supply line, the Croton Aqueduct, were discussed earlier in this Chapter. The chief design engineer for the aqueduct was John Bloomfield Jervis, and four years after the Croton was completed he began work on another project. Supplying the growing Boston region, the Cochituate Aqueduct fed water into the Brookline Reservoir, to the west of the city. In 1902 the City of Boston sought to sell the reservoir and surrounding land. A group of neighbours contributed US$50 000 of their own money towards purchasing the site, in order to preserve it from what they considered might be inappropriate development. One of the neighbours lived barely 200 m from the reservoir, at a property known as Fairsted. His name was John and from Fairsted, together with his brother, he ran the landscape architecture practice they took over from their father, Frederick Law Olmsted.

Cleaning water in order to drink it is not the only thing we do with this precious resource. After water, stable sources of power are among the fundamental requirements of contemporary human settlements. The power supply for most cities, like the water supply, comes from remote sources. Coal-fired or nuclear power plants, wind turbines or hydroelectric dams are usually, like most of the public utilities and land uses discussed in this chapter, out of sight and out of mind. The spaghetti systems that deliver the power generated at these heaving hidden places is also largely hidden.
While overhead power lines are still common, our preference as both citizens and designers is for 'undergrounding' to remove the unsightly structures from view. The natural conveyance mechanisms for water – rivers and streams – are often among the first casualties of urban development. Research by Curtis Millay, for example, demonstrated how the McMillan Reservoir in Washington D.C. was not just a monumental civil engineering project dropped far outside the then city border, which is what a casual observer of today's city plans might deduce. Instead, it was precisely located because of its place in the wider network of streams and springs in the catchment. While not the fastest flowing, the Smith Springs were at the highest elevation, and therefore best able to gravity-feed water to the growing city to the south. Millay also uses insurance claim data to map the presence of the now buried streams of the capital; the buildings in districts that suffer most from basement inundation and combined sewer problems are also those built on top of the once-flowing streams and springs.[205]

The reliance on local springs also eventuated in a major reappraisal of municipal water supply for New Haven, Connecticut, which quadrupled its population between 1800 and 1850. By this time the city was a hub for both transit and industry, with many buildings in the centre reaching five storeys in height, but no organised systems for sewage treatment, rubbish collection or drinking water supply. Clean water was eventually distributed in 1862, after nearly a decade of protracted electoral and contractual debate, and many more preceding decades of typhoid and cholera epidemics. Central to the story was Eli Whitney Jr, whose father was one of a group of mechanically innovative, entrepreneurial-minded men who pioneered American technical development. Whitney Sr first purchased property on the outskirts of New Haven in 1789. He had won a federal government contract to manufacture 10 000 muskets for the army, despite having no factory, staff or experience in making guns. Armory Street, New Haven is today one of the few reminders of Whitneyville, the self-contained factory town he built on the banks of the Mill River, which powered many of the manufacturing processes on site.

Many of the original buildings were demolished during the period when Eli Jr ran the Armory. A year after taking control in 1842 he contracted with Samuel Colt to produce 1000 Colt revolvers for a Captain Walker, of the Texas Rangers. In 1860 he commenced the raising of the existing Mill River dam wall by five times its existing height. This not only created Lake Whitney, which today still contributes to the local water supply system, but enabled him to substantially increase manufacturing production, and to deliver on his contract with the local Water Co. to design and build a waterworks and distribution system for New Haven. While personal financial gain was an obvious motivator, it's possible that Whitney was motivated by a strong New England civic impetus to 'do well by doing good'.[206] Even after Eli Whitney Jr sold his rights in the Armory to the fabled Winchester Co., he retained his interest in the Water Co. for which he was a major stockholder.

In 1901 a major typhoid outbreak in New Haven prompted construction of a plant to treat the Lake Whitney reservoir water before distribution: a slow sand filtration plant was constructed to the west of the Whitney Armory grounds and operated successfully from 1906 until 1991, when it was decommissioned. Unlike the McMillan Plant in Washington, the Lake Whitney plant was undistinguished architecturally, although functionally it featured a different configuration and method for cleaning sand than many other slow sand facilities. What it had in common with McMillan was a sunken structure, covered with turf, which was adopted by local residents as an informal parkland. Undated black and white photographs of the treatment plant show much the same bucolic rolling hills and wooded backdrop as captured in an 1828 painting of Whitneyville.[207] Children visiting the Eli Whitney Museum and Workshop, established in remaining Armory buildings to celebrate the spirit of innovation and technical challenge of the early industrialist, would come across the road to fly paper planes on the unfenced grassy field or to have informal outdoor lessons at the small wetland beside the sand filtration plant. Once it was demolished in 2001 this spirit of community accessibility and engagement was something that the design team for the new water treatment plant was keen to continue.

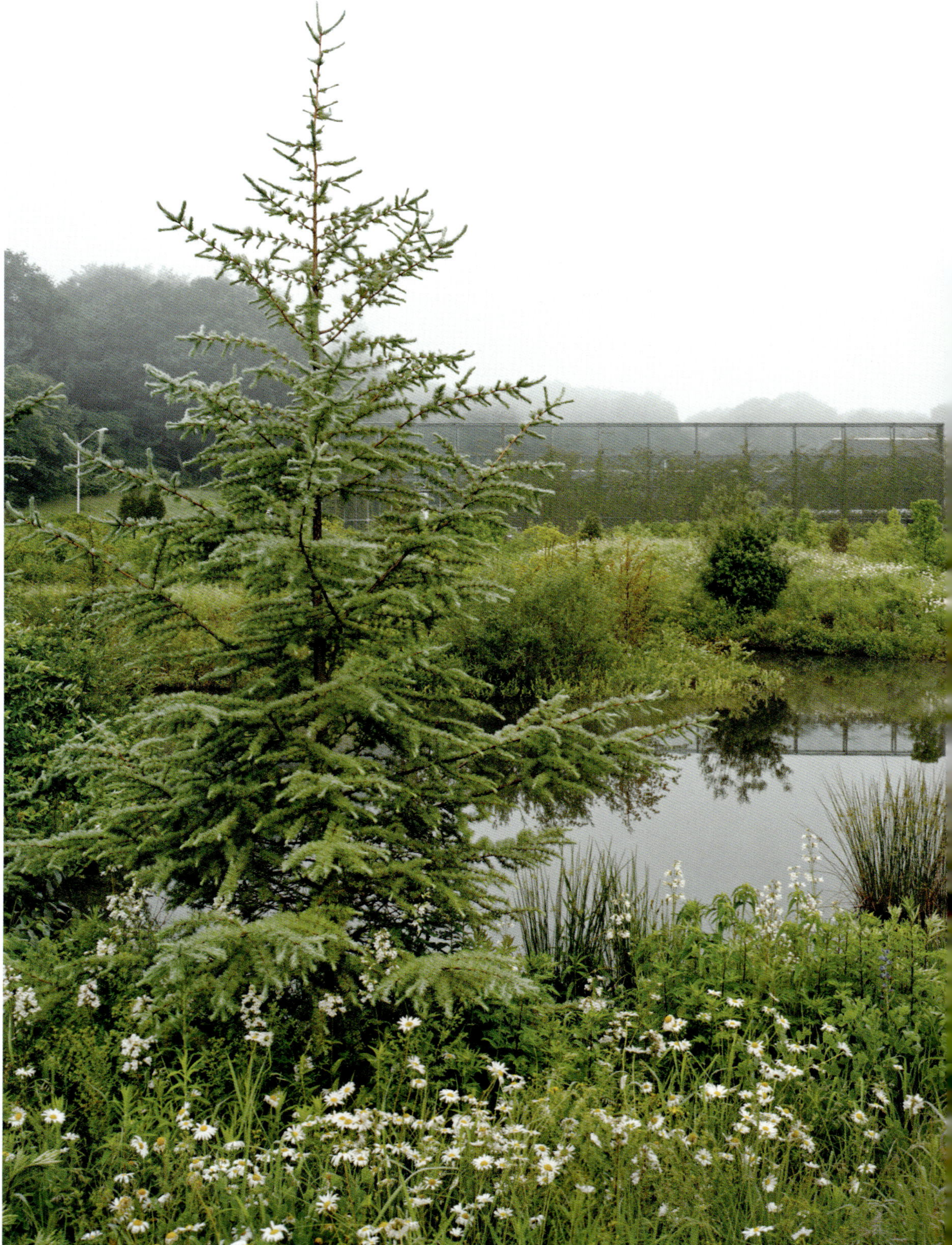

New Haven: view of the Whitney Water Treatment Plant main building, green roof and landscape works before planting has established. The security fence was not part of the original scheme. (Elizabeth Felicella)

The new Lake Whitney Water Treatment Plant was designed by Stephen Holl Architects and constructed over three years between 2002 and 2005. The landscape works were completed in 2006, and five years later an artificially constructed representation of the New Haven watershed is well established on the site. Holl's building covers 13 000 m², of which 70 per cent is underground. The most visible element is a long extruded form supposedly resembling an upside-down water drop clad in sleek stainless steel slates. Full height glazing at the ends affords long views into the surrounding landscape, and it was originally intended that this openness be physical as well as metaphorical, with the plant open and available for school children and members of the public to visit and see how drinking water arriving in their kitchen taps. Unfortunately, this notion was rapidly abandoned post-September 11, and only recently has the water authority begun permitting strictly controlled visitor access.

What is available though, from dawn to dusk, is the 5.6 ha landscape that covers the site and the 2800 m² green roof of the treatment plant. Sinking the building not only provided the green roof opportunity but enabled water to be gravity fed into the plant from Lake Whitney, and created the fill that was used to create the varied topography of the watershed-in-miniature. Today, locals can enjoy more than just a pleasant green lawn. From street-level entry points pathways meander beside a newly constructed wetland, past a gorge, through a stream valley and around an agricultural garden planted with lines of hedges and circles of smoke trees, before ascending a spiral path to the top of a sculptural mini-mountain. From here the whole system is revealed, and it's possible on the way back down to follow the path of stormwater as it moves through the landform and terrain before reaching the wetland, where it is filtered before recharging the water table below.

The Whitney Water Treatment Plant is both civic and civil, perhaps subconsciously influenced by Eli Whitney Jr's earlier 'do good by doing well' approach. Looking at the areas of rapidly establishing vegetation it seems amazing to comprehend that the regional water board temporarily abandoned the project at one stage, instead considering locating the plant in a different, poorer community, where residents might have been less inclined to complain. In the end the water board did engage proactively with the vocal New Haven locals, addressing serious concerns about water quality in Lake Whitney, and asking the community to form several committees. Of these, the design committee was instrumental in achieving the final outcomes. It not only released requests for proposals for an integrated built and landscape response, the process by which Holl and Van Valkenburgh became involved, but it advocated strongly for the water board to recognise the opportunity to create a landmark piece of civic infrastructure.[208]

A community design process was also central to the success of the Willamette River Water Treatment Plant Park in Wilsonville, Oregon, which is open to the public round-the-clock. This was achieved by close collaboration between Miller Hull Architects and Murase Landscape Architects. The design team developed a long, linear concrete wall running north to south through the centre of the site. For much of its length the wall is solid, and provides a secure line of enclosure for the treatment plant. As it moves south, and closer to the Willamette River, it begins to break down into a series of frames and blades that are interspersed with lower stone walls that allow views into courtyards and structures within the plant. The arrangement of the wall syncopations reflects the different stages of water treatment occurring beyond. The wall also forms a dramatic backdrop and organising device for a water feature, more than 150 m long, that drops over low stone weirs, cascades over a waterfall, laps at pebble-lined banks and reflects the overhead sky. Stormwater run-off from the 4 ha park is collected and treated in the water garden, and pathways and bridges allow visitors to journey through or stop at rest points and picnic tables, before connecting to the Morey's Landing Trail and continuing on to adjacent neighbourhoods.

All images this spread – Willamette River Water Treatment Plant. The administration building. (Aboutmovies via Wikimedia Commons)

The watercourse and fountain outside the administration building. (Aboutmovies via Wikimedia Commons)

*The pumphouse.
(Aboutmovies via Wikimedia Commons)*

*Right – the stream and picnic area in the park.
(Aboutmovies via Wikimedia Commons)*

*Below – the Treatment Plant in its parkland setting.
(Aboutmovies via Wikimedia Commons)*

Co-locations **209**

Around the same time that the Lake Whitney plant was starting construction, the local water authority in Phoenix, Arizona was getting ready to open its own landmark, designed as a centrepiece for its sustainable energy program, and, as in New Haven, created as the next in a long line of infrastructural evolution. As introduced in relation to the Rio Salado project, the canal system built to serve Phoenix, Arizona, has survived in one form or another for centuries. The earliest Arizonan canals were built by the pre-Columbian Hohokam tribe and are believed by some to have comprised the largest irrigation system in prehistory. Centuries later many of the Hohokam canals were appropriated and expanded by European settlers desperate to ensure a reliable water supply for Phoenix.

For more than 100 years the Salt River Project (SRP) has managed the 214 km long system, which is owned by the US Bureau of Reclamation. As the pressures of water and power supply have increased, the once naturalistic and tree-lined corridors have been increasingly converted into concrete channels and are now 'all but vanished from the cultural landscape of the region'.[209] In one part of the system the canal contained a waterfall dropping 6 m, the height of a two-storey building. Known as Arizona Falls, it has been used to generate hydroelectric power on and off since the late 1800s. A photo from that time shows a family, tightly buttoned neck to ankle in dark sober clothing, enjoying a day out beside the falls. The most recent Arizona Falls project is an attempt to re-engage local Scottsdale residents with the canal system. As part of its decision to re-establish hydroelectric power generation at Arizona Falls, SRP partnered with the city's Phoenix Arts Commission to create a showpiece for its renewable energy program, EarthWise Energy. Local landscape architect Steve Martino and east coast artists Lajos Heder and Mags Harries collaborated to produce WaterWorks, which references the past public uses of the place for dancing, the five dams that supply the water that ultimately ends up in the Falls, the colours and texture of the Salt River, and remnant industrial infrastructure from the earlier power plant into a combined public space, artwork and educational facility.

What results is a meaningful yet honest place that doesn't pretend to be anything other than what it is: a hydroelectric generating plant. In fact, embracing the engineering reality has given the design team, the project and ultimately the public its most appealing feature – the ability to once again come face to face with the thunderous roar and cooling air generated by megalitres of rapidly cascading water. While the new high performance generator remains concealed, it is clothed in publicly accessible space. And even though this space is made of concrete and stone, with very little vegetative material, the presence of all that water makes it as much, if not more, of an inviting proposition than the exposed and unshaded 'real' park next door.[210]

Phoenix: Arizona Falls. (Cygnusloop99 via Wikimedia Commons)

Co-locations 211

Images this spread – Kempten: Iller River Hydroelectric Plant. (Alofok via Wikimedia Commons)

212 future**park**

One other notable feature of Arizona Falls is its size. Normally discussions about hydroelectric power bring to mind images of behemoths like the Three Gorges Dam in China, whose construction displaced one million people, or complex systems of infrastructure such as the Snowy Mountains scheme in Australia, with its 16 dams and seven power stations. In comparison, Arizona Falls is tiny. Many organisations currently working with communities in developing nations are promoting the benefits of 'micro-hydro' as a way of providing a sustainable local power source. Among the benefits of micro-hydro are the reduced landtake and environmental devastation that accompany urban or regional-scale hydroelectric dams. Micro-hydro also means that rivers and streams are managed at the local level, the potential problems and opportunities of decision making are locally and immediately evident, and the infrastructure itself can physically fit more comfortably within settlements. In many ways it is easy to dismiss such ideas as a return to the past, when all households were responsible for finding and maintaining the energy they required. On the other hand, this is just as worthy of exploration as a way of increasing the resilience of our cities and communities, as are local power supply, water sensitive urban design, multimodal transport, wind turbines and urban agriculture – many of the catchcries of 'relocalisation' – that are already being embraced in shrinking cities. Of course the other benefit of such initiatives is the opportunity they present for integration into thriving, ecologically healthy networks of publicly accessible park-like places.

'Riverfront park' may not be the description that immediately leaps to mind on first seeing the Iller River Hydroelectric Plant in Kempten, Germany. Built to replace an existing 50-year-old station, the new plant is a sinuous swoosh of curving concrete that looks as if the warp drive from the Starship Enterprise has broken away and come to rest beside the handsome but benign gable roofed brick buildings that line the river. While there's not a tree in sight, the plant does display a welcoming civic gesture in its embracing curves, cobbled walkways and elegant integrated pedestrian and cycle bridge. What the Iller River Hydroelectric Plant does best is represent the dynamic surge of water that powers its engines, thereby celebrating its important function and inviting onlookers to acknowledge the celebration.

The overt celebration of water used in its hydraulic engineering function is something that Arizona Falls shares with Parque del Agua in Bucaramanga, Colombia. Unlike Arizona Falls, Parque del Agua is a partially functioning water treatment plant. What unites them though, is oversight by the local water authority, a past use of the site for public recreation, and a contemporary renaissance that re-engages with the community and celebrates the engineering uses of water to create delight.

Bucaramanga is about a one-hour flight from the Colombian capital, Bogota, and passengers have been known to find the Palonegro airport runway approach somewhat unnerving, perched as it is on what seems like an impossibly narrow piece of flat land teetering above two vertiginous cliff faces. The typically nerve-jangling taxi descent into town seems almost relaxing in comparison, especially when the driver rounds a bend to reveal Bucaramanga nestled below, between the enveloping mountain ranges. A Lonely Planet travel guide describes an 'air of vibrancy' but advises that there's 'little to see in the city itself'.[211] Such rousing endorsement, combined with the relative lack of exposure of South American projects in English-language publications, has ensured that Parque del Agua remains little known outside the city. Within Santander province, however, the park is a popular site for both local and regional visitors.

Parque del Agua is owned by Acueducto Metropolitano de Bucaramanga (AMB), the city's water supply authority. At its establishment in 1916 the AMB was charged with supplying water to Bucaramanga and two other nearby towns. As demand grew, so did the need for additional facilities, which the AMB developed and operated until 1975, when it was bought by the local council. From its early days the primary water treatment plant was located at Morrorico, on the eastern fringe of the city. The actual treatment facility occupied only a small portion of the large landholding, and local residents became used to enjoying the spontaneous tropical landscape and lawns of the park-like grounds. Expansion of the plant reduced the amount of land available, and after the council buyout a shared company took responsibility for water treatment and supply. Public use of the land dwindled and the once vibrant community gathering place became neglected. In 2001, AMB Manager Victor Azuero Diaz proposed moving the company's administrative functions back to Morrorico. With the support of the Mayor a park was proposed for the site, in homage to the former public appropriation of the land for recreation.

The design team of Lorenzo Castro, Michele Cescas, Alfonso Leyva and German Samper took advantage of the now mature stands of vegetation, as well as the 20 m level change from north to south, to create a cool and inviting park that celebrates water. When used in hydraulic engineering, water takes two forms: wide and still, and rapidly moving. Both of these are used throughout the Parque del Agua, as gravity drops water from the top of the site over cascades and falls, to mid-points where it is intercepted and held in pools. Water forms a constant companion for visitors moving up from the entry along either the broad, stone paved, stepped promenade to the north, or the narrower gravel and timber path that hugs the curving southern perimeter. Both connect with a timber deck at the top of the site, along which extends a long, long bench to lie back into and look up into the heavy arching canopy of the 9 m high bamboo that frames the space.

Bucaramanga: Parque del Agua.

On a warm June morning youngsters disport themselves insouciantly along the bench, while a grey-haired gentleman in crisply pressed shirt unfolds and arranges his own straight-backed chair on top of the timber, the better to negotiate the logistics of sitting and then standing again. Opposite, the face of a high sloping bank is covered with almost indecently rampant masses of bromeliads, heliconias, philodendrons, liriopes and other startling green foliage, the whole thing sliced through by a series of rippling cascades. On the muggiest day, the air in the park is cool, and although the AMB charges a small admission fee (2500 pesos – around AUD$1.40) for entry, visitors of all ages are drawn in. In the midst of the paths and ponds, the climbers and the cascades, the AMB continues to provide clean drinking water to Bucaramanga.

All images this spread – Bucaramanga: Parque del Agua.

still operate on the site. Where the park could undoubtedly go further is in pushing its diverse biomass and abundant water to be more than just ornamental. True, they do make the park invitingly cool for visitors, but they do not actively show how rainwater could be detained and slowly released to reduce local flooding, or how biological treatment could assist the cleansing of water before its release back into the catchment, both worthwhile exercises in a tropical environment. Despite these missed opportunities, the Parque del Agua convincingly demonstrates how land associated with a municipal authority use can be effectively made available for public use as a park-like place.

Maintaining and improving urban water quality is also the primary objective of the staff at Portland's aptly named Water Pollution Control Laboratory.

drinking water supply but on the health of the overall catchment. While this places it slightly outside the types of public utilities and land uses discussed in this chapter, it is worthy of discussion for it actively engages with the adjacent riverfront parkland, inviting passers-by to explore the laboratory building, car park and external areas, all of which overtly demonstrate the synthesis between high-performing technical and civic functions. Apart from a small fenced lot at the rear of the building where boats and major pieces of equipment are stored, all space outside the building is publicly accessible. Collected stormwater run-off rumbles through a rubble lined trough before pooling in a circular basin wrapped in a sloping stone wall. In late summer the water level is low and staining on the wall reveals where it has peaked and hovered in past seasons. Tiny filaments of moss fluff their way along the top. Two walkways project out over the detention basin, placing visitors right into this thriving learning landscape. Planting has almost obscured the north-west side of the building, but a squirrel easily finds the corn cob placed for him on a specially crafted timber holder attached to a tree.

To the east of the building run-off from the car park is directed into biofiltration treatment trenches, and roof water is also directed into gardens via hanging chains, rather than being piped away in gutters and downpipes. For all intents and purposes the Water Pollution Control Laboratory is a building in a park. This is largely achievable because the main work of the laboratory occurs either inside the building itself, or out on Portland's waterways.

Situated at the confluence of two rivers, the city is geographically defined by water. The Willamette River is further south, and the city centre looks north across its banks. The Columbia River defines Portland's northern limits before continuing deep into Oregon, and it's into the Columbia Watershed that all the local waterways drain. Enjoyment of the river and responsibility for its care are things that Oregonians share with their neighbouring State, Washington.

All images this spread – Water Pollution Control Laboratory.

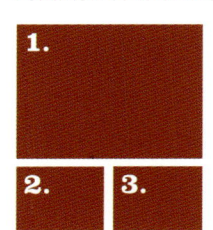

Opposite Page
1. *Aerial view from St John's Bridge showing the laboratory building, water treatment pond and connection to riverfront parkland.*
2. *Water sensitive car park design catches and treats stormwater run-off.*
3. *Public artwork in front of the laboratory building.*

Facing Portland across the Columbia River is the city of Vancouver, Washington, and almost directly opposite the Portland International Airport is the centrepiece of Vancouver's waterway health program, the Water Resources Education Center. Opened a year before the Water Pollution Control Laboratory, this facility also contains water sciences laboratories, but the main focus is on community engagement and education, delivered via the on-site theatre, gallery, exhibition space and classroom. Close to the main building is a deck that allows visitors to immerse themselves in 'one of [the] few remaining natural Columbia River riparian areas in the Vancouver-Portland Metro area'.

The detention basin with curving stone wall.

The Water Resources Education Center came into being at the same time as the neighbouring Marine Park Water Reclamation Facility, and was initiated by the City of Vancouver council as a means of moving beyond just the efficient delivery of water and sewer infrastructure and into a 'leadership role in educating and advancing stewardship of the community's high quality water resources'.[212] The Center is also part of a broader project, the Columbia River Renaissance, and the still-evolving Renaissance Trail passes alongside the natural riparian wetland and viewing deck. While the intent is inherently civic, and the external spaces can definitely be utilised in a park-like manner, some aspects of the Center itself are less successful than at the Portland Water Pollution Control Laboratory. The building and its landscape are less didactic, making the Center seem outside of, rather than deeply embedded in, the urban water system. It is also less visible. The Water Pollution Control Center can be seen from the St Johns Bridge way overhead, and the closest houses are little more than a block away. By contrast, dense screen planting means that the Water Resources Education Center cannot be clearly seen from Lewis and Clark Highway on its northern border, and despite the Renaissance Trail, for the most part visitors must rely on cars. The closest residents are again only a couple of hundred metres away, separated not only by the highway, but also the Burlington Northern Railroad line and a significant change in grade.

Another facility in a parkland setting is the Pierce County Environmental Services Building. A local wedding service promotes the site as 'a unique and beautiful setting for your wedding and reception. The outdoor courtyard features a covered patio and a lawn with spectacular views of Puget Sound and the Olympic mountains.'[213] The building, designed by architects Miller Hull, does indeed sit in an enviable waterfront location, with paths, boardwalks and riparian planting by Bruce Dees and Associates creating an inviting parkland setting. Also designed by Miller Hull is the LOTT Clean Water Alliance Regional Services Center, in Olympia, Washington State. The facility combines water treatment, reclamation, and a water education and technology (WET) centre, and 'shows the sexier side of water treatment', at least according to some.[214]

What all these facilities do is put a public face to municipal water treatment – by humanising something that for a long time has been dealt with by 'others' operating behind closed doors, it becomes easier for everyone, from schoolchildren up, to understand how clean drinking water gets to their kitchen taps, and the damage dirty water can do to riparian and aquatic ecosystems. In some places the push to improve water quality is driven by the existing water infrastructure, in particular combined sewers.

Water Pollution Control Laboratory: public parkland and riverfront pathway alongside the laboratory building.

For largely economic reasons, many Western cities initially installed this type of infrastructure, where pipe networks carried both stormwater and sewage. For most of the time the combined sewer system was efficient, bringing both types of wastewater to a central plant for treatment. In times of heavy rainfall the result was different, and in order to cope with the influx of surface run-off a portion of the wastewater in the system was discharged directly into lakes, rivers or oceans without treatment.

Co-locations

In the United States it is estimated that around 40 million people, in over 700 communities, are served by combined sewers, mainly in the longest settled regions of the Atlantic north-east.[215] In the United Kingdom over 20 000 combined sewer outfalls (CSOs) discharge into receiving waterways,[216] with around 500 having outlets on or close to public beaches. Although some combined sewers were constructed in Australia, they are very much in the minority, with most cities and towns operating separate stormwater and sewerage systems.[217]

When centralised sewerage treatment plants are bypassed in heavy rain, the overflow from either combined or separate sewer systems can be fairly accurately described as revolting, not to mention potentially harmful to both human health and the environment. However, credit must be given where credit is due, and it's worth remembering that sewerage treatment plants were originally constructed in order to prevent all waste flowing into waterways all of the time. In Portland the first sewer was a simple timber trough, a few blocks long, that collected (let's face it) poo, and emptied it into the Willamette River. Built in 1864, it was extended over time and the system upgraded to first terracotta, and then concrete pipes. By the 1930s the river was so polluted by sewage and agricultural and industrial run-off that salmon fingerlings released into the water died within 15 minutes.[218] In response to increasing public anger, the Columbia Boulevard Waste Water Treatment plant was opened in 1952, after voters approved a US$12 million bond for its construction. By 1972 the federal Clean Water Act augmented Oregon State laws regulating the sources of water pollution. In 1991 Portland embarked on its Combined Sewer Overflow Program, one of 10 targets in its Clean River Action Plan, enabling the city to simultaneously tackle multiple problems to meet multiple regulatory requirements. The Columbia Boulevard Wastewater Treatment Plant plays an ongoing role in this integrated approach.

The plant was built with public health and water quality objectives at the forefront. Integrating the plant within an accessible park-like setting was not an initial goal, but it has become an increasing reality as the city renegotiates its relationship with the Willamette and Columbia Rivers, and as public expectation of both enhanced water quality and access to the river edge has grown. In 1997 a new headworks facility was built to replace one of the oldest parts of the existing plant, and was surrounded by carefully considered landscape works by Murase Associates, including ponds and native planting sustained by disinfected secondary effluent reclaimed water. Unfortunately the gating of the driveway means this garden is now off-limits to casual visitors.

Appointments can be made to tour the plant, but otherwise the best way to comprehend the vast scale of the place is by taking the Columbia Slough Trail through the parklands that fringe its eastern boundary. The Columbia Slough is one of the largest urban wetlands in the United States, containing six lakes, three ponds, 80 km of waterways, 50 km of flood control levees and more than 50 km of secondary waterways. It once supported an indigenous population and was noted for its plentiful wildlife by the Lewis and Clark Expedition. Located between the Willamette and Columbia Rivers, the Slough once flooded annually, but urban growth pressure saw its waterways piped and channelised to allow agricultural, residential and industrial development. Today around 54 per cent of the Columbia Slough watershed is impervious.

Appreciation of the recreational and amenity value of the Slough has come full circle. In 1903, the Olmsted Brothers, presumably at a bit of a loose end having sorted out the future of Washington's park system, presented their *Annual Report of the Park Board* for Portland, in which they identified the Columbia Slough as one of the 'great landscape feature[s] in the region'. They proposed 'a great meadow reservation...to preserve the beautiful bottom land scenery', going further to explain that 'No other form of park has ever proved so attractive and so useful to the masses of the people... particularly when there can be associated with it long reaches of still water as a landscape attraction and for boating purposes'. The masses of the people in the early twenty-first century seem to agree.

Portland: the Slough Trail passes adjacent to the Columbia Boulevard Wastewater Treatment Plant.

Co-locations

Beside the Columbia Boulevard Wastewater Treatment Plant the Slough Trail passes through a scrap of woolly wilderness, created by Murase Associates to reference the pre-existing riparian landscape. Photos reveal just how extravagantly the vegetation has grown in less than a decade. Boys with fishing lines dawdle, and ubiquitous Portland cyclists zip on their way to the pedestrian bridge across the Slough. Students with iPods jog, and Portland mothers with Portland-weather-proof baby strollers do the rounds. The people who left the girly magazine behind the boulder near the entry path no doubt find other uses for the park, and while some of the interpretive signage suffers from exposure and spray paint, the integrated artwork and sculpture looks at home among the fallen leaves and riverbank mud. Concrete steps leading down to the water are inlaid with carved granite panels illustrating fish, birds, tides and the phases of the moon. It's beautiful without being prissy, exactly the right sort of public art for a city where tattooing is a recession-proof industry and the best donuts are Voodoo.

Above – Detailed artwork along the Slough Trail references the indigenous cultures.
(Richard Buchanan)

Opposite page above – Slough Trail with treatment plant to the right and Columbia Boulevard to the left.

Opposite page below – Looking back towards the treatment plant from the Slough.

Co-locations 225

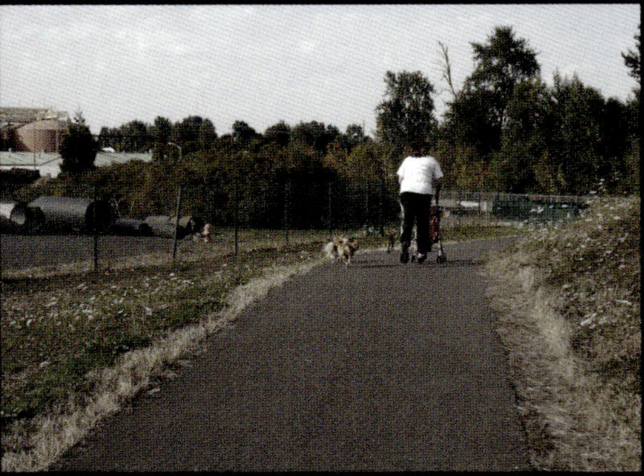
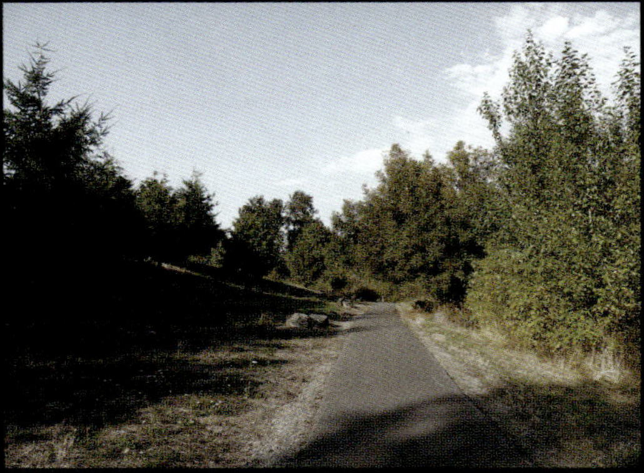
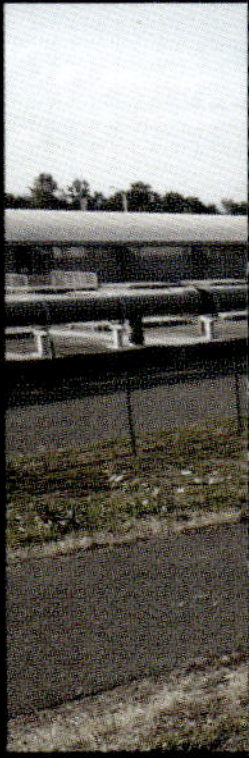
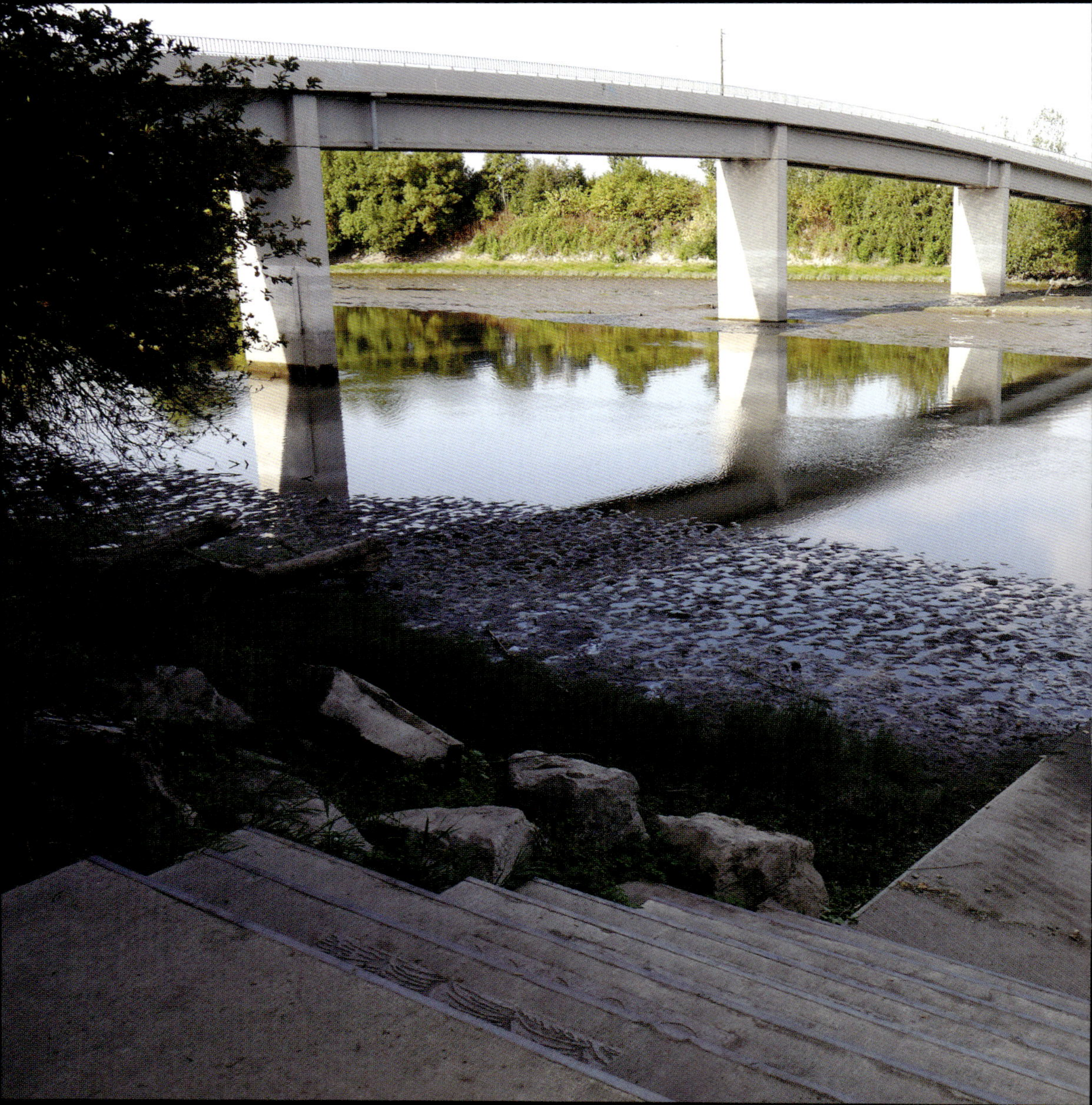

The Columbia Boulevard Wastewater Treatment Plant is not hard to get to, but neither is it exceptionally easy. It is bordered to the south by North Columbia Boulevard, and to the south, west and east by rail lines. The connectivity provided by the Slough Trail means it's possible the parkland setting is used more by those travelling through on their way to somewhere else, than by residents from neighbouring communities.[219]

1. Columbia Boulevard Wastewater Treatment Plant: heading towards denser planting beside the Columbia Slough.
2. Parkland planting draws from the Slough watershed landscape.
3. Portland: the Slough Trail passes adjacent to the Columbia Boulevard Wastewater Treatment Plant.
4. Steps down provide Slough access, while the trail continues on a shared pedestrian/cycle bridge.

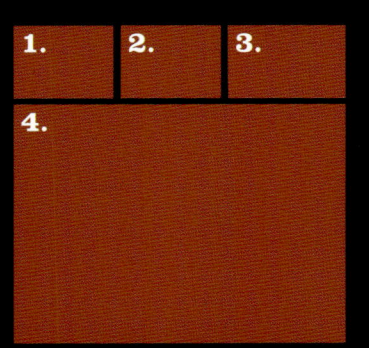

Co-locations

Trail connectivity is perhaps the only thing the Water Pollution Control Plant in Arlington, Virginia, has in common with the Columbia Boulevard plant, although initially the aspiration for public art was just as high. Artist Mary Miss was commissioned in 2003, early on in the long and complex project to upgrade the Arlington plant. In response she developed an art concept master plan to 'transform an existing 30-acre infrastructure site into a public space', and through art to connect 'the daily lives of Arlington neighbourhoods with Chesapeake Bay'. The proposition was based around three interconnected elements: a Process Diagram, whereby a series of black-and-white banded pipes, numbers and supergraphics, and information kiosks would reveal, in life size, the step-by-step process of water treatment; Living Surfaces, where green elements such as planted roofs and trellises, porous paving and rain gardens would provide educational, ecological and visual benefits; and Public Nodes, where the complexity and extent of the plant would be brought down to a comprehensible scale at kiosks, rest points and viewing areas.

Almost a decade later there is no sign of banded pipes or green planted roofs at Arlington, and planned landscape 'improvements' will provide peripheral flourishes of species diversity and colour, rather than the educational 'park of sorts'[220] envisioned by Miss. In March 2012, Tejo Remy and Rene Veenhuizen were announced as preferred artists to 'create a unique design enhancement' for the nearly 500 m long chainlink fence that separates the plant from the Four Mile Run Trail.[221] The principles and framework for public art along the trail are guided by a citywide master plan that was also prepared by Mary Miss.

Images this spread – Newtown Creek Wastewater Treatment Plant. Above: Viewed from the Nature Walk.

Below: Dramatic night time illuminations (Victoria Belanger)

Co-locations **229**

Newtown Creek Wastewater Treatment Plant and Nature Walk, with the Midtown skyline behind Newtown Creek industry.

Mary Miss is based in New York, and many of her earliest and best-known works were made in that city. In 1986 her work was acknowledged in a group exhibition at the La Jolla Museum of Contemporary Art. Entitled *Sitings* it also featured the work of fellow landscape and environmental artists Alice Aycock, Richard Fleischner and George Trakas. In 2011 Trakas and Miss worked together leading cross-disciplinary teams exploring options for the Long Island waterfront as part of the project 'Civic Action'. Trakas has twice received National Endowment for the Arts Fellowships and is a medal winner for sculpture from the American Society of Arts and Letters, which honoured his unique 'vision of landscape'. Like his contemporary, he has long experience working in complex waterfront sites, including the Newtown Creek Nature Walk in Brooklyn. This project not only ekes out a sliver of public access to a contested waterfront, but brings visitors face-to-face with the biggest sewerage treatment plant in New York City.

HORSETAIL
(Equisetum hyemale)
Survivor of the Carboniferous Period
(354 to 290 million years ago).
The plant, also known as Scouring Rush,
was used to polish arrow shafts.
Early spring sprouts were eaten
raw or cooked as greens.
Roots cooked with whale oil and
salmon eggs were eaten as a delicacy.

Above – Detailed interpretive signage is located throughout the Nature Walk.

Right – Glimpse through bowed wall of The Vessel into functioning treatment plant behind.

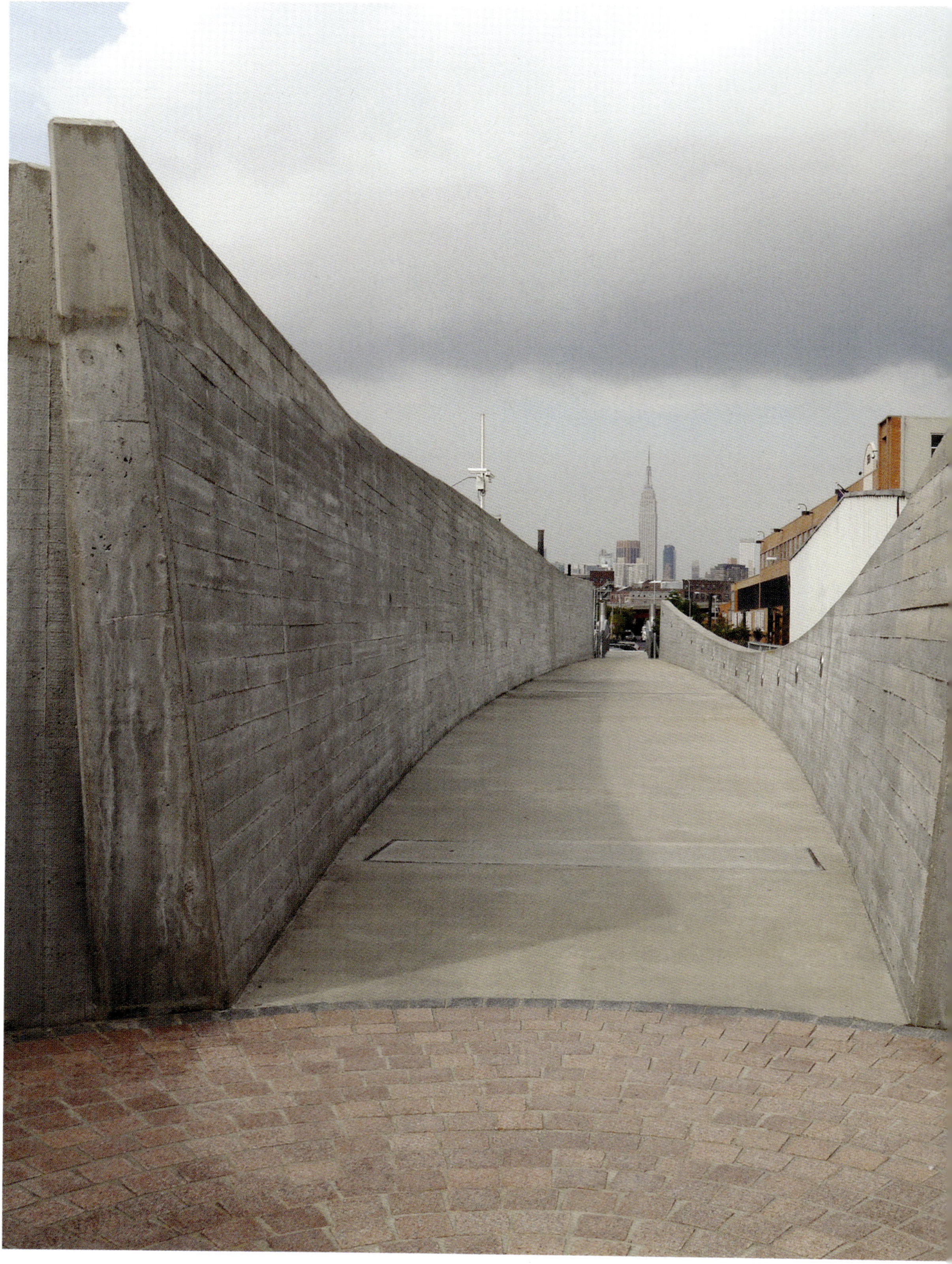

Newtown Creek Wastewater Treatment Plant is a dramatic and exciting assembly of pipes and tubes and shiny things, lit an otherwordly purple at night, and all dominated by four enormous pieces of industrial-Fabergé-chic. These are the symbolic and literal centrepiece of the plant: referred to in the industry as 'digestor eggs', this is where the business end of sewage treatment takes place. They loom over the waterway, linked together at the top with a glass-walled walkway, like a setting from *Metropolis* or *Gattaca*, and the public applies in droves to see the eggs up close whenever the plant advertises tours.

If the treatment plant looks like a vision from the future, the park opposite references a time past, one where Newtown Creek flowed fresh and clear, as it did when the indigenous Lenape people made their home here. Trakas' artwork is multilayered and comprehensive. Particular plant species were chosen for their cultural or historic significance, which is relayed on small plaques. The wood of the Kentucky Coffee Tree (*Gymnocladus dioicus*) was used for boat ribs, and its seeds are not only eaten by beavers, foxes and groundhogs, but were roasted by Native Americans and used as a coffee substitute during the Civil War. Rubbish bins are made in the shape of old water barrels; steps down to the water represent geological epochs, as do rocks placed among the planting. These were brought to Newtown Creek from Van Cortland Park in the Bronx. They were blasted into existence during excavation works for the new Croton Filtration Plant, which was constructed in the park after local residents protested its proposed location in the Jerome Reservoir site.

The Vessel with view on axis of the Empire State Building.

Co-locations **233**

Newtown Creek Nature Walk is tough and robust, like the gritty waterfront precinct it fronts. Yes, there are some trees in place now, but the overwhelming view is of industry: big barges with cranes on them moving crushed-up metal onto smaller barges with old tyres round their waterlines; big light towers, the undersides of big bridges, big billboards, big warehouse buildings – everything big and tough. The Nature Walk itself is more popular than one would at first expect, given its near neighbours. Mid-morning on a desperately muggy late September Monday brings a friendly man hauling camera gear, then a woman in a white blouse with a bow at the neck, wearing thongs and carrying her heels. Others come and go. Retracing the path to the entry, visitors pass once more through the swollen concrete walls of George Trakas' 52 m long *Vessel*. Holes punched through the walls allow glimpses of the mechanical equipment and processes going on behind. The view straight down the centre of *Vessel* aligns with the Empire State Building, seemingly a world away from the unexpected tranquillity of this park-like space next to the sewage treatment plant.

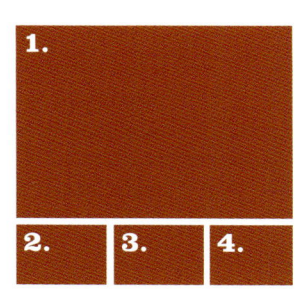

1. *This restricted space offers a variety of experiences.*
2. *In some places dense planting screens the immediate context.*
3. *Breaks in the planting show the riverfront industry of Newtown Creek.*
4. *Industrial scale water access and seating.*

Co-locations

The compelling combination of soaring design hidden in plain view is something the Newtown Creek Wastewater Treatment Plant and Nature Walk have in common with the West Point facility in Seattle. The genesis of the project was ironic: Seattle's residents had lobbied hard in the 1950s for a municipal sewage treatment plant, which was duly built at West Point on Puget Sound. The site passed from military ownership to the city, and developed into the lushly forested Discovery Park. The treatment plant, however, was highly visible from within the park, which had become a much-loved local and regional destination. Seattle's then-mayor thought he was onto a winner when he proposed feasibility planning for the demolition of the plant.

Brightwater Wastewater Treatment Plant: aerial view taken October 2011, showing the extent of accessible, park-like treatment integrated with the treatment plant. (King County)

236 future**park**

What he didn't count on was that nature had designed the waters around West Point to be ideally suited to receiving and dispersing treated water. The treatment plant had to stay. It also had to be expanded. And it was to be hidden from view. The solution conceived by Danadjieva and Koenig Associates was a series of undulating terraces, densely planted, that screened the plant from the waterside, and integrated it into Discovery Park. The roadways and pedestrian paths on the south side of the plant allow some glimpses of the treatment plant infrastructure, but the focus is on concealing, not revealing, the processes inside.

Whereas the West Point Plant has received praise and curiosity for its investment in civic architecture, the Brightwater Wastewater Treatment Plant down the road from Seattle in Snohomish County, has been criticised for being 'too nice'. In an interview on Fox News, Toby Nixon, a former Republican State Representative for Washington, opined about the 'Sewage Taj Mahal' that, 'It doesn't make sense for it to become a major educational centre, a conference centre, a place where people go as a destination for their Sunday afternoon stroll. We have parks for that.' Brightwater took years to build, and encountered numerous challenges during construction, including a 4 m deep sinkhole that opened up in the early dawn hours in a local driveway. Resident Jeff Rochon drove over the same spot only hours before, gratefully observing that it 'would have been quite the wake-up to drive right down a hole'. Despite its reported US$1.8 billion price tag, not all residents were against the project, and many were involved in its creation. Consultation with more than 60 stakeholder groups drove the incorporation of education and community space as well as public parkland. When it officially opened in September 2011 the festivities ran over the course of a weekend and included talks by public artists, a traditional blessing of the waters and live music, all presided over by the delightful Princess Sparkling Clear. Shuttle buses delivered visitors eager for their first glimpse of the 46 ha site, over half of which is given over to a sculptural, educational and functional landscape of wetlands, rolling landforms, trails and forested areas all of which demonstrate water-cleansing processes and habitat creation. Although the Princess Sparkling Clear's appearance was a one-off, the 5 km of parkland trails will be open from dawn to dusk.

Co-locations

Opening weekend tours of Brightwater were also offered as part of the inaugural Seattle Design Festival. Under a theme of *Beneath the Surface*, festival organisers aimed 'to reveal and celebrate aspects of design that are often overlooked or hidden from view'.[222] A similar motivation drove the creation of the Waterworks Gardens, located to the south of Seattle at 1200 Monster Road, Renton. Open since 1996, the public success of Waterworks Gardens helped embolden King County's ambition for Brightwater. Waterworks Gardens was never meant to be beautiful: three simple ponds surrounded by fences and screening trees were originally planned to discreetly treat stormwater run-off from 16.2 ha of hardstand as part of the upgrade of the South Treatment Plant. Instead, Waterworks started with 1 per cent – the mandatory percentage of the overall construction budget required to be spent on public art under King County's program for public construction projects. As sewage treatment plants are expensive to build and upgrade, 1 per cent of the budget amounted to US$650 000. The project team cleverly combined this with the US$300 000 allocated for detention ponds and US$250 000 allowed to restore an existing wetland, resulting in a US$1.1 million budget for the Waterworks Gardens. Under the leadership of artist Lorna Jordan, landscape architects Jones & Jones and engineers Brown and Caldwell, what emerged on site was an 'earth-water sculpture and a living landscape that integrates esthetics, infrastructure and ecology'.[223]

All images this spread – Waterworks Garden.

Opposite page above – Part of the chain of settlement ponds and wetlands. (Joe Mabel via Wikimedia Commons)

Opposite page below – The Grotto. (Joe Mabel via Wikimedia Commons)

This page – Entry. (Joe Mabel via Wikimedia Commons)

Co-locations 239

What these projects reveal is an increasing acceptance by both local authorities and communities of how public utilities can add value to their neighbourhoods by providing park-like places that are integrated or close by. Most of them also show an increased willingness to put water treatment processes 'on display', most commonly in wetland systems that catch and treat site run-off. Workers have no qualms spending their lunch hour in a park where water drains off the roofs and paths and car parks and is cleansed by special types of plants before flowing to a river. Parents are happy to send their children on school trips to see the frogs and fish that live in the wetlands. Would those same parents have second thoughts though, if the frogs and fish were instead living in water pumped directly from inside the sewage treatment plant itself? Far from being a potential public relations disaster, this is exactly the way that three very large-scale park-like places have come into existence in three very different locations.

The first is called the Talking Water Gardens, and it is located not far from several other projects described in this chapter. The cities of Albany and Millersburg are both located in upstate Oregon, and within the watershed of the Willamette River. Further west the Willamette passes through downtown Portland on its way to join the Columbia River, and some portions are so degraded that in 2000 they received federal Superfund designation (falling in the Comprehensive Environmental Response, Compensation, and Liability Act category needing environmental remediation). Upstream, the condition is not so dire, but human settlement has still had an impact: today there are substantially fewer secondary channels, sloughs, islands and riparian forests in the reaches of the Willamette near Albany and Millersburg than there once were. The cities share a sewage treatment plant, the Albany–Millersburg Water Reclamation Facility, that discharges into the Willamette, as does the ATI Wah Chang manufacturing plant to the east. Recent changes to state water quality legislation would have required compliance upgrades for both facilities, and the conventional engineering response, favouring least-cost solutions for the individual dischargers, would have seen an additional effluent diffuser being built in the river.

Albany and Millersburg elected to take a different approach. The cities expanded their own partnership to include ATI Wah Chang, and create a mutually beneficial public/private partnership, the first engineering project of its kind in the United States. Nearly 15 ha of constructed wetlands have been built in a location central to all three partners.

Talking Water Gardens: cascade at Lower Cool Creek. (City of Albany)

While the wetlands do provide some tertiary water quality treatment, their main function is cooling effluent water before it is discharged into the river. Water from the three facilities is pumped to the wetlands over a series of aerating waterfalls – the sound of water passing over gives the gardens their name. Paths and trails connect to existing links, and additional community facilities including a Visitor Center, additional landscape works and public art, are planned.

Talking Water Gardens. (City of Albany)

Talking Water Gardens effectively demonstrates the possibilities of mutually beneficial partnership between private industry and local government. The project not only enables regulatory requirements to be met, but provides net social, environmental and economic benefits. Despite the holistic and long-term view adopted by the local council leadership, USA Senators John McCain and Tom Coburn both included Talking Water Gardens on their list of 100 federal stimulus projects on which they claimed funding has been 'directed towards silly and shortsighted projects'.[224]

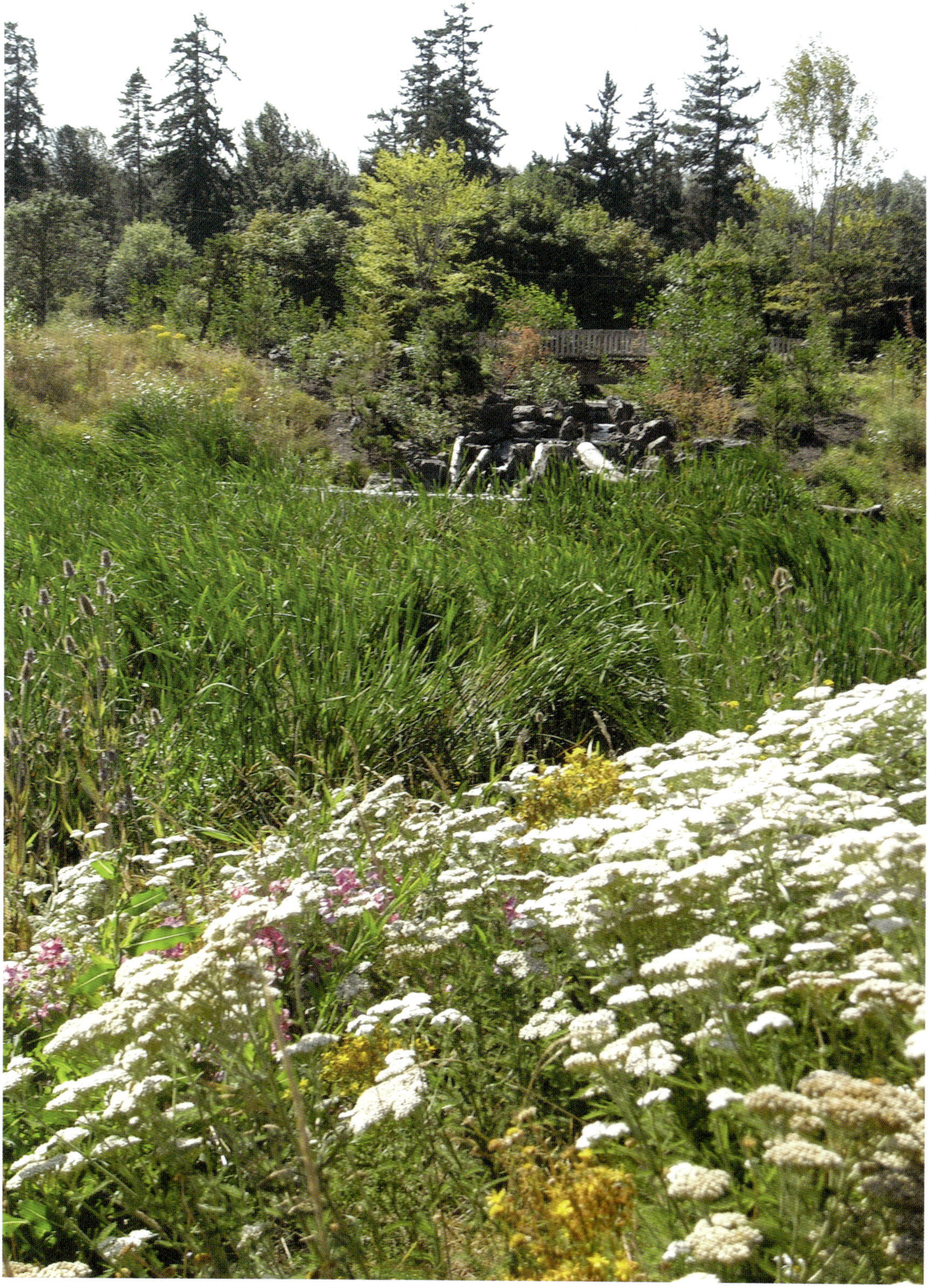

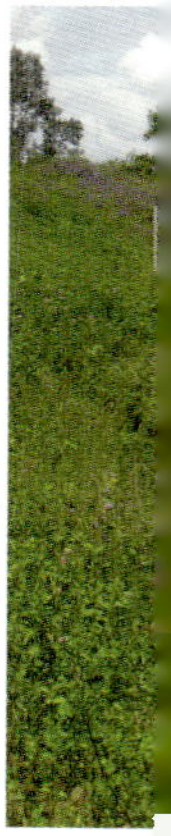

All images this spread – Talking Water Gardens.
1. *Cascade at the southern influent point. (Photo provided by the City of Albany, Oregon)*
2. *Bridge over Cool Creek. (Photo provided by the City of Albany, Oregon)*
3. *Entry on the Willamette River at Albany and Millersberg. (Photo provided by the City of Albany, Oregon)*

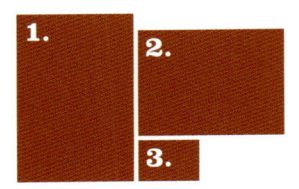

Co-locations **245**

Phoenix: Tres Rios project flow regulating wetlands.
(US Army Corps of Engineers)

The Tres Rios project in Arizona operates on a vastly larger scale. Its nearly 200 ha wetland helps enhance an 11 km long, 600 ha stretch of the Gila and Salt Rivers – the Rio Salado, again. As at Talking Water Gardens the wetlands at Tres Rios provide tertiary treatment to effluent from the municipal wastewater treatment plant, and this function drove the initial explorations into alternative, cost-effective treatment methods. As feasibility progressed it became clear that the wetland-based system could also provide flood control, achieve habitat and river restoration, enable water reuse and effluent conveyance, manage disease vectors and mitigate the urban carbon footprint by reducing the energy demand that additional mechanical water treatment requires. Federal, state and local agencies were involved in bringing Tres Rios to fruition.

This page – Aerial views of the Tres Rios project. (US Army Corps of Engineers)

After a long gestation and construction period, the wetlands received their first intake of effluent water in 2009. Operations and Maintenance Supervisor, Ron Elkins, observed, 'I realized I would never witness a beginning of this magnitude again.'[225] Tres Rios is a place that functions on many levels – solving technical and regulatory requirements is only one of its achievements. Tres Rios also provides community benefits. In the dryness of Arizona the wetlands are visibly alive and green. The river restoration projects have brought a rich array of birdlife into the city. Bird viewing platforms are among the new community facilities, along with paths, shelters, bridges and public art that are woven into this park-like place.

248 future park

In a different kind of desert, Wadi Hanifa, in central Saudi Arabia, is the final example of a project that embeds the wastewater treatment process into a landscape or park-like response. The Wadi Hanifa project is larger again than Tres Rios, with a 120 km long, 4000 km^2 catchment. A wadi is a valley, often an ephemeral streambed, and Wadi Hanifa was the historic water source for Riyadh, which now pipes desalinated water over 350 km from the coast. As Riyadh grew, the wadi changed. It was quarried for sand and stone, agricultural land was paved over for new development and illegal dumping was rife. The lower reaches flowed continuously, the result of rising groundwater and the discharge of sewage effluent from the rapidly growing city. A new landscape emerged, 'a luxuriant ecological corridor, almost 100 km long… with small waterfalls, lakes and islands, supporting a rich variety of flora and fauna'.

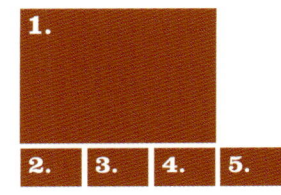

1. This project is already successful in providing water treatment while creating a one-of-a-kind natural facility and open-space public attraction. *(Arriyadh Development Authority and Moriyama Teshima Planners)*
2. Developing a major part of the Wadi Bed Naturalized Parkland and Recreational and Interpretative Trail, to get early public participation and use of the Wadi environment. *(Arriyadh Development Authority and Moriyama Teshima Planners)*
3. The parks are designed in a way that provides family compartments, in the form of semi-enclosed areas, that each family can use for the day, without being disturbed by neighbouring families. *(Arriyadh Development Authority and Moriyama Teshima Planners)*
4. The Bio-remediation Facility is one of the most impressive features of the project. *(Arriyadh Development Authority and Moriyama Teshima Planners)*
5. Wadi Hanifa: aerial view in 2009. *(Arriyadh Development Authority and Moriyama Teshima Planners)*

Co-locations

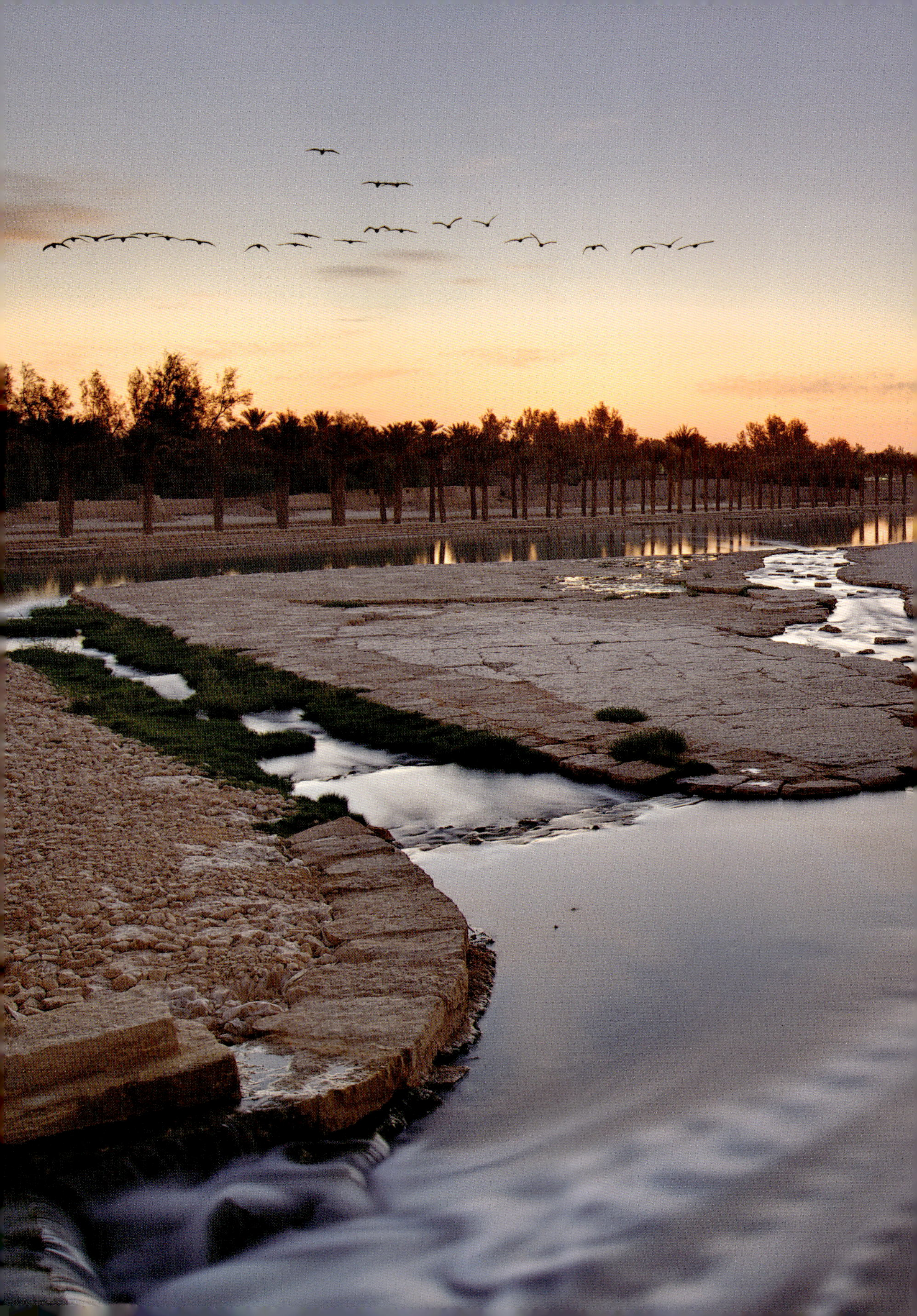

Re-establishing the natural landscape in the desert tablelands and rangelands of the desert catchment area above the Wadi bed, including construction of check dams. (Arriyadh Development Authority and Moriyama Teshima Planners)

Recognising that something needed to be done to safeguard the wadi, the Arriyadh Development Authority commissioned Buro Happold, engineering consultants, and architects Moriyama and Teshima to prepare the Wadi Hanifa Comprehensive Development Plan 2002. The resulting master plan and program of ongoing enhancement and restoration projects was based on securing the wadi as an 'environmental, recreational and tourism resource'. In 2010 the Wadi Hanifa initiative was honoured at the Aga Khan awards. Among the projects completed to date is a new wastewater treatment plant that provides treated water resources for both rural and urban Riyadhis, and uses an extensive wetland system.

The entire wadi is a park-like system, with agricultural land retained and enhanced, existing wildlife areas conserved, and new recreational facilities and amenities developed along its length.

As discussed, parks associated with water and sewage treatment plants share the advantage of waterfront locations. This makes sense, as the plants themselves are generally located so they can capture and treat incoming urban wastewater and then release it, clean, back into the waterway system. Ongoing community and government focus on waterway health continues to drive an emphasis on access and connection, education and stewardship of urban waterways. Coupled with this is an ongoing human desire to be close to 'nature', which in increasingly urbanised environments puts added pressure on the rivers, lakes and coastlines of our cities.

What the above examples show is that parks in, beside or close to water and sewage treatment plants, and other pieces of civic infrastructure, can succeed. Not everyone is put off by big public utilities. Tours of many treatment plants, reservoirs and the like are quickly oversubscribed when they open for bookings. Random 'Googling' of most of the facilities described above will bring forth at least one blog post from a regular person (not a scientist or engineer or plumber) who has decided to book in for such a tour, just to see what it's all about. For those who are put off by the realities of municipal infrastructure, however much they rely on them, co-location offers a way to render infrastructure more 'appealing'. If a parkland setting brings a community closer to a wastewater treatment plant, then it brings them closer to thinking about how such facilities work, how much energy they use, how much space they require, how much money they cost and what alternatives there might be. Successful co-location projects show that municipal need, cost effectiveness and community benefit can co-exist, and they demonstrate that bringing together different parties with different problems can deliver results that are greater than the sum of their parts.

... parks associated with water and sewage treatment plants share the advantage of waterfront locations.

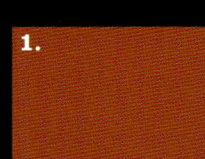

1. Picnic area along the Wadi. (Arriyadh Development Authority and Moriyama Teshima Planners)
2. Interpretative trails wind their way throughout the Wadi allowing the public to access the area easily and directing them to places of interest. (Arriyadh Development Authority and Moriyama Teshima Planners)
3. A series of natural stone weirs were built in order to introduce oxygen into the water as it passes over and through them, helping to reduce the amount of pollution in the Wadi. (Arriyadh Development Authority and Moriyama Teshima Planners)
4. Riyadh: Wadi Hanifa before implementation of the project. (Arriyadh Development Authority and Moriyama Teshima Planners)

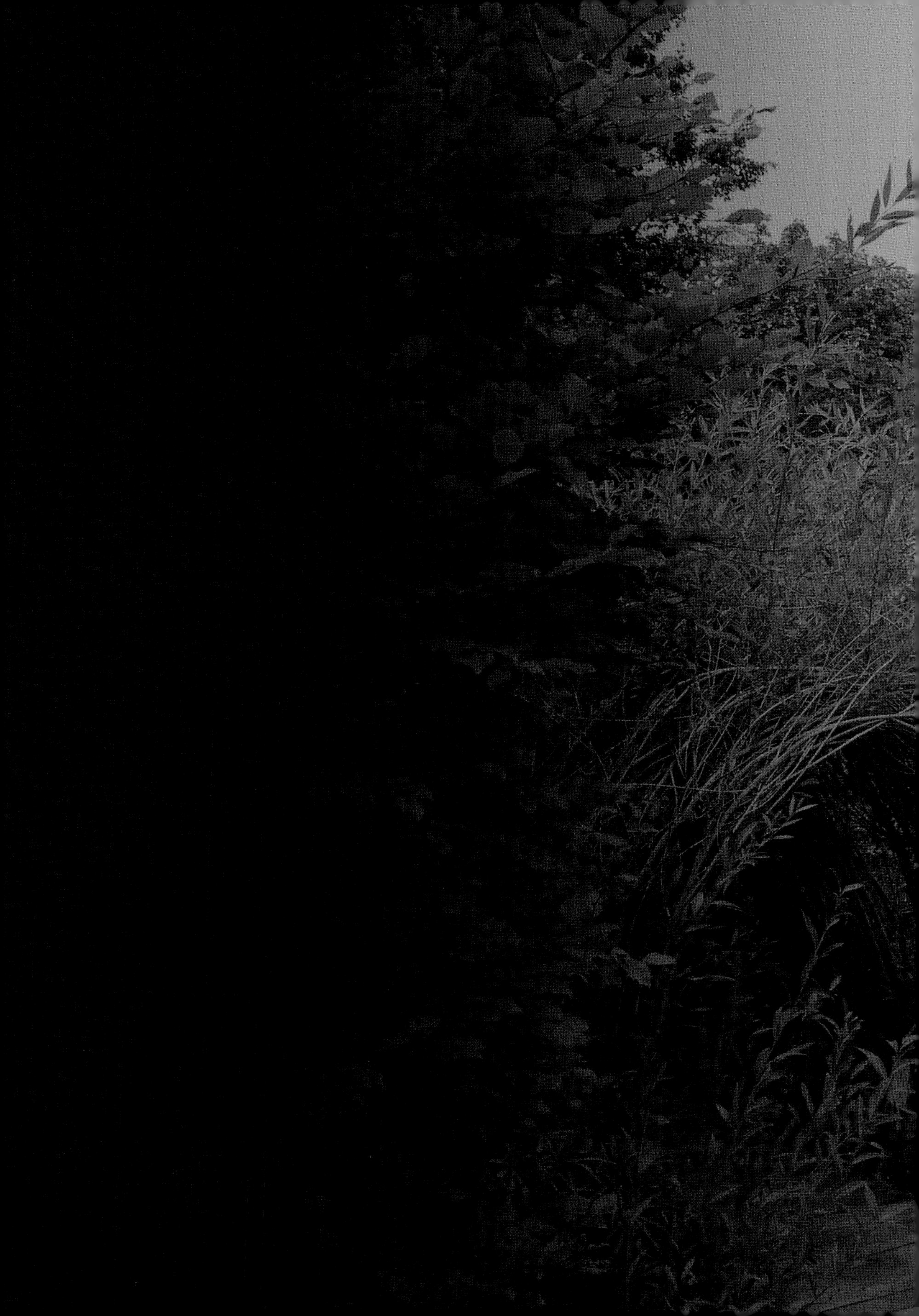

04
Installations

Installations

In the summer of 1982 an artist planted a field of golden wheat in lower Manhattan, only a few blocks from Wall Street on a landfill site with views to the Statue of Liberty. Nearly 10 years later a different wheat field appeared on the Champs Elysées in Paris. Travel forward another decade and images of fields and cows were projected onto a brick wall in Brooklyn by a landscape architect. Children tried to climb over the log rail fence and fake turf she installed to get a closer look. Five or so years after this, the same New York borough had design bloggers rushing to their keyboards to report about people frolicking in swimming pools made from garbage skips, or dumpsters, and installed in a top secret location.
On the other side of the world people prepared to lounge for the tenth year in a row not next to dumpsters, but on a sandy beach by the banks of the Seine. The beach appeared only a month after the Champs Elysées was closed again, transformed into a 1.5 km-long garden that was visited by 2 million people.

These intriguing urban happenings, occurring over a timeframe of several decades, appear random and unconnected. I believe, however, they form landmarks on an exciting journey of exploring a new type of urban public space. This exploration has steadily gained momentum as it interrogates and draws from the possibilities of unlocking private lots, repurposing public streets, learning from 'guerilla' events, challenging the status quo at festivals, and experimenting and empowering through land art. Installation parks provide our fourth and final way of thinking about what parks could be and how we make parks in our cities.

Of all the emerging park typologies discussed in this book, this one is perhaps the most elusive.

That is not to say that installation parks occur less frequently than co-location parks, or are more difficult to achieve than linkage parks: in some cities the opposite is patently true. It is also not a problem with definition. Installation parks can be most simply understood as those that are implemented for a limited time: an installation park is a temporary park. What makes this type of park-making approach so intriguing is, instead, the diversity of activities, motivations and inspirations that are represented and intertwined in the concept.

> *Of all the emerging park typologies discussed in this book, this one is perhaps the most elusive.*

This chapter provides, therefore, a sampler of installations, ranging from those that are quite recognisably park-like, to those of the 'sort-of-if-you-squint-very-hard' persuasion. What unites all projects is, first, a response to time and, second, a commitment to encouraging viewers and participants to think differently about what they consider a 'normal' park. And it is this aspect that binds installation parks to the other park-like approaches we have explored. Like them, installation parks challenge and invite us to think differently about what parks are, how we use them, what they do and what they could become in the future.

She couldn't have known it at the time, but the exposed and barren site Agnes Denes had spotted in downtown Manhattan was going to make her famous. Historic Battery Park was the location of the city's southernmost defensive fortifications. Located at the very bottom of Manhattan Island, the site of the original battery is now a park, built on top of a substantial nineteenth century landfill, and as you progress further below the surface, on top of car parks, roads and subways. Battery Park City lies around the corner, just up and to the north-west. Today it is home to some 10 000 residents who live in the many highrise buildings, work in the barely chastened global epicentre of trade and finance, enjoy the views of the Hudson River from the 14-plus ha of parkland and waterfront esplanades, and do it all in the vast psychological shadow cast over their neighbourhood by the absence of the World Trade Center. When Agnes Denes found her site in 1982 none of this existed.

If you look at old maps of lower Manhattan the shoreline is almost completely encircled by a fringe of bristly piers. Like a giant zip these piers formed a new transition zone between the land and the water. Claimed from the water with material discarded from the land, the piers and their denticular pattern, reaching out into the waters, gave physical form to the importance of the sea in creating, building and sustaining New York. The famous Manhattan street grid pattern responds to this central fact: when the map was created the numbered cross streets were more closely spaced than the avenues to enable ease of movement between the shorelines.[226]

Over time many piers fell into disuse. As shipping declined in importance and manufacturing moved elsewhere, piers that had once formed the stage upon which the first acts of the New York story had been played out were closed, then abandoned, and finally reclaimed by the sea. In many instances the tops of the supporting piles were all that remained, delicately pinpricking the waterline and the memory. It was from such an ignominious end that Battery Park City was born, created a truckload at a time by filling over, around and in-between disused piers. The bristly city edge was smoothed out into a new bulge of land, its westernmost edge defined by the furthest reach of the piers.

Nearly all the fill material came from excavation of the World Trade Center site.[227] Contemporary photographs show a ground surface containing bricks, pieces of broken concrete, wire, rusted pipes and metalwork.[228] And it was in this curious and confronting landscape of destruction and creation that Agnes Denes planted wheat.

Planning took many months. Denes and an *ad hoc* team of volunteers spread eight truckloads of soil over hundreds of truckloads of landfill material, covering a 0.8 ha site with scant centimetres of topsoil, and hand clearing landfill waste from 285 furrows. Seeds were sown by hand and over a four-month growth period the field was tended; irrigated, weeded, and kept free of disease. Harvest day yielded just over 450 kg of wheat.[229] The location of *Wheatfield – A Confrontation* is not marked on any map. No signs or plaques indicate its presence. Contemporary photographs show one view with the Statue of Liberty rising above a vast foreground of golden wheat, and another, equally iconic, with the twin towers of the World Trade Center looming in the background. So vast are they and so completely do they fill the frame that only a small strip of grain field remains visible in the image.

What was the point, and what does this have to do with parks? For a start, Denes chose her site because, however bedraggled at first glance, the land being created at Battery Park City was worth US$4.5 billion. It was paradoxical to grow something as simple as a field of wheat on such valuable land, and by doing so Denes sought to represent 'the ideals of this country, and money' by drawing attention to 'mismanagement, the use of the land, the misuse of the land, and world hunger'.[230] In that respect *Wheatfield* can be seen as one of the evolutionary antecedents from which many contemporary installation parks descend. It demonstrates one of the fundamental tenets to which most parks in this book subscribe; it challenges us to think about things differently, in this case to think about the value of land and the uses we put it to. As for being a park, *Wheatfield – A Confrontation* was not one, and was never intended to be viewed as such. But it did provide a visual counterpoint to the constructed concrete landscape of downtown. As be-suited power brokers looked down on the field from their high-rise windows, they saw something that, if not 'nature', or even 'natural', was undeniably organic and definitely picturesque. The wheatfield thus provided, at least psychologically, the Olmstedian requirement for a respite from the travails of city life.[231] Finally, the field was only there temporarily. After one growing season it was gone. And yet the knowledge that it would grow inexorably day-by-day, for a certain number of weeks, until ready for harvest, and then not be seen again in this landscape of concrete and steel, conferred an additional power and poignancy to the otherwise unremarkable field.

Wheatfield – A Confrontation is today regarded as one of the seminal works of land and environmental art.

Emerging during the 1960s, this movement responded to a period of awakening social consciousness, intense questioning, and 'longing – for a future that broke with a complacent present and for a past that transcended both'.[232] By the time Agnes Denes' wheatfield had vanished under apartment towers, this notion of questioning and longing had already been deeply embraced by another artist. His artwork, at once provocation and response, would make him as famous in the art world as Denes, and it had already been quietly growing for four years, just up the road from hers.

Alan Sonfist started planning *Time Landscape* in 1965, but he didn't get to start making the piece that would become his defining work until 13 years later. Sonfist sought out ordinary sites in the city, which he proposed to transform into reconstructions of the pre-settlement landscape of New York. This ambitious project was most visibly realised on a 0.75 ha site on the corner of Houston Street and LaGuardia Place in Greenwich Village. When first planted, *Time Landscape* was intended to portray the three stages of forest growth, from open grassland to pioneer forest of saplings and finally mature grown trees. According to the New York City Parks Department, which now manages the site, the three parts of *Time Landscape* are slowly evolving into an oak forest, and today display the following elements:

> 'The southern part of the plot represented the youngest stage and now has birch trees and beaked hazelnut shrubs, with a layer of wildflowers beneath. The center features a small grove of beech trees (grown from saplings transplanted from Sonfist's favorite childhood park in the Bronx) and a woodland with red cedar, black cherry, and witch hazel above groundcover of mugwort, Virginia creeper, aster, pokeweed, and milkweed. The northern area is a mature woodland dominated by oaks, with scattered white ash and American elm trees. Among the numerous other species in this miniforest are oak, sassafras, sweetgum, and tulip trees, arrowwood and dogwood shrubs, bindweed and catbrier vines, and violets.'[233]

Like *Wheatfield – A Confrontation*, *Time Landscape* has never been 'open to the public' in the manner of a conventional park. It is enclosed on all four sides by a slightly dilapidated fence and we can only touch as much as can be reached between the bars, or which hangs overhead. The forest is planted on 'public' land, owned by the city, and is part of the Greenstreets program, which plants and turfs 'leftover' pieces of the city's road reserves. Volunteers carry out maintenance duties such as rubbish removal, which is a jarring incongruity that can only serve as a reminder that, however well researched the species, however well created the soil profiles, *Time Landscape* exists not in the seventeenth century but the twenty-first.

Within its small footprint it engages directly with the contemporary environmental and landscape architectural discourse. Is it a complex ecology with diverse habitats, or merely a symbolic gesture, a 'designer ecology' reminding us of a lost past without helping to build resilient ecosystem communities for the future?[234] Does it have 'a metaphorical impact and moralizing intent' that sets it apart from the function of other city parks?[235] The way Alan Sonfist sees it, we use statues in our cities to create monuments to great heroes, victories and battles. Why not also create living monuments to great terrains and geologies?[236]

Time Landscape is an installation conceived by an artist, not a landscape architect. It is managed by a municipal parks department, not an art gallery. It is made from the stuff of parks; trees, shrubs, soil and flowers, not paint on canvas. Its name confirms that this work of art deals with time. It does not do this passively, by deteriorating over the years like a painting exposed to the light, but intentionally and centrally, by evolving and transforming with us and the city around it, and by doing so, it uses the present to evoke the past. Most poignantly, *Time Landscape* is also a park-like place and installation confronting time on a daily basis. It may look older and more established than a field of wheat but perhaps because it is made of the stuff we are used to seeing in parks and cities it is more invisible and more vulnerable.

*Images this spread –
New York: Time Landscape.
(ephemeralnewyork.
wordpress.com)*

Unlike the downtown wheatfield, *Time Landscape* is not weeded, watered, fertilised or kept free of pests. A prolonged drought or aggressive invader could reverse Alan Sonfist's intentions in a season. While the site is managed by parks people, the land itself falls under the ownership of the transportation department. Trees the world over have made way for roadworks, including many much older than the 30-year-old babes on this roadside. Finally, the negligent custodianship of living trees by cash-poor parks departments and risk-averse asset management services has resulted in increasingly poor outcomes for both the trees and the public realm.[237] This is the challenge faced by *7000 Eichen*, the final land art installation that directly intervenes with the physical fabric of the contemporary city using the stuff of park-making, in this case trees and stone.

There are many in the art world who regard Joseph Beuys as, frankly, a bit of a joke. One of his most famous works consisted of the artist spending three days clad only in a grey felt cape and hood, and locked in a gallery space with a coyote, so I'll let you form your own conclusions. Others regard Beuys as one of the great twentieth-century artists, and, with Anselm Keifer, as one of Germany's finest exports. Landscape architects, whether we know it or not, also owe a great debt to Beuys, and in particular to his great civic installation *7000 Eichen*. This work was created for the seventh running of documenta, the influential contemporary art festival held every four years in Kassel, Germany. In the northern hemisphere summer of 1982, documenta 7 was held, the same time as the Battery Park wheatfield bloomed. Unlike Denes, though, Joseph Beuys was interested in exploring a longer time frame than a single season, and to do so he turned to the same material that Alan Sonfist had used: trees.

Like Sonfist, Beuys was interested in the absence and disappearance of 'the forest' from contemporary cities. He was concerned with reconciling the place of nature in an increasingly technological world. And he wanted to enable this reconnection with nature to occur within the everyday life of a city.[238] Unlike Sonfist, though, he did not seek to recreate the past, or symbolically remind citizens of what had been lost. Instead Beuys used the types of trees that were conventionally planted within European cities; planes, beeches and slow-growing oaks (the 'eichen' of the work's title), to reintroduce 'nature' into the barren streets of Kassel. By so doing Beuys initiated a deeply contested debate over the role and form of the contemporary city, the place for trees in such a city, and the best ways to plant and maintain urban trees to ensure long-term health and survival.

These are all concerns that are familiar to contemporary landscape architects, arboriculturalists and 'asset managers'. Street trees remain a starkly polarising part of urban life today, so it perhaps comes as no surprise that Beuys encountered strong opposition to his proposal for a work of art that required the planting of 7000 trees throughout the streets of the city. Anti-tree arguments included the need to preserve road corridors for future widening, the presence of underground utility services, the lack of suitable subgrade, and the general unsuitability of inner-city streets as a location for trees (sound familiar anyone?). Beuys ploughed ahead, addressing each obstacle by consulting with a team of specialists and conducting his own fundraising campaign, even appearing in a whisky commercial on Japanese television. Joseph Beuys succeeded in initiating his grand Stadtverwaldung (afforestation of the city) but did not live to see it completed. His son planted the last oak in 1987, the first anniversary of the artist's death.

Today, like *Time Landscape*, what was once considered an artist's folly is a protected landmark. However, because Beuys used everyday trees and planted them in everyday streets, it can be hard to recognise the 'works of art'. The way this is achieved is by locating the stelae, or basalt columns, that were placed adjacent to each tree as it was planted. These markers not only identify the 'Beuys trees', but form an integral part of the exploration of time that is central to *7000 Eichen*. The stone stelae represent the ancient world, and stability and strength in a time of change. Placed next to small saplings they were, in the beginning, the dominant physical component of the artwork. As the trees grew, the trunk size began to exceed the dimensions of the stelae; the stone provides a permanent benchmark against which the growth of each tree is registered and made particular. The stelae themselves were originally stored in a vast stockpile in one of central Kassel's biggest public squares. As each successive tree was planted a single basalt block was removed to accompany it.

Left – Kassel: 7000 Eichen. Period photograph c. 1982 showing the stone stelae stockpiled before installation. (J. Bunse via Wikimedia Commons)

Right – 7000 Eichen. The two trees in front of the museum were the first and last of the 7000 oaks planted. (Belinda Smith. Smith and Plummer)

Once all 7000 trees had been planted most were left to fend for themselves, despite Beuys' concerns with maintenance, and his desire that they survive for at least 300 years. Recent studies have examined the results of 25 years of *ad hoc* maintenance. If anything they serve to bind many works of Land Art even more closely to the practice of landscape architecture and to the use of installation practices to create new forms of public space. For me the most intriguing story from the three artworks discussed here is one about blurring boundaries. First the land artists moved their zone of influence out of the gallery, which enabled them to see the possibilities in a multitude of new 'canvases'.

Installations **263**

Agnes Denes, Alan Sonfist and Joseph Beuys saw the city as their canvas, but were then clever enough to use their positions as artists to negotiate the access, knowledge and politicking required to realise their visions. Most importantly, these three artists used their art to challenge others to see the city in a new way: to think about the relationships between culture and nature, between economy and ecology, between past and future, and between permanence and impermanence. Others have come after them to also blur the boundaries and create hybrid spaces with an in-built social commentary. Their work develops some of the central tenets of land art and gives them form in a way that advances our options for installed park-like places.

Louis G. le Roy is a garden artist who began working on his 4 ha site in the 1970s. Since then he has been engaged in a continual, self-described 'battle' between himself, space and time. The result is a hybrid space that le Roy calls *Ecokathedraal*, and the battle is at once simple and complex. Various plants introduced to the site by le Roy have become well established, and they compete vigorously with the structures he assembles. These are painstakingly created by piecing together bricks, stones, pieces of concrete and other elements from among the truckloads of construction debris dumped on the site each year in an agreement struck by le Roy with the local authority. Since le Roy began work 2500 ten-ton trucks have dumped the region's building waste on the site.[239] Through this annual procession the northern Dutch town of Mildam becomes part of *Ecokathedraal* and part of the story of time for visitors to the project. Not only do they experience the constant change in vegetation and the continually evolving built structures, the project can only proceed as quickly or as slowly as Mildam recreates itself.

1. 2.

1. *Mildam: Ecokathedraal. (Pwouda via Wikimedia Commons)*
2. *Ecokathedraal: detail of walls and path. (Pwouda via Wikimedia Commons)*

Ecokathedraal blurs the boundaries between artwork and public park. Like *Time Landscape* and *7000 Eichen* it continues to evolve as a living artwork. Unlike *Time Landscape*, visitors are able to experience the site from within, where they may actively engage with the walkways and undergrowth, and the way they have been manipulated into a visual commentary on the relationships between consumerism and waste. Or they may see *Ecokathedraal* as a picturesque ruin and contemplative retreat from contemporary life. Similar questions and challenges are presented to people visiting the *Rock Garden* in Chandigarh, India.

Installations

Like *Ecokathedraal*, the *Rock Garden* is made completely from the stuff a city no longer wants. It is the creation of one man, Nek Chand, who crafted by hand, in secret, using material that he transported night after night on his bicycle to a deeply forested location outside the city. Chandigarh is one of the great monuments and sacred sites of modern architecture and city planning, symbolic twin to South America's Brasilia in its deployment of monumental axes, heroic roadways and iconic built form. In the way of such designs it offers everything that an ambitious new city might need, except humanity. Chandigarh was planned and designed by the ubiquitous French architect Le Corbusier, and it was the employment opportunities available in the massive city-building exercise that drew Nek Chand from his home village post-Partition. Working as a roads inspector opened Chand's eyes to the great beauty of the local geology, including intriguing rock forms that seemed to him to contain an inner presence. He also witnessed the destruction of countless local settlements in the way of the new city, and the resulting piles of rubble and construction waste left behind. It was these interesting rocks and this leftover waste that Chand began to claim, and to move, piece by piece, on his bicycle after work.

For nearly 20 years he worked alone, at night, and in secret, fashioning a new landscape integrated into the forest, and filling it with thousands of beings, bejewelled women, traffic inspectors, tea vendors, human-like figures, and animal-like humans, all made from concrete, stone, construction rubble and a vast array of other discarded items. The *Rock Garden* was discovered by accident and only the foresight of several supporters within the local administration prevented its immediate destruction. Today the *Rock Garden* is protected by a non-profit foundation and is open to the public. Prosaically, it represents one of Asia's largest recycling schemes, but just as importantly it shows how new hybrid forms of public space – Is it a sculpture garden? An art installation? – can result from blurring the boundaries between landscape architecture, art and artist.

All images this spread – Chandigarh: Rock Garden.
1. Figures look down from the top of a very high wall. (Nagesh Kamath via Wikimedia Commons)
2. Detail of individual figures made from recycled pottery. (Giridhar Apparji Nag Y via Wikimedia Commons)
3. Window overlooking cascade. (Nagesh Kamath via Wikimedia Commons)

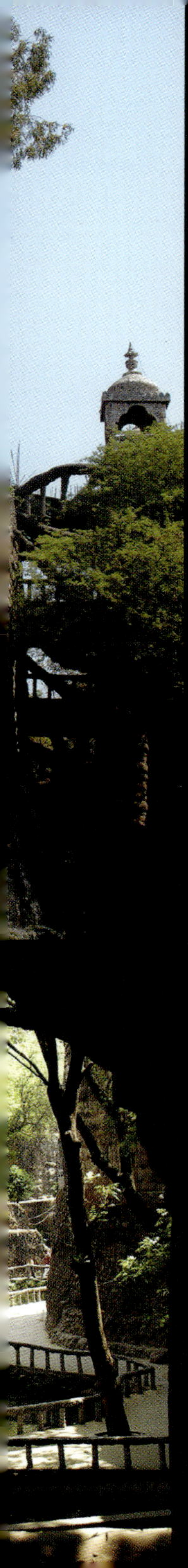
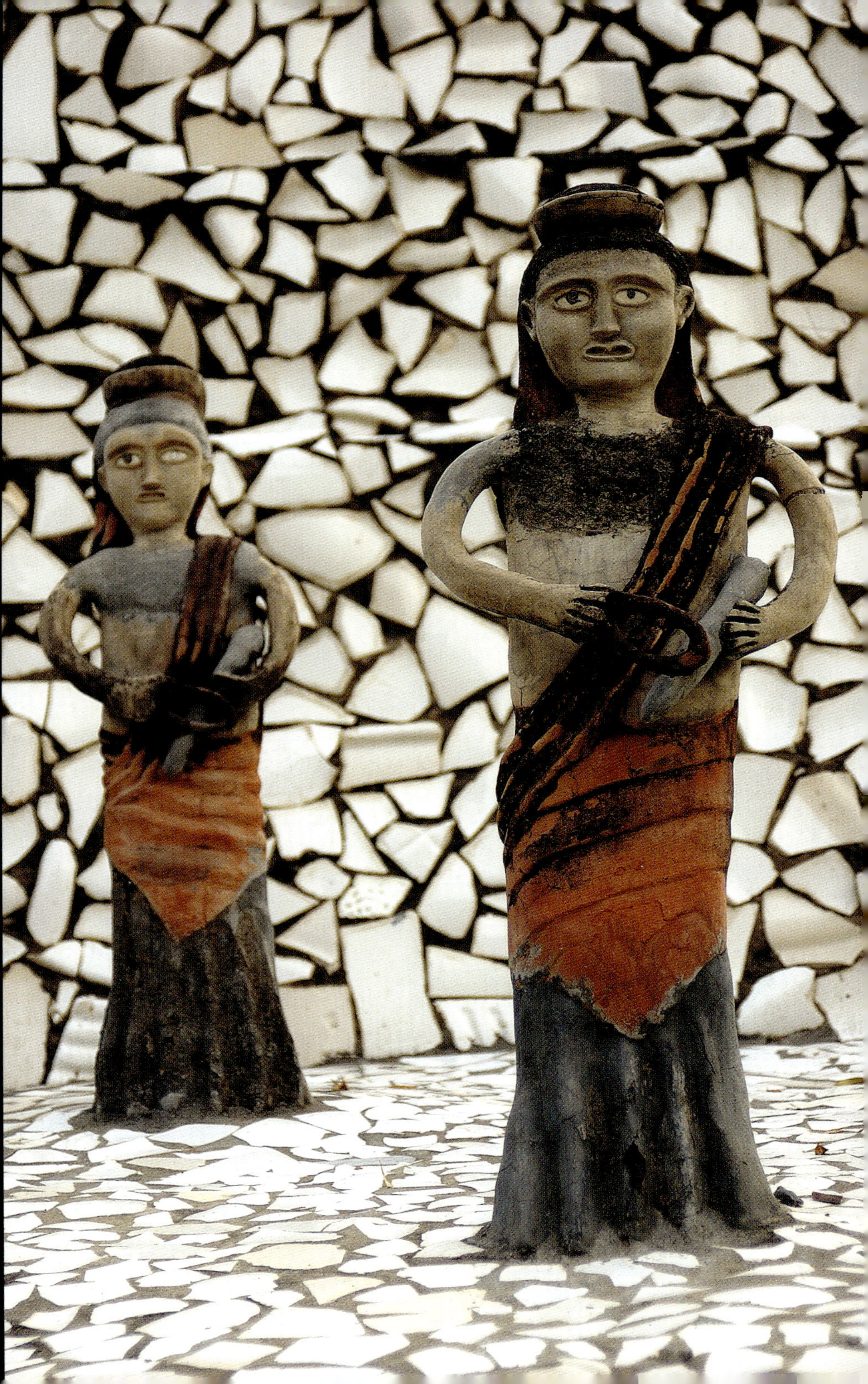

Over a million people have visited the *Rock Garden* in the past 35 years, drawn by the combination of otherworldliness, and skillful composition.[240] I suspect that people are drawn initially to the *Rock Garden* by the story of its creation, but they go back or tell their friends about it because they have found the spaces and experiences created by the humble 'amateur' to be genuinely moving and unique. Thus the divisions between 'professional' and 'amateur', and private vision versus public process are two final boundaries that have been blurred in the creation of recent park-like places.

There's a room in Wooster Street, New York, that's filled with dirt. The *New York Earth Room* forms part of the collection of Dia, a foundation established in the early 1970s to enable 'visionary artistic projects that might not otherwise be realized because of their scale or ambition'.[241] Among Dia's collection are such seminal works as Robert Smithson's *Spiral Jetty*, Walter De Maria's *The Lightning Field*, and a New York outpost of Joseph Beuys' *7000 Eichen*; five trees and their attendant stelae planted on West 22nd Street in 1988. Seeking to house its permanent collection of large-scale works, Dia undertook the purchase and renovation of a former Nabisco box printing warehouse in Beacon, a small town 90 minutes' train ride from New York. Continuing its commitment to and support of artists, Dia engaged Californian artist Robert Irwin to lead the design vision for Dia: Beacon. While design professionals did form part of the overall project team, landscape architect Brian Tauscher acknowledged that he was there 'not to install a landscape but to fabricate an exhibit'.[242] Leadership and authorship of the design response in terms of visitor arrivals, progress through the exhibition space, placement and sequencing of artworks, and landscape character and arrangement were all Irwin's direct mandate.[243] Although not a landscape architect, Irwin had designed a landscape before. His Central Garden at the Getty Center in Los Angeles was completed in 1997 and is one of the most visited parts of that complex.[244]

Despite Irwin's self-described motto for the garden, 'always changing, never twice the same', he himself was challenged to accept the placement of a Léger sculpture within his artwork. Criticised at the time for many aspects of the garden design,[245] a similar level of controversy did not seem to follow Irwin across the continent to Beacon.

Images this spread – Los Angeles: The Robert Irwin gardens at the Getty Centre.
(Nev Connell)

Installations

Dia Beacon: internal garden spaces designed by Robert Irwin. (USA Velvet via Wikimedia Commons)

Dia Beacon: showing the building in its park-like setting, as designed by artist Robert Irwin. (Rolf Muller via Wikimedia Commons)

Beacon is one of the most economically depressed parts of New York State, and officials latched on keenly to Dia's plans for the old factory. Things began in earnest once Dia negotiated a deal in which it would be gifted the building by Nabisco in exchange for undertaking the almost US$1 million site remediation required. The local railway station received an US$11 million upgrade, and extensive investment has been made both on riverfront land and within the town itself. Dia: Beacon does not represent the first time investors and communities have relied on the catalyst potential of a significant public art institution to reinvigorate a town; the 'Bilbao Effect' is coveted by mayors the world over.

What is curious about this project is the lack of reliance on a 'starchitect' to produce the necessary wow-factor building to draw in the punters. Curiously, Michael Govan, the Director of the Dia Art Foundation, commented expressly on the 'undesigned' nature of the project. In a 2003 interview he observed: 'It's supposed to look raw and simple… The building didn't need to be redesigned. It just needed to be tweaked and humanized.'[246]

Given the success of the Getty's Irwin garden in drawing visitors, Govan was surely being disingenuous in not admitting that the Foundation hoped at least some of the same magic would rub off on his project. The relative inaccessibility may be one factor contributing to Dia: Beacon receiving 65 000 visitors per year[247] compared with the Getty Centre's 1.8 million across its two campuses.[248] The other may be the type of landscape created by Irwin for Dia. Whereas the Getty's Central Garden is both an obvious 'garden' and destination, Irwin's landscape work for Dia: Beacon is more restrained. In fact, despite being responsible for the overall site master plan and the sequence of visitor movement from the moment of arrival by car or foot, the most obvious components of the work occurs within the visitor car park, building entry plaza, and the West Garden, a contemporary *hortus conclusus* built on the site of the old rail spur and loading dock.

Visitors may be through the forecourt and inside the building without noticing the first part of Irwin's work, and may be so overwhelmed by the expansiveness of the building and the collection that they run out of puff before making it to the West Garden. Certainly, reviews of Dia: Beacon do not single out the project landscape for as fulsome praise as they do for the Getty. Descriptions of the greater surrounding landscape do, however, feature loud and clear. Train travellers are advised to sit on the left-hand side of the carriage to take full advantage of the Hudson River views, while aerial photographs show the massive building deposited squarely in the midst of an abundantly treed watershed. On the ground this exterior landscape remains largely invisible, and the river cannot be seen from any point within the museum.

In renovating the building, Irwin chose to replace only a very few of the opaque glass panes on the long window wall with clear glass.[249] This serves to ensure visitors are not distracted by 'the scenery' and are able to concentrate on the art, bringing some of the land artists full circle, and back to the primacy of the gallery from which they once fought so hard to escape. It also reinforces, however subtly, that Robert Irwin's gardens are artworks and belong within the museum compound, the place of art.

New York: Looking down on the MoMA roof garden. (Peter Mauss / Esto)

    The idea of creating a piece of landscape as a work of art was also behind the new roof garden at the Museum of Modern Art (MoMA) in New York. Like Robert Irwin's work at the Getty Center the MoMA roof garden brought controversy and criticism raining down on its designer, Ken Smith. In this case it wasn't because Smith was an artist designing a landscape. At the time of accepting the commission Smith was in fact a celebrated mid-career landscape architect who started his eponymous practice in New York in 1992 after working for industry luminaries Peter Walker and Martha Schwartz. Instead, Ken Smith drew fire because he conceived of the roof garden as a temporary installation that did not contain a single living plant.

    Somehow the fact that Smith complied with pretty much every aspect of his client's constrained project brief seemed not to matter to the critics. MoMA wanted something that functioned as an art installation as well as a garden to be viewed from above, they forbade any structural fixing points or penetrations of the roof structure, they required a lightweight solution that would not impose structural loading problems, they didn't want to do much maintenance, or provide irrigation, it would not be open to the public to visit, and they required the incorporation of black and white gravels that had already been purchased.[250] Despite this long list of requirements, a clearly upset correspondent on the Archinect blog bemoaned the presence of something fake, plastic and 'always look[ing] the same' instead of a 'wonderful, blooming, LIVING garden',[251] while on the TreeHugger site Smith was damned with faint praise as a 'fantastic' landscape architect who had simply made a mistake, in helping MoMA commit 'the crime of the century'.[252]

So how did it all come to this? MoMA is a much-loved cultural institution, with a rich architectural, design and artistic heritage, and a slew of wealthy and influential patrons and neighbours. When the museum announced plans in 1995 to expand its premises, it seemed like everyone weighed in with an opinion. Some found the proposal by successful architect Yoshio Taniguchi too bland and safe. Others called it disrespectful for removing the black-clad façade facing the Phillip Johnson–design sculpture garden. Tony neighbours in the adjacent residential buildings disapproved of the height of the proposed six-storey addition (yes, even those in the 40-plus storey tower block), but they were eventually placated by the museum's commitment to providing a 'viewing garden' on the rooftop of the new building. Due to the protracted negotiations, Smith was not engaged to start work on the project until the building had been built, engineered and waterproofed, leaving him no opportunity to create a 'LIVING garden' even if MoMA had wanted one.

Several schemes were developed and reviewed with the museum. The neighbours objected, until Smith started playing with the idea of camouflage. The patterns from a pair of skateboarder pants were traced, and then, eventually, transferred to the roof surface, where they were outlined in laser cut foam borders and filled with blocks of shredded old tyres, rubber chip, plastic 'shrubs' fixed to PVC pipe and plastic grating, and finally several hundred painted fake rocks, of the sort used for hiding spare house keys in suburban gardens.

Being human, Smith probably prefers the praise his design has received, including an Honor Award from the American Society of Landscape Architects, over the criticism. Perhaps if the scheme had been called the Roof Painting, or even Installation, the expectations and reactions of the critics would have been different. However, even a cursory reading of his statements about the project demonstrate a much deeper level of thinking about landscape and public space than the sound-bite focus on fake rocks implies. The idea of camouflage appeals, for example, because it is so close to what landscape architecture does, uncritically, on a daily basis.[253] The 'shrubbing up' of vast developments and levelling and replanting of industrial sites is completely to do with replacing the view of one thing with the view of something different, but 'more attractive'.[254] The garden sort of camouflages the roof and its penetrating services, but it certainly does not conceal the building from view from above, quite the opposite. For some observers the roof garden simply represents one version of Smith's 'engagement with the notion that nature in our time is entirely constructed',[255] while others have pointed to the much-venerated example of manufactured landscape that we now view as 'nature' created at Central Park.[256] As for his roof garden always looking 'the same', achieving this and ensuring a consistently high quality 'visitor experience' is the aim of parks and gardens maintenance crews the world over.

Other critics have commented on the 'non-sustainable' qualities of the MoMA Roof Garden compared with its greener counterparts. It does not reduce the urban heat island effect or improve the thermal performance of the building below. This is true, but with Smith coming so late to the project it is a criticism that should surely be laid at the feet of the architects, engineers and museum stakeholders whose inputs preceded his by many months and years. Smith points to the use of many post-consumer recycled materials on the roof, including the rubber tyre chips that replaced the Mexican river pebble preferred by the architect.[257] This response only goes part of the way though, and does not clarify what will happen to those materials once the lifespan of this installation is reached. This aspect of temporary parks and public realm places is one that has to be addressed by designers, fabricators and commissioning agents if the idea of installation projects is to grow in application and acceptance.

It is of course ironic that the largest artwork in MoMA's collection is one that no visitor can see.[258] The museum intends that Smith's design be replaced in due course, and it will be interesting how his replacement handles the challenge. For our purposes, the MoMA Roof Garden has not only blurred the boundaries between artist, landscape architect, art and nature, it has proposed a new way of thinking about public space,[259] a way that challenges what we believe a garden or a landscape should be. In this regard Ken Smith's approach at MoMA is closely aligned to the aims and objectives of contemporary garden festivals.

'Ce ne sont pas des jardins, ceci n'est pas un paysage!'

This quote, which roughly translates as 'These are not gardens, this is not a landscape!'[260] was overheard by landscape architect, academic and author Susan Herrington at Métis, an international garden festival held every two years on an expansive property north-east of Montreal in Canada. The number of landscape and garden festivals has grown in Europe, North America and Australia over the past 10 years. Garden festivals supplement the ever-expanding range of landscaping expos, flower shows and citywide carnivals that attract huge numbers of visitors every year. In 2010, Australia alone held 16 major public events, ranging from the Tropical Garden Spectacular in hot, wet Darwin, to the annual Floriade festival in cold, dry Canberra. The Toowoomba Carnival of Flowers, in south-east Queensland, has been run for over 50 years, and in 2010 more than 80 000 lined the streets for the traditional parade through the city.

Chaumont-sur-Loire: International Garden Festival 2011.

Canberra's Floriade has been around for less than half that time, but now attracts around 400 000 people during its month-long running season. Expos such as the travelling roadshows put on by ABC television's *Gardening Australia* attract similar numbers of people wanting to not just look at plants, but also learn about maintenance and horticultural tips, as well as the latest in paving, outdoor furniture, barbecues and other 'lifestyle' items. Although the Australian public has actively embraced a more creatively waterwise approach to its gardening pursuits, following years of punishing drought and subsequent water restrictions, it would be fair to say that most people are not attending *Gardening Australia* shows to challenge their perceptions of what a landscape can be. This, however, is the objective of Métis in Canada, of its equally famous French counterpart in Chaumont, and of many other contemporary garden festivals.

Métis and Chaumont both opened their doors to the public again in 2011. Of the many teams who applied to create one of the three new show gardens for Métis was Terragram, the firm led by Australian landscape architect Vladimir Sitta.[261] Terragram's 2011 garden comprised a stretched and morphed layer of geotextile fabric covered with a landscape of soil and plants, and held aloft by a series of posts and trees. Visitors entered below the landscape and then popped their heads up through holes in the fabric to find themselves standing eye-to-eye with the plantings. Coming eye-to-eye with unexpected things and superlative-exhausting plantings is also the name of the game at Chaumont. I visited Chaumont on a resolutely miserable day and it took me over three hours to get there, from the time I left my hotel in Paris to the time I walked through the ticket gates. The International Garden Festival is not something that one just 'stumbles across'.

This process of deliberate arrival, of choosing to removing ourselves from the everyday in order to experience something 'new', is only the first of several aspects of time that are fundamental to the festival garden. The idea of time lies at the heart of the festival garden. For a start, these are temporary gardens, lasting from a season to a year or two. This means that we cannot experience the same type of relationship with festival gardens as we do with traditional gardens and parks; we can't go back for repeat visits, we can't see them change with the seasons, bloom, grow and mature. Many of the temporal experiences of traditional landscapes are provided by vegetation and, as the timeframes of trees and plants do not generally align with the timeframes of annual or biennial events, they tend to play very much a supporting role in festival gardens. Instead, garden festival exhibits blur the boundaries between traditional garden design and installation art, favouring set pieces of hardscape and built elements.[262]

There are exceptions to this general rule, and recent years at Métis have included gardens dedicated to the integration of landscape and architecture, and the rehabilitation of degraded sites through planting. *The Mobile Landscape Intervention Unit* by Charlotte Gaudette and Emmanuelle Tittley first appeared at the festival in 2004 as a mobile container filled with all the equipment and supplies necessary to remediate a (fictional) piece of degraded land. Visitors in 2005 could see the 'restored' and rehabilitated site, replete with lush vegetation. Similarly a sprawling aerial meadow was the centrepiece of *Head in the Clouds*, by Atelier Big City (Randy Cohen, Anne Cormier and Howard Davies). Visitors entered a shady undercroft space of columns before ascending through the structure of tilting elevated planes to the meadow, halfway between the ground and the sky.

Chaumont-sur-Loire: International Garden Festival 2011.

Installations **277**

Chaumont-sur-Loire: International Garden Festival 2011

A connection with time may still be established in the more sculptural gardens. Taylor Cullity Lethlean's Metis installation paired a meandering line of young eucalypts with a series of gently curving, laser cut, weathered steel panels. The screen pattern showed an enlarged version of the cell structure of the eucalypts. Although the plants did not grow much during the course of the festival, daily visitors could have enjoyed the shadowplay through the screens, at times forming a link between the two elements before breaking apart again.

Whether using organic matter or not, the one thing festival gardens demonstrate above all else is the hand of their creators. These are gardens designed by people and they visibly reinforce the idea of landscape as 'artifice, an environment artfully shaped by humans'.[263] By doing so they invite the viewer to consider his or her own relationship with, and role in creating the contemporary landscape at every scale. In this way the temporary installations at garden festivals provide a strong precedent for many installations seen at recent cultural festivals.

Garden festivals, while popular, appeal to a particular cross-section of the population. Cultural festivals aim to appeal to everyone. It is true that many of the world's great cultural festivals have grown up and around an ancient community event, such as the Palio horse race in Siena. It is also true that the purpose of many contemporary festivals is as much outward-facing as inward; an opportunity to showcase the city and market it to the world. As Sharon Zukin puts it, cultural strategies such as 'public art installations, modern art museums, and festivals have become a pervasive part of cities' toolkits to encourage entrepreneurial innovation and creativity, cleanse public spaces of visible signs of moral decay, and compete with other capitals of the symbolic economy of finance, media, and tourism'.[264]

While many cultural festivals explore or draw attention to contemporary themes, and invite public participation and questioning, they tend to utilise installations that are more conceptually approachable than those seen at garden festivals. In the past decade a variety of festival installations have engaged with topics that dovetail with ongoing explorations of what a public space, a garden or a park can be. Many installations have focused on the idea of urban agriculture as a way of transforming their installations from passive ornament or cerebral game, to active and productive enterprise.

In Washington D.C. the Smithsonian Museum hosts an annual summertime Folklife Festival. In 2005 the line-up included a garden of edible herbs, flowers and vegetables planted in the National Mall by school children from Berkeley, California. They represented the Martin Luther King Jr Middle School, which for 10 years had been part of the Edible Schoolyard Project established by Alice Waters, chef and owner of legendary local restaurant Chez Panisse.[265]

In San Francisco activist art and design group Rebar led a team of volunteers to produce the Civic Center Victory Garden in collaboration with the Garden for the Environment's Victory Garden Program, Slow Food Nation. After removing the turf from a 929 m² portion of the city's Civic Center Plaza, the team created a temporary productive garden which, at its peak, resulted in around 45 kg of fresh produce per week.[266]

The ideas expressed in these installations are not new, and the works of many land and environmental artists in the 1970s tackled similar themes. Helen Mayer Harrison and Newton Harrison's works, *Portable Farm: The Flat Pastures* (1971–72) and *Portable Orchard, Survival Piece No. 5* (1972), represented the orchards of California that were under pressure from pollution and development, threatening both the plants themselves and the communities dependent on the orchards for their livelihoods.[267] Where these festival installations have the most chance of changing public perception is when they have been placed in an existing and well-known piece of urban public realm. The National Mall is one of the United States' democratic urban set pieces. It is visited and loved almost to death in some places along its 1.6 km length. What message does it send for the Mall to grow vegetables rather than turf? The symbolic power of transforming a national icon was recently exploited by Michelle Obama when she reinstated a vegetable garden at the White House.

Art installations in familiar locations also ask us to look at the existing landscape differently. At the large end of the scale, Christo and Jeanne-Claude's *The Gates* provided a short-term opportunity for visitors to hit the refresh button on their perception of New York's Central Park. More than 3000 saffron curtains hung from sturdy rectangular frames, tracing the park's elaborate network of paths, roads and trails. Elements of the park that were previously part of the background were now framed for newfound appreciation. The contrast of the bright orange fabric against the winter landscape hinted at the autumn just past and the warmth of spring to come. At the small end of the scale, Julie Farris' *Temporary Landscape: A Pasture for an Urban Space* allowed Brooklyn residents to think about life and landscape beyond the city.[268]

Many of the festival installations described above occurred on pieces of public land that were already used or understood as park-like places. They invited visitors to look anew at those places, and to see the potential for adapting or using them in different ways. The following examples show how this invitation has been taken a step further. They have looked at the pieces of public land we call streets and roads, and undertaken temporary installations to transform them into park-like places.

Right – San Francisco: Civic Centre Victory Garden, Slow Food Nation.
(David Silver via Wikimedia Commons)

Below – New York: The Gates.
(Delaywaves via Wikimedia Commons)

Installations **281**

Paris: Nature Capitale, with the Arc de Triomphe at the end of the Champs Elysées. (Citron via Wikimedia Commons)

In 2010 the Champs Elysées was closed to traffic for two days and over two million people came to play on the street.[269] The closure was orchestrated by artist Gad Weil who worked in conjunction with French farmers' associations to cover the 10 lanes of asphalt with agricultural and horticultural installations. Called *Nature Capitale*, the project highlighted the plight of the country's farmers and rural workers. A year later it happened again, though perhaps not as dramatically, in Lyon, and a similar event was planned for Rio de Janeiro. Weil was familiar with the Champs Elysées, the 'elysian fields', having installed *La Grande Moisson*, a field of wheat, in the same location a decade earlier. *Nature Capitale* was praised by some for showing that major streets such as the Champs Elysées could become more than just places for cars. Others argued that the Champs, with its incredibly wide and popular footpaths, mature trees and enclosing built form and vistas, was already more than just a place for cars, and that removing traffic would diminish its vitality.

When the Sydney Harbour Bridge was closed to traffic in 2010, numbers greatly in excess applied to fill the 6000 places available for *Breakfast on the Bridge*, part of the annual Sydney International Food Festival. Why would people pay to sit on a crowded, exposed bridge when some of Sydney's most beautiful waterfront parks were only strolling distance away?

Is lawn the lure? Lawn is certainly one of the weapons of choice deployed by *Breakfast on the Bridge* organisers, and it makes for an appealing image on the 6 o'clock news; a vivid green stripe connecting the north and south shores of the sparkling blue harbour.

The lure of the 'country in the city', or the 'garden in the city' that unexpected turfing provided has been identified not just by event planners and festival organisers but also by advertising agencies. In 2010, several railway platforms at Britomart Station in Auckland were temporarily covered in turf for the filming of a television commercial for the dairy industry. Although this transformation was dutifully covered on green design blog *Inhabitat*,[270] in reality the exercise contributed nothing to the debate on urban public space options. What it did confirm were the complexities and contradictions inherent in allowing private money to buy the exclusive use of public space.

Breakfast on the Bridge is a private event that generates income and publicity for the event organisers, the sponsors and the owners of the bridge. For the pain of a two-hour road closure the owners benefit from guaranteed news footage of thousands of happy people revelling in the morning sunshine in the middle of Sydney Harbour. Organisers can claim that, however superficially, they are supporting 'sustainable' transportation (trains run as normal on their separate level of the bridge) alongside 'organic', 'slow' and other buzzword sustainable food options. Guerilla gardening founder Richard Reynolds observed that the temporary grassing of Trafalgar Square in 2007 allowed then-Mayor of London Ken Livingstone to make 'a rather pointless, expensive and ecologically dubious gesture about "greening" the city'.[271] Similarly, the temporary protest/installation by eco-warrior group Reclaim the Streets for a May Day event three years later, was viewed by Reynolds as nothing more than 'renewable graffiti'.[272]

London: Trafalgar Square with temporary turfing. (Andrew Skudder via Wikimedia Commons)

Installations **283**

Commercial interests definitely facilitated the three-day closure of Michigan Avenue in downtown Chicago for filming of the Oprah Winfrey show in 2009. Critics observed that an application to close the same road to traffic for three hours for an anti-war demonstration was denied. The power of Oprah will come as no surprise to Sydneysiders who similarly saw many publicly accessible parts of their city off-limits when Winfrey visited the city during her Australian tour in early 2011. The forecourt, steps and approaches to the Sydney Opera House were closed to the public for hours while Oprah's team bumped-in, admitted 6000 ticket-holders (350 000 applied),[273] filmed Winfrey pressing the flesh with Hugh Jackman, Russell Crowe and Nicole Kidman, and then moved out and on with the juggernaut. For Australian politicians, promoters and sponsors the whole 10-day extravaganza was worth the AUD$5 million Tourism Australia tipped in to get Winfrey to and around Australia.[274] For weeks before, during and after the event the press busied itself quoting the '145 countries' whose eager citizens would watch the show when it aired, and the millions in tourist revenue that 'could' be generated. In this light, upsetting a few disgruntled members of the public and overseas visitors who were kept away from the Opera House during the Oprah visit was an unfortunate side effect from the greater necessity of showcasing Sydney and Australia as destinations on 'the world stage'. As Sharon Zukin has observed, 'For the past few decades Destination Culture has offered a general model of a city's new beginnings in postindustrial production and leisure consumption… Like The Gates, [in Central Park, discussed earlier, and the Oprah Winfrey Show Live in Sydney] all forms of Destination Culture are judged according to their financial results.'[275]

Other short-term street closure events do invite participation by the general public. Early in 2012 part of Ballarat Street in Melbourne's Yarraville was turned into a 'pop-up' park.[276] Although presented as part of the Yarraville Arts Festival, it was hoped that the street closure would encourage local residents and traders to think differently about the role of parks and the public realm in their city. This is also the chief intention of PARK(ing) Day. Since its inception in 2005, September has been the month in which PARK(ing) Day is held around the world. In its first year PARK(ing) Day was the single act of San Francisco design collaborative Rebar, who fed a parking meter with enough coins to buy a couple of hours use of an on-street car park, and then used that time to install some seats and a ground covering, creating in effect a mini 'park' by the side of a street. They took a couple of photos and made a short film which appeared on (it seemed) every design blog in the world, and that was that; last year 975 temporary, car park-sized parks were created around the world during PARK(ing) Day.[277]

Parking Day. (G. Garitan via Wikimedia Commons)

Installations **285**

PARK(ing Day) appears to have done what many public art events have failed to do: attract media attention, public popularity and longevity.[278] Perhaps PARK(ing) Day works because it appeals to a particular market of students and design professionals who relish the opportunity to 'break the rules' for a day, and to be part of an event that can generate publicity for their creative design endeavours. Not many architecture/landscape students get the chance to literally stop the traffic with something they've assembled with their own two hands. Sometimes the temporary 'parks' are themselves so beautiful, clever or intriguing that they attract attention for themselves, and the underlying message of PARK(ing) Day, that there are many opportunities to provide park space in our cities if only we're prepared to look hard enough, can sometimes get lost in the noise.

Another criticism of PARK(ing) Day is that it distracts attention from existing urban parks, and the many benefits and opportunities that they already provide. There is validity to this claim, as parks in many cities go unloved and unvisited. Conversely many cities are blessed with many successful, diverse and well-used parks. In both cases it's easy to view a couple of kids sitting on old timber pallets covered in fake turf as noise, as a stunt getting in the way of the real work to be done. But that's how it goes with things that ask us to question the status quo. One thing that's undeniable is that PARK(ing) Day does not exist in isolation. Instead it is just one in a whole range of one-off events, and short- and medium-term transformations that repurpose segments or even whole street uses other than for vehicular traffic, and are eagerly patronised by the public.

Does the popularity of such short-term road closures suggest that people have a genuine interest in seeing and experiencing their cities in different ways? If you normally cross the Sydney Harbour Bridge in your car, concentrating on the other five lanes of traffic, it could be intriguing to see what it feels like to amble, to pause in that same place. If you normally only ever see oblique glimpses of the Arc de Triomphe through the trees along the Champs Elysées footpaths it would be dramatic to experience the same monument front and centre of your view, if only for a day. This ability to reframe the view of a familiar environment and experience a street without traffic noise and fumes, is one of the reasons for the sustained success of Paris-Plage.

Paris-Plage is both the best known and one of the most successful in a string of Urban Beaches located, usually, in land-locked cities around the world.[279] Unlike PARK(ing) Day or *Breakfast on the Bridge*, where parts of the road network are closed to traffic for an hour or two, or a couple of days, Urban Beaches create new forms of parkscapes by closing roads for a month or more.

Does the popularity of such short-term road closures suggest that people have a genuine interest in seeing and experiencing their cities in different ways?

During Paris-Plage the Georges Pompidou Expressway is closed to traffic and converted into a beach, park and pedestrian esplanade beside the River Seine. Temporary park-like spaces are also created in other parts of the city, including temporary swimming pools along the river, beach volleyball courts in front of the Town Hall, and a secondary outpost along the waterfront at La Villette. Paris-Plage provides a wide variety of summery spaces and places for people to experience, right down to cooling water sprays and misters. The first Paris-Plage was held in 2002 and was an initiative of the Mayor of Paris, who had a strong social agenda for pursuing the event. That is one of the many reasons why Paris-Plage works.

First, Paris in summertime is famously hot, and the ability to be beside the water is attractive. Parisians who can afford it leave the city for their summer holidays. Paris-Plage provides an affordable, accessible alternative for those who stay in the city, and has become a piece of 'Destination Culture' that draws tourists who would not otherwise visit at this time of year.

Second, with many people on holiday the central city traffic is reduced. Closing the expressway at this time of year causes less disruption. Third, Paris-Plage also brings a whimsical hint of Riviera glamour to the serious capital, and public space that is fun is public space that is used. Next, the temporary nature of the park means that it is relatively easy to extend or modify the installation each year, to accommodate greater numbers or different types of activities. Finally, the fact that it is seasonal creates anticipation, unlike permanent parks, which are perhaps easier to take for granted. All of these aspects contribute to the ongoing success of Paris-Plage.

Paris Plage. (slasher-fun via Wikimedia Commons)

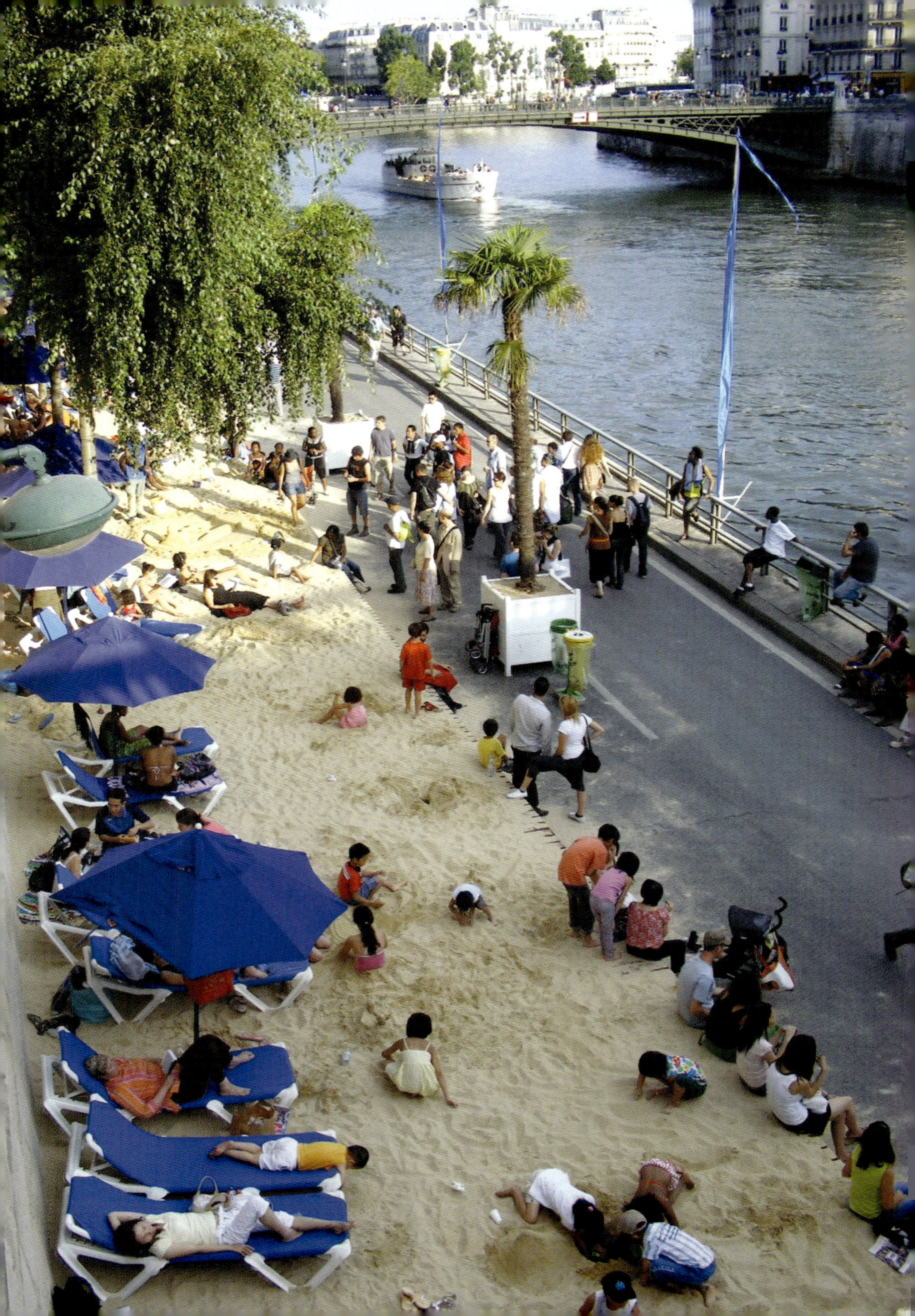

Opposite page – Paris Plage: Beach volleyball in front of the Town Hall. (Shizhao via Wikimedia Commons)

Seasonal installations can be good options in cities that actually have distinct seasons. In Brisbane it's feasible to have a permanent, constructed urban beach because we have relatively mild weather all year round. In Paris such a facility would be closed for at least six months. One common criticism of temporary installation projects is that of environmental recklessness. The annual importing and then disposing of the tonnes of sand required to create Paris-Plage is criticised for reinforcing the values of 'throwaway society' at a time when we should be encouraging longevity, incorporation of embodied energy and resource awareness. The City of Paris takes pains to publicise the use of river craft, rather than road transportation to move its sand. It also claims that the sand is entirely recycled after use.[280] Even so, addressing issues of embodied energy, waste and sustainability will be critical to ensuring longevity for the concept of Installation Parks, if not for the parks themselves.

Nature Capitale appears to be just as unsustainable as Paris-Plage, but the organisers believe the concerns have been addressed. *Nature Capitale* lives on beyond the lifespan of its weekend festivals, as pieces of the landscape mosaic are distributed across the city to enhance streets, parks, schools, riverfronts and other public places. In 2010 the contents of a 'food pyramid' display were donated to a local restaurant that helps feed the homeless. Segments of the 8000-piece green display were also sold off to bidders through the event website; 700 euros – around AUD$950 – could purchase a plot 1 × 1.2 m, delivered to your door, a limited-edition print, symbolic keys to the pre-event viewing and so on. A cheaper package was also available.

This is a similar approach to that taken by artists Christo and Jeanne-Claude, who sell drawings, prints and pieces of dismantled exhibitions to finance their next work. It is not clear, however, what happens to those pieces of *Nature Capitale* that aren't sold or claimed.

A concern with more sustainable use of urban resources does underpin other installation-based approaches to new urban parkland. The 'Pavement to Parks' initiative in San Francisco deliberately focuses on underused parts of the urban environment, identifying underused car parks and road reserve, disused rail tracks and other 'leftover' space for repurposing as parkland. Small-scale installations, called 'Parklets' are created by temporarily reclaiming these underused spaces. The Parklets are completed with substantial contribution of community labour, *pro bono* professional advice and recycled or second-hand materials. If successful, the city continues the process to make the Parklets permanent. To date, eight projects have been created.

'Castro Commons', at 17th Street and Castro, in San Francisco looks as settled in its community as it's possible for a park to be. Created out of excess road reserve at a trolley car terminus, Castro Commons is a place to see and be seen. Planters filled with sculptural groundcovers and shrubs hug the space, enclosing and protecting it from an enormous and busy intersection. The rainbow flag flies overhead. Movable metal chairs slowly migrate back and forth as people arrive, see people they know, stop for a chat, read the paper and then move on. A naked man with an all-over tan has a cushion on his chair. He too is chatting and watching, occasionally stopping to have his photo taken with a disbelieving tourist.

San Francisco: Castro Commons, a Pavement to Parks project.

292 future park

San Francisco: Castro Commons, a Pavement to Parks project.

TIMES
Prudential
HSBC
The world's local bank
HSBC
SAMSUNG
LG
Corona
Light
swatch

Above – Green Light for Midtown: temporary road painting and barriers near Columbus Circle

Opposite page – New York: Green Light for Midtown, the temporary transformation of Times Square. (Tiago Fioreze via Wikimedia Commons)

'Green Light for Midtown' is also a scheme that reclaims public space from road traffic, but at a much larger scale. An initiative of the New York Department of Transport (NYDOT), Green Light for Midtown is an ambitious scheme to improve both pedestrian safety and vehicular traffic flow through midtown Manhattan. Using extremely low-cost measures such as road paint, concrete planters and barriers, and street furniture, the width of road carriageways was substantially reduced along Broadway and other major streets. In some locations tables and chairs spill out from the footpath into newly created plazas filled almost to capacity with people strolling, window shopping or watching the world go by over a cold drink. Further north, close to Columbus Circle, the increased pedestrian space is delineated by huge green circles painted on the road. After a carefully monitored trial period over the summer of 2010, data collected provided the evidence that both aims of the project had been achieved,[281] and a capital works budget was to have been allocated to complete a permanent transformation.

We have seen that some cities have started to explore the creation of new public space by temporarily transforming their street and road infrastructure. Although the results may vary, and the impetus can range from festivals and events through to trialling proposed modifications, this approach is in some ways picking the low-hanging fruit. Most roads are already public assets, so changing from one type of public use to another should theoretically be reasonably straightforward. San Francisco, for example, owns and operates its own roads, parks and public transport system, and Pavement to Parks is a collaborative effort between the Mayor's Office, the Department of Public Works, the Planning Department, and the Municipal Transportation Agency. Identification of citywide goals is clearly articulated and interdepartmental cooperation is strong. When it works, transforming public space from traffic usage is a powerful way to add to the quantum and variety of city parks. What is more challenging is incorporating privately owned land into the equation.

Roads take up a lot of land. Even so, the largest proportion of land in most cities is privately owned. Many others have written about the opportunities and challenges of creating new public parkland as part of new development. Among the benefits is the ability for a city to increase its parkland space without cost to rate-payers. Parks can be built in exchange for development rights such as increased building heights or gross floor area.

Private development of parks in desirable residential or commercial locations frees local councils to spend their limited budgets in less affluent areas. On the downside, developer-driven parks may not deliver the type of parkland asset that a city may seek. Where a local council may want a park to contain large shade trees, a developer may prefer low planting that doesn't obstruct good views. When the discussion moves beyond just delivering the park and on to long-term operation and maintenance, the pros and cons of private involvement multiply.

A potentially easier place to start is with a piece of privately owned land before it is developed. Brisbane in the late 1980s was full of securely fenced blocks of inner-city turf. Developers had purchased sites and demolished the existing buildings, but whether through delays in development approvals or financial difficulties, many months and sometimes years elapsed before construction commenced. Brisbane City Council did not allow the land to remain as building sites, so the ground was turfed. Then, to keep people out, the lots were fenced. Lush lawns that were shady in summer and sunny in winter appeared as inviting urban refuges, mini parks, from which the public was excluded.

A decade ago, when Brisbane City Council was preparing to build its own new central offices on the banks of the river, a slightly different process occurred. It started the same way, with BCC acquiring its site and demolishing the existing buildings. The turf then appeared, but with it a few other things. There were a few trees, randomly distributed, and a couple of *ad hoc* paths were laid. Critically, there was no fence. In a short time this piece of land became valuable for the way it opened up new views of the Treasury Casino in its historic building, and the Brisbane River. It also provided a more direct way for pedestrians to get from the Queen Street Mall to the Victoria Bridge. But that, unfortunately, was it. When evidence of historic occupation was found on the site, the ensuing archaeological dig was kept off-limits and not publicised. Opportunities to manage the site as a temporary green stepping-stone between the bustling Queen Street Mall and the Brisbane River were not explored. Even the pedestrian desire lines dug into the turf were not taken forward into the final design for the site as lessons learnt.[282] As a pro-development city that seeks to position itself on the world stage, the management of its private development sites as an evolving series of temporary parks would be one way Brisbane could stand out.

The Lent Space project in downtown Manhattan provides one example of how the process can work. Lent Space is a privately owned development site, 2508 m² in size, located across the road from the cinema where Robert De Niro's Tribeca Film Festival is held each year. I stumbled across Lent Space on a cold and windy May morning, without knowing about the project, but drawn to the intriguing mixture of public art, robust built-in furniture and fencing, and the semi-permanent nature of what was obviously a place open to the public. It turned out that, in conjunction with the Lower Manhattan Cultural Council (LMCC), the owner of the site had agreed to it being used as a temporary cultural space, until the planned development went ahead. While the site was fenced it was open from dawn to dusk, and had hosted a series of artists who had made temporary artworks. The LMCC involved design firm Interboro, who had responded to the site and nature of the project with a plywood kit of parts of seats, benches, openable walls and planters, in which were planted advanced tree stock that would eventually be placed as street trees around the neighbourhood.

New York: Lent Space temporary cultural and parkland space in Tribeca.

Installations   **297**

New York: Lent Space temporary cultural and parkland space in Tribeca.

The whole design language of Lent Space speaks of a temporary park. The plywood benches look like they will only last a few years. The trees look like they're in a holding nursery. The ground plane looks like it's just been levelled and covered in gravel. The fence looks like you aren't meant to go in when the gate is shut. Lent Space treads a fine line between being designed enough that it makes a meaningful contribution as a public space, but not so much that there will be a huge protest when it is eventually dismantled. It will be interesting to see what, if any, of the successful elements of the park might be incorporated into the final scheme for the site.

Looking more permanent than temporary created a different challenge for the owners of Rottenrow Gardens in Glasgow. The Gardens are located in central Glasgow and owned by the University of Strathclyde. The site was bought for redevelopment by the university after the Glasgow Royal Maternity Hospital planned to replace its existing building with a new modern facility elsewhere. The old building was duly demolished and, in good faith, the hospital engaged landscape architects GROSS.MAX to prepare a design for transforming the steeply sloping site into a temporary park. The designers jumped at the opportunity to work with both the terrain, the remnant structures, and the very idea of a temporary place. The design involved a deliberately restrained palette of hardy and quick-growing emergent plant species. The idea was to get a lot of green happening in a short period of time. Pieces of concrete and walls that were left behind after demolition were quickly covered by rampant creeping vines. Rottenrow Gardens very quickly developed the look of 'a forgotten garden that never was'.[283]

People loved it. So much so that when time was up and the university was ready to plan its new building, a public outcry ensued against the removal of vital green space. Some visitors to Rottenrow Gardens genuinely had no idea that this was anything other than a long-established piece of green parkland. The university was fortunately in the position of being able to adjust its plans and build elsewhere on campus, allowing the Gardens to remain as parkland. Visiting Rottenrow Gardens today one still feels that sense of a place forever caught between what was and what could be.

What is the difference between Lent Space and Rottenrow Gardens? For one thing, the designers of Rottenrow wanted it to look 'established' as quickly as possible, with dense stands of vegetation, whereas Lent Space looks a bit rough-and-ready, almost home-made. This is a quality that adds to the park as a unique place. In both cases it is possible that the designers approached their tasks differently knowing the products would only be in existence momentarily. Would GROSS.MAX have used those fast-growing trees and climbers for a permanent park on the same site? Has the constraint of designing a temporary park actually provided an opportunity for both designers to be more adventurous or whimsical?

What about the public? Even without knowing the histories of the two parks do visitors to Lent Space and Rottenrow somehow react differently? Was it the fact that there were so many plants that saved Rottenrow? Does the slightly ramshackle presentation and lack of overwrought detailing somehow result in visitors feeling more relaxed in these places than they would in a more manicured park? What does this tell us about the fine line between low maintenance and neglect?

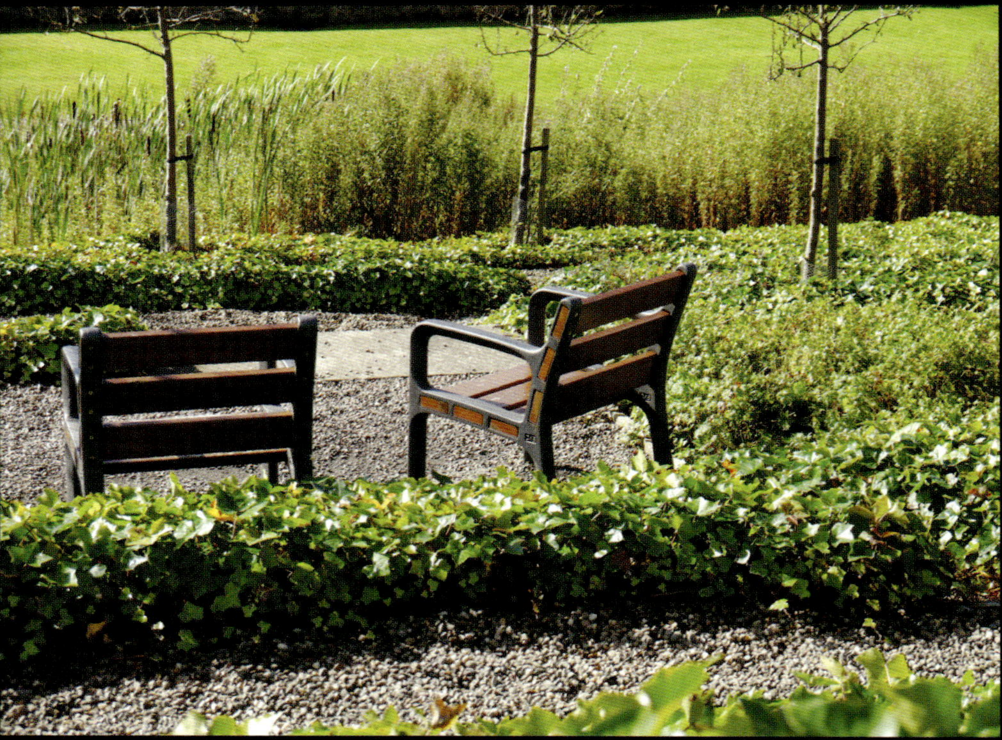
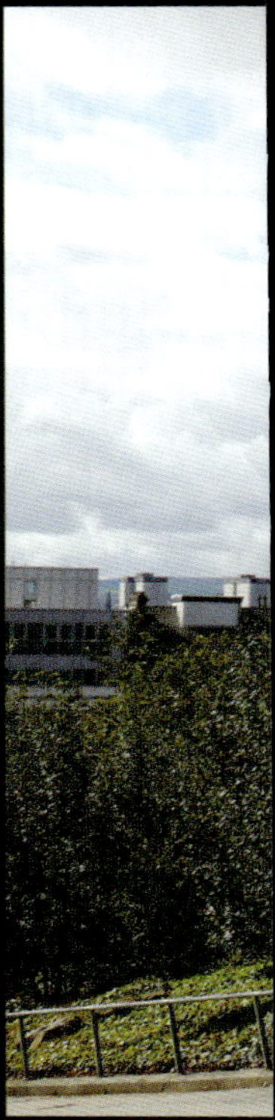
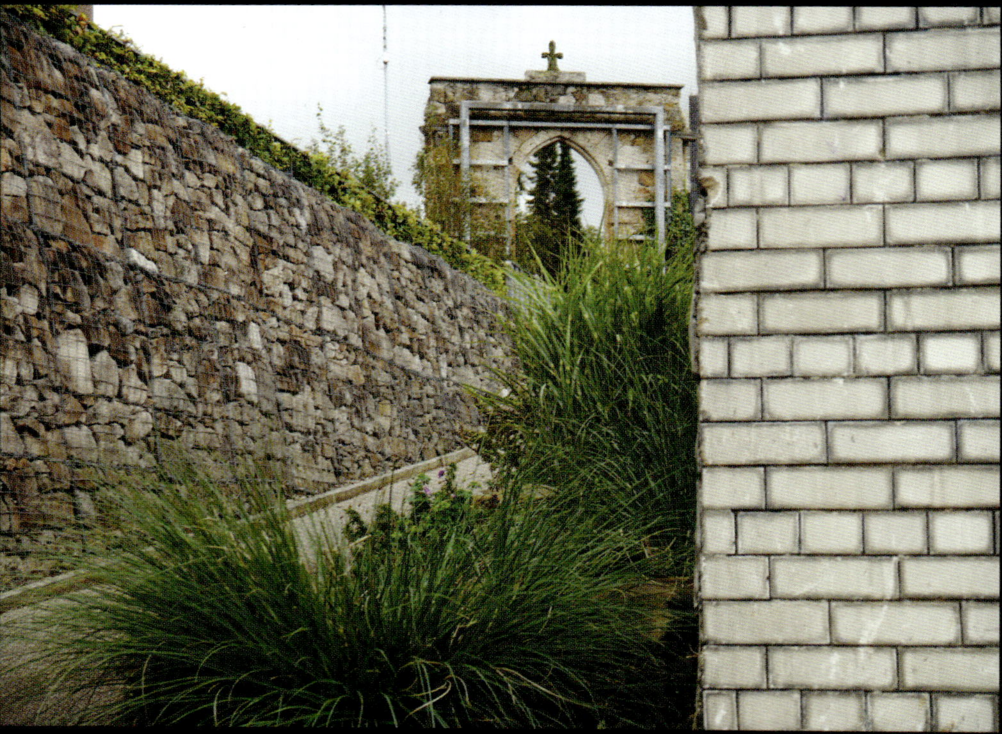
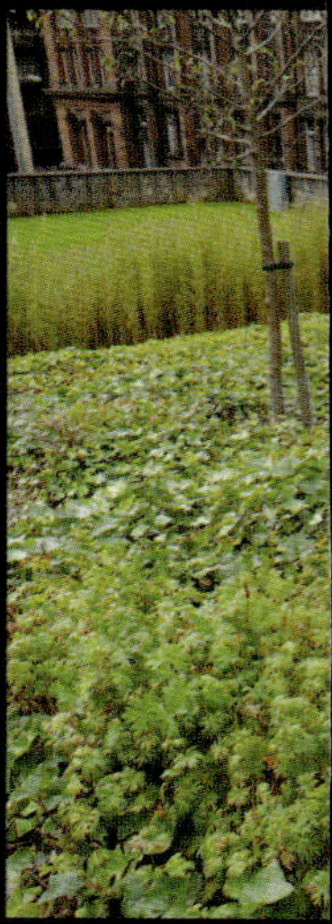

All images this spread – Rottenrow Gardens.
1. Solitary spaces.
2. The retained hospital entry gate.
3. Walls from the old hospital are integrated into the par[k]
4. Fast-establishing plants cover the site.

Retained hospital walls and new construction create a layered tapestry of materials and textures interwoven with the planting.

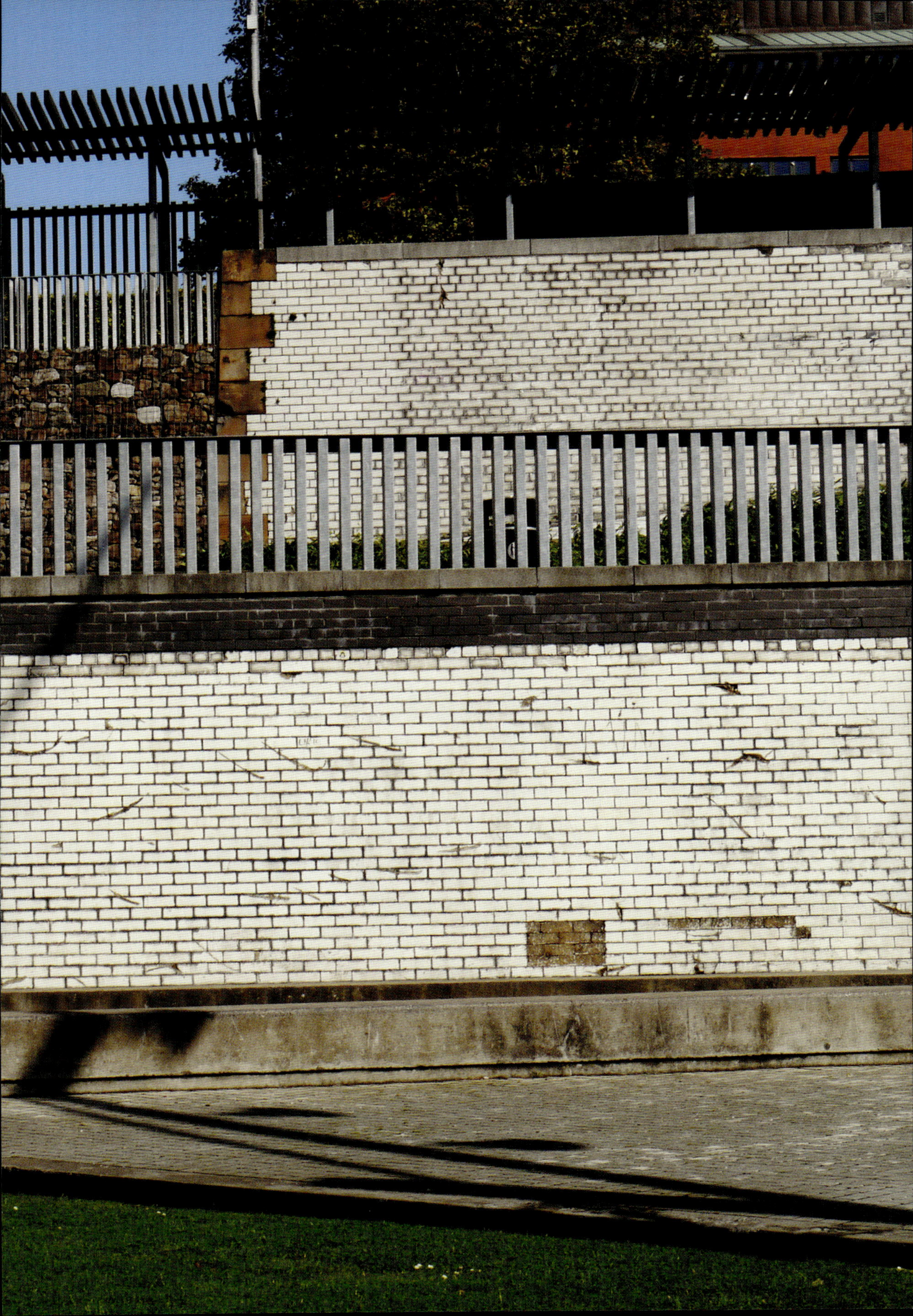

Rottenrow Gardens.

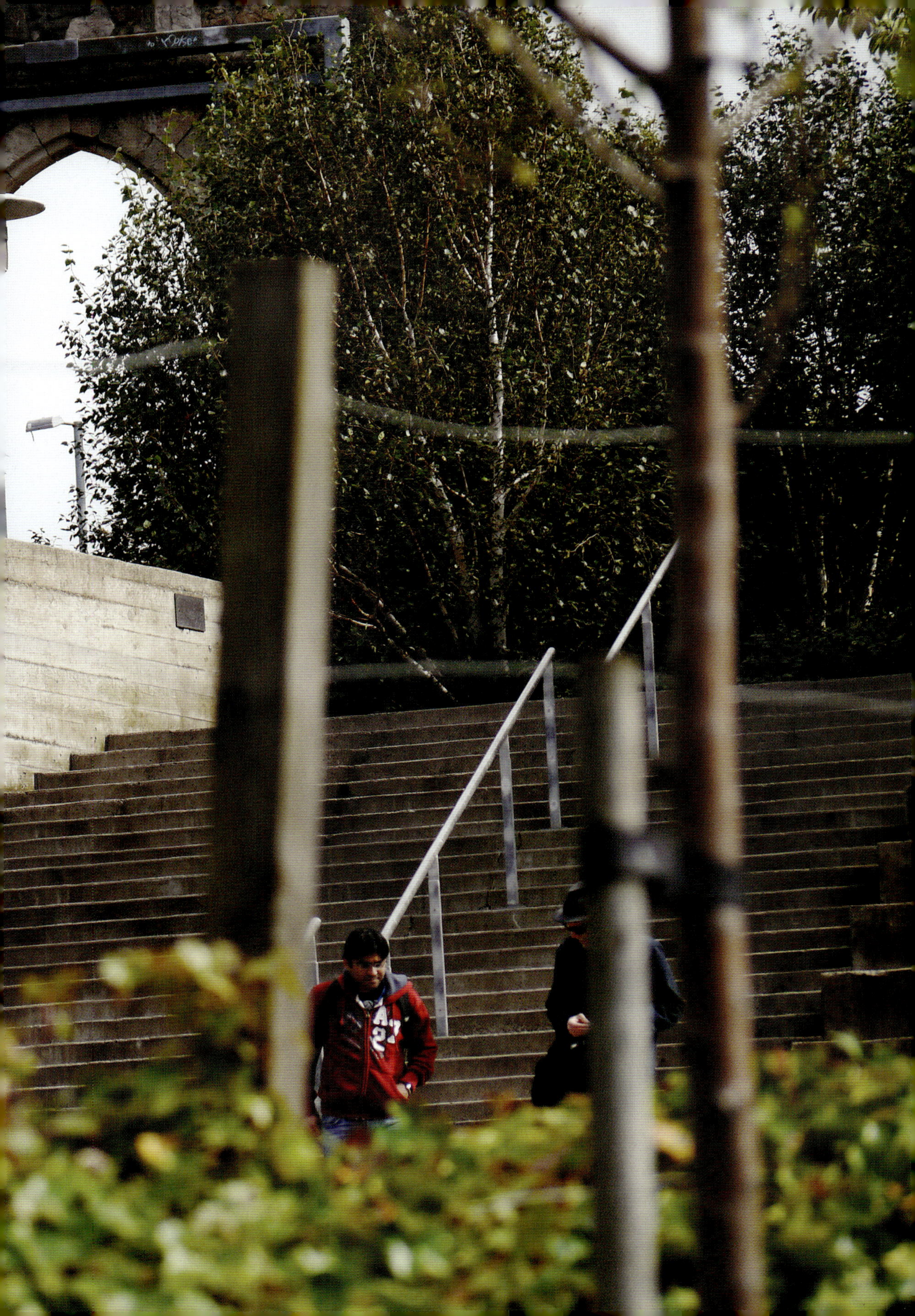

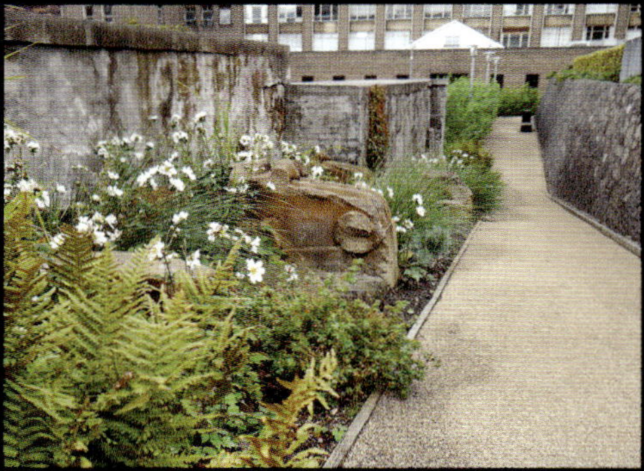

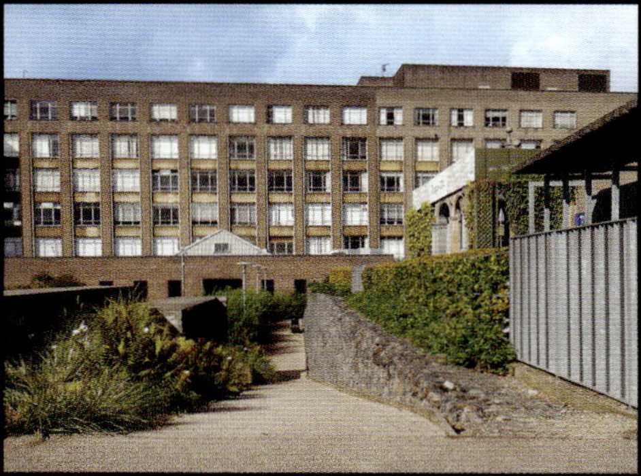

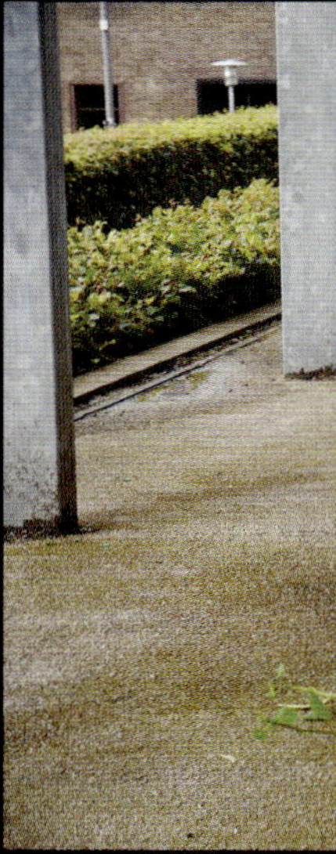

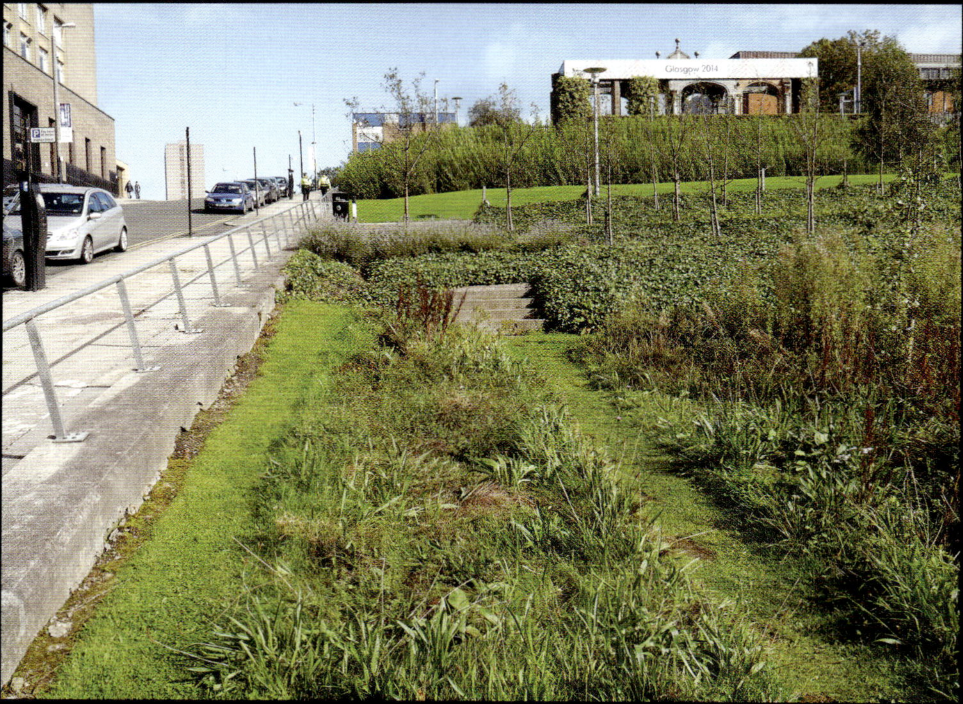
Glasgow 2014

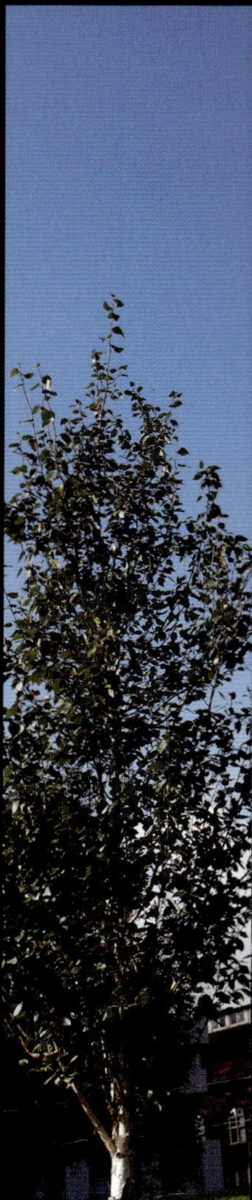

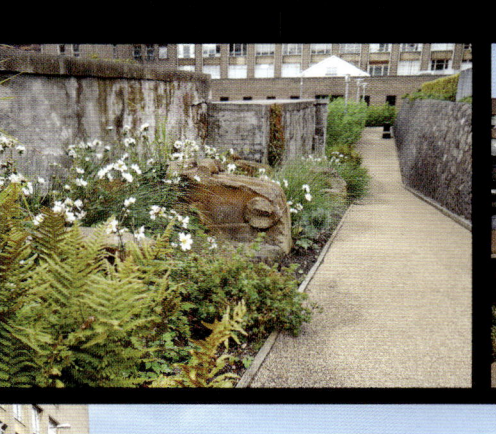

And finally, what about the owners of the parks? The University of Strathclyde could find a way to achieve a win-win outcome. Developing a new educational building and creating – no, saving – a much-loved piece of parkland are two voter-friendly achievements that any politician would be clamouring to be associated with. How different would the story have been if there was no other option than to build on the site of the Gardens, as originally planned?

These same contradictions will be played out at 18Broadway in downtown Kansas City. The steeply sloping half-hectare site could have been left vacant, turfed, and at risk of significant erosion after the GFC killed a planned residential development. Instead, developer DST Systems engaged 360 Architecture to develop a scheme that would manage stormwater run-off across the site. This approach fitted well with the municipal initiative to reduce combined stormwater outflows by better managing urban stormwater. According to the designers '90% of all rain events in Kansas City produce an average of 1.37 inches of rainfall. 18Broadway's stormwater control infrastructure can capture, clean, and store the water of four such events without sending any to the city's sewer system.'[284] As the design progressed, the idea of a productive garden evolved, and raised planters now cover the site. A crop harvest of nearly one tonne was projected for 2011. A wind turbine powers the perimeter lighting, photovoltaics help power the pumps, and much of the material used to build the garden is recycled. This is very much a temporary site installation conceived as a productive public park.

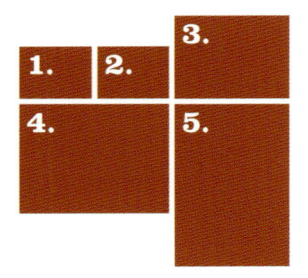

All images this spread – Rottenrow Gardens.
1. Remnant stonework among verdant planting.
2. Loose gravel paths mark the way through the park.
3. Solitary lunch spot among the nasturtiums.
4. A block of green hidden in the centre of the city.
5. The giant nappy pin sculpture commemorates the site's former occupant, the Glasgow Royal Maternity Hospital.

Installations

The informal and *ad hoc* qualities of 18Broadway, Lent Space and Rottenrow Gardens create an undeniably picturesque visitor experience. The lure of the ruin remains strong, whether it is visitors to Rottenrow glimpsing the remnant stone archway and then finding a garden unfolding below, or those stumbling across Lent Space and not knowing if they've found something in the process of being built or demolished. Lent Space almost looks like it was built illegally; planned for months, thrown up overnight, and potentially closed down and gone tomorrow. This sense of flirting with permanence was one of the reasons people responded so enthusiastically to images of a secret swimming pool in Brooklyn that had been made from old garbage skips, or dumpsters. An urban beach of the most rudimentary kind, this water-filled steel box turned an asphalt car park into a park-like place that New Yorkers were desperate to discover. Once the designers were 'outed' their project was legitimised with a commission to create a publicly accessible dumpster pool, although the slip-resistant surfaces, path widths, and lengths of access ramp and handrails required to ensure compliance with regulatory codes somewhat diminished the sense of truck-it-in, spontaneous transformation inherent in the initial project. Other designers have also explored the potential for repurposed skips to enhance the public realm. In the United Kingdom, architecture group Oliver Bishop-Young developed the Skip Conversion project. Among its installations was a skip garden with protected seating and planting that could be moved using conventional equipment to different locations as required.[285]

These skip projects, along with 18Broadway, Rottenrow Gardens and Lent Space, reveal links to Guerilla Gardening, a movement that responds to the issues of land scarcity and neglect, according to founder Richard Reynolds.[286] Reynolds believes that while scarcity of land motivates guerilla gardening, it also threatens the survival of the gardens created. Once the land-owner has a better use, the garden is no longer tolerated.[287] In Rottenrow Gardens, Lent Space and 18Broadway the land owners were active participants in the process of creating park space on their property. The neglect of absentee land owners was one of the factors early community gardeners used to their advantage. In their quest to establish a beachhead in green-poor neighbourhoods, community garden leaders saw the potential in pieces of land that, like Rottenrow and Lent Space, had the potential to contribute positively to the lives of local residents, instead of dumbly waiting 'to be developed'.[288]

...installation parks encourage us to continue exploring, learning, questioning and trying to change things for the better.

The story of the early community gardens thus brings our discussion full circle to 1970s New York. Alan Sonfist was releasing a parcel of roadside land back into primeval abandonment with his *Time Landscape*, at the same time that Adam Purple was rescuing a rubbish-strewn lot from abandonment to create *The Garden of Eden*,[289] the two of them straddling a fine line between rescuing something from abandon and freeing something into abandonment.

As we begin to explore the verdant family tree of installation parks a couple of themes recur. First, most installation parks evolve from or are inspired by concerns for environmental issues, and how people and nature coexist. This appears to be true of all but the most superficial installations. Second, park-making is not 'owned' by landscape architects. Installation parks emerge out of a blurring of boundaries between traditional professions and disciplines – between landscape architecture, art, architecture, ecology, horticulture, activisim and installation. Third, installation parks, by their very nature, express a particular relationship with time. If change is the only constant, as the saying goes, then installation parks encourage us to continue exploring, learning, questioning and trying to change things for the better.

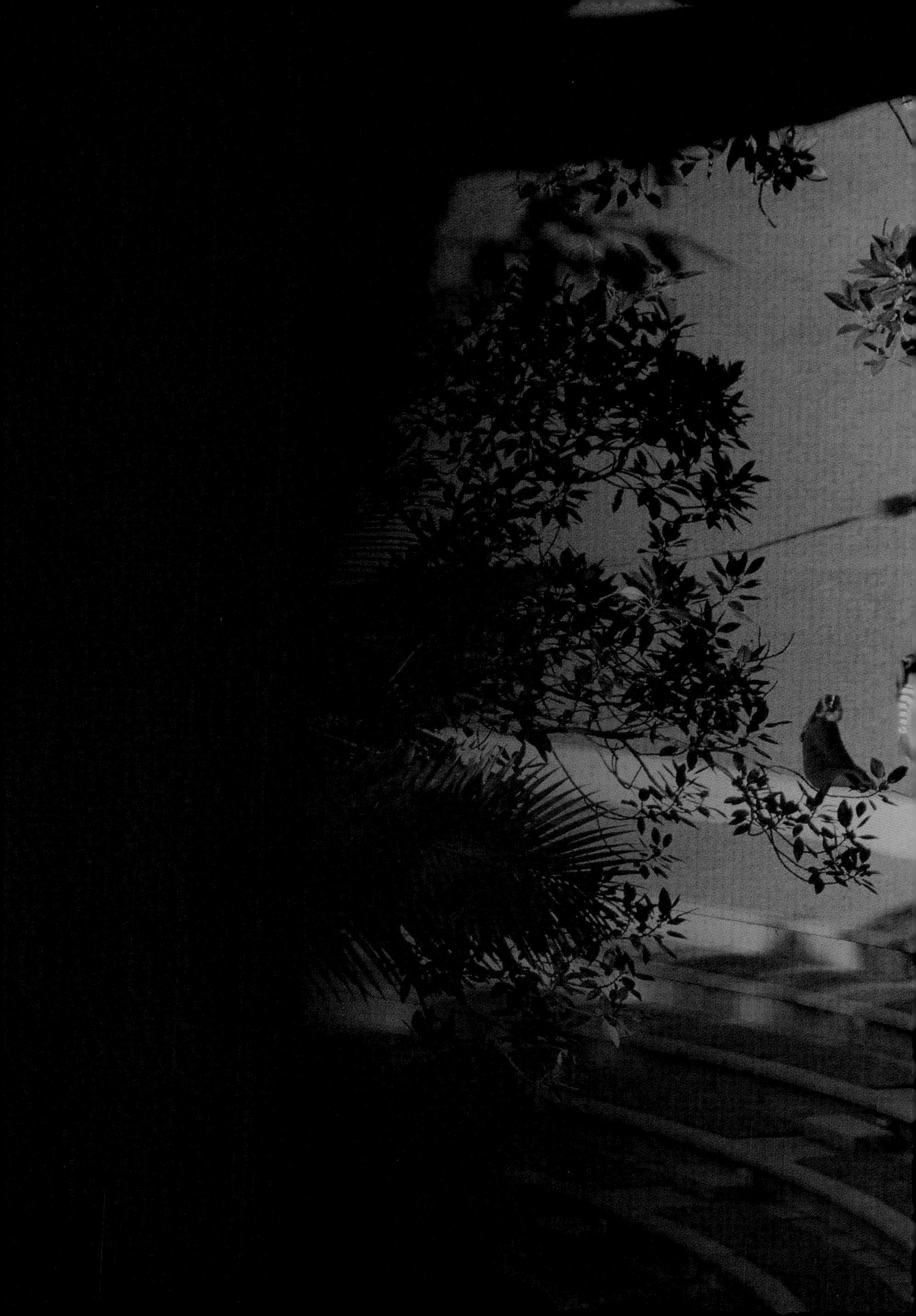

Where to from here?

Where to from here?

Near my home in Brisbane is a small park. It has all the trademark elements we would recognise at a 'typical' park: a few trees, two seats, some play equipment, some shrub planting – flowering, Australian species. Money has been spent on the equipment and construction, yet during the decade I've lived in this neighbourhood I've never seen a single person visiting this park. There are plenty of obvious reasons why. The park is off the main streets and hidden from view. It is at the low point between two ridge lines, and becomes a boggy mess after not much rain; its location also ensures a near-continual lack of sunlight – not so bad in summer, but a deal-breaker in the cooler months. The lack of sun means no lawn will grow under the trees. Instead a grim puddle of dark red softfall pools like congealed blood under the playground equipment. Sadly, there is not a huge resident population of children nearby to use the swing, it's too small for a dog to run around, and in any case, a large notice forbids their entry. Although one of its near neighbours is a hospital, there is no convenient access, not even a footpath alongside. It is surrounded by a substantial metal fence, and does not project a welcoming air. The two chairs, which could be used by countless nearby residents or workers, are the final straw. One overlooks the large rubbish bin, while the other addresses the decaying fence of the adjoining apartments. They are both of the variety that features a central armrest, that mean-spirited gesture that prevents even the local homeless from making use of the place to stretch out.

I've pondered whether using one of the four approaches described in this book could make something more of this forlorn park. Creating a linkage could help. Nearby is the great belt of inner-city parkland that includes King Edward Park, Albert Park, Roma Street Parklands and Victoria Park. If you know the way, they can all be accessed by following the contour line that describes itself along Wickham and Gregory Terraces in that part of the city. Many of Brisbane's older terraces appear as wiggly lines on street maps, slicing across neatly ordered grids at odd angles, and doubling back on themselves. They do so because European settlers quickly discovered that the winding Aboriginal paths provided the driest and most expeditious route through the crinkled landscape.

Brisbane: trees and a seat do not a successful park make...

The ridge line terraces connect the city park belt, but within the parks themselves the topography is varied and dramatic. Outside the parks the local neighbourhoods also lay themselves like carpeting up and down the slopes. If you live at the bottom it can be a disheartening climb up to the bus stop in the morning. Perhaps some of these cross-contour streets could be re-imagined as green links, creating a welcoming way of negotiating the hilly streets bordered by the serenely flat terraces. My local park could then have a purpose; it would be a stepping stone on a slow, pleasant and quiet journey of homecoming, and a knot on the green guide rope connecting back up to the terrace summits.

Where to from here?

Obsolescence is trickier. The suburb of Spring Hill was named after the source that provided early drinking water to the township, and it was one of the first to be settled after the riverside central city area. Lots in the street where our small park is today were surveyed in the 1870s, 30 years after the convict gaol closed. Spring Hill quickly became a densely populated, working-class neighbourhood, retaining a slightly down-at-heel reputation until well into the 1980s, when gentrification slowly took hold. At that stage students, artists and musicians enjoyed its low rents and proximity to the city. Celia McNally, 'The Duchess', ran the annual Spring Hill Fair, which provided the name for the third album by Brisbane band The Go-Betweens. Stalls spilled off the main location on Leichhardt Street and down into the steep streets and backyards.

The pro-development environment fostered by the Bjelke-Petersen state government saw Spring Hill suffer a similar fate to other older parts of the city. The tall, pink, faux-latticed Hotel Grand Chancellor replaced a sprawling corner pub. Other medical, commercial and residential towers appeared on the terraces, throwing deep shadows over the houses below. Workers' cottages were bought up by those rediscovering the potential of inner-city life, and those seeking to build smaller apartment complexes. Diagonally opposite the small park is a two-storey building, visible in old photos, with a long-closed corner store downstairs. Today Spring Hill still manages to accommodate boarding houses across the road from some of the city's most prestigious private schools, and students still live in the cold, dark valleys behind the doctors and lawyers and fine old buildings that are now heritage listed.

Our park does not feature in the first edition of the Brisbane Street Directory, released in 1955, nor had it appeared by the mid-1980s. It would seem to be a product of Spring Hill's late twentieth century evolution – a bit of the street too flood-prone or unprofitable to build on, an obsolescence. Could its use in any way tell a part of this story?

How might co-location work? The park occupies too small an area to share with a school or a water treatment plant. Maybe it could provide both recreational value and public utility in another way. I've already described how this tiny park is built in a low point and becomes all but unusable after rain. If we were to get rid of the rarely used swing and create instead a landscape that was intended to catch water, and hold it, and get boggy, and then dry out again, we might find a way to re-imagine the place as a water park. There is no reason we couldn't still have a seat or two, and we would still have planting, but now, it would be providing a function as well as visual interest. By encouraging stormwater run-off and detention, the pressure on local hard stormwater infrastructure would be reduced, even slightly, and the park would now contribute positively to, rather than adversely suffering from, its location.

Using an installation approach could be another way the park could respond to and evolve with its location. While there are not many swing-set-using children in the immediate vicinity, there are more than a few students. Crammed, as finance demands, into tiny flats and draughty houses, they can be seen in the afternoons and evenings crouched in the gutters, smoking and talking, using the kerb as a seat. Maybe our park could accommodate them. Again we could remove the swings, take down the fence and prune the trees to let a bit of light in. Then we could install some plywood platforms, like Lent Space, or some big flat rocks for seating, and a bit of lighting so it feels safe at night. Our cold, unused playground could be temporarily re-imagined as an outdoor study nook and living room.

Wherever I look in inner Brisbane I see evidence that we are more than willing to embrace and use forms of public realm well beyond the traditional concept of parkland. School kids distribute themselves along the walls of planters and rubbish bins in the Albert Street arms of the central mall, and readily spill down and onto the pavement once there's no more room on the seats. They could all go to the Botanic Gardens and sit comfortably and spaciously on the lawn. Groups of young men meet every weekend to practice parkour on the steps and the old World War II bomb shelter bordering King Edward Park. It's standing room only in Reddacliff Place for the monthly Suitcase Rummage, where trash and treasure changes hands from suitcases placed on the ground.

Brisbane: the monthly Suitcase Rummage, held in Reddacliff Place.

Where to from here?

These spaces are all physically and visually different, but once we look beyond those aspects several commonalities become readily apparent. Among other things, they are all places that are well linked or connected, they provide other features or services, and they allow for varying use and occupation over time. J.B. Jackson said of his long curiosity and many investigations, 'The greater the number of landscapes I explored, the more it seemed that they all had traits in common and that the essence of each was not its uniqueness but its similarity to others.'[290] My own exploration of different landscape and park responses to very different urban paradoxes also ended up revealing many overlaps and similarities. The threads of each story frayed out beyond the edges of its own category boundaries to interweave with other stories. It was as if kin recognised kin, and reached out to connect across the borders of space and time.

And so we get the community gardens on Philadelphia's vacant lots talking back across time to Agnes Denes' field of wheat. Her commentary on the politics of food, on hunger and resource mismanagement is now played out as those left behind by the swinging pendulum of industrial development work to supplement their food desert neighbourhoods. We see the becalmed canals and hunkered concrete forts of the New Dutch Waterline talking across continents to the torrents gushing through WaterWorks in Phoenix. As a species made largely of water, living on a similarly watery planet, our response to water remains emotional and powerful, even as we bend it to our service. We see vegetation reclaiming the once-mighty Duisburg Nord blast furnace into the greater Emscher Landschaftspark, but also see the tiny first steps at Newtown Creek to create a new landscape that negotiates a relationship with functioning industry, and not just mitigates or hopes for its departure. These places all seem grounded in an attitude to landscape that Jackson described as 'Landscape 1', a system in which everything is jumbled together, and things are impermanent, flexible and mobile. During the twentieth century we evolved and finetuned a different system, Landscape 2, wherein everything was ordered, separated and permanent. Landscape 2 was a manifestation of the worldview in which the planet and its resources were to be bent to our will and controlled. As we move into this century, more people have realised that, on our planet, change is the only constant. Our efforts to more tightly control weather, climate, food, energy, economies, nations, information, property, politics and each other has resulted in unforeseen side effects or even unmitigated disaster.

Many of the projects described in this book achieved what they did, and simply came into existence, because a group of people was prepared to step, just for a minute, into a place more like Landscape 1. Given questions and impossible challenges and rules, they reframed them. 'We can't do that because…' turned into 'What if we did this…?'

In Australia we continue to have an uneasy relationship with our landscape. As soon as we 'conquered' the bush we began leaving it, yet the outback is the archetypal landscape we claim affinity with. We lament that the bush is dying, but in a romanticised, aestheticised way – we don't want to live there ourselves. We love the land enough to have fought to save the Franklin River in Tasmania, and the Mary River in Queensland, yet we demand the right for our communities to make their livings from sand mining, forestry, coal seam gas extraction. And we love our 'outdoor lifestyle' yet demand as a birthright a vast home, requiring continuously metastasising new neighbourhoods with bigger houses jammed onto smaller lots, from which we drive further distances to schools, shops, workplaces and entertainment.

Although we are embracing and using a wider variety of public places we still love the best of our traditional parks. When not at the one-day festival, Brisbaneites love the rest of South Bank – the arbour, the lawns, the waterplay and the lagoon – all the bits that are more conventionally 'park-like'. It's the same story at Roma Street Parklands, New Farm Park and the Botanic Gardens on a perfect Brisbane winter afternoon. There are gatherings of 20 and 30 people, visitors from overseas, local families at the playground and young couples canoodling in the privacy that only a thronging crowd can provide.

Brisbane: young love at Roma Street Parkland.

Where to from here?

All images this spread – Brisbane.
1. *Brisbane's oldest park, the Botanic Gardens in the city.*
2. *Opened in late 2011, The Cove at South Bank was instantly popular.*
3. *Late afternoon at the Roma Street Parkland amphitheatre.*
4. *Spring in the air at The Cove, South Bank.*

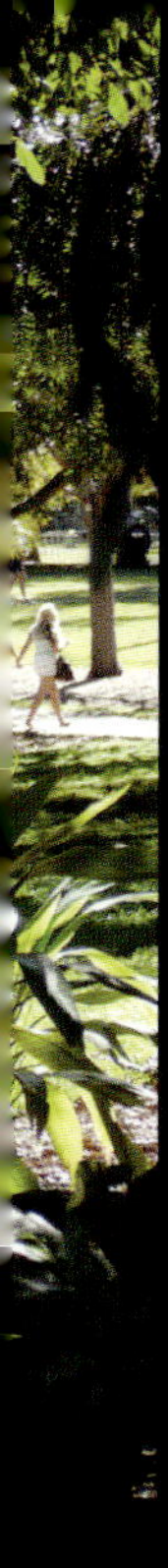
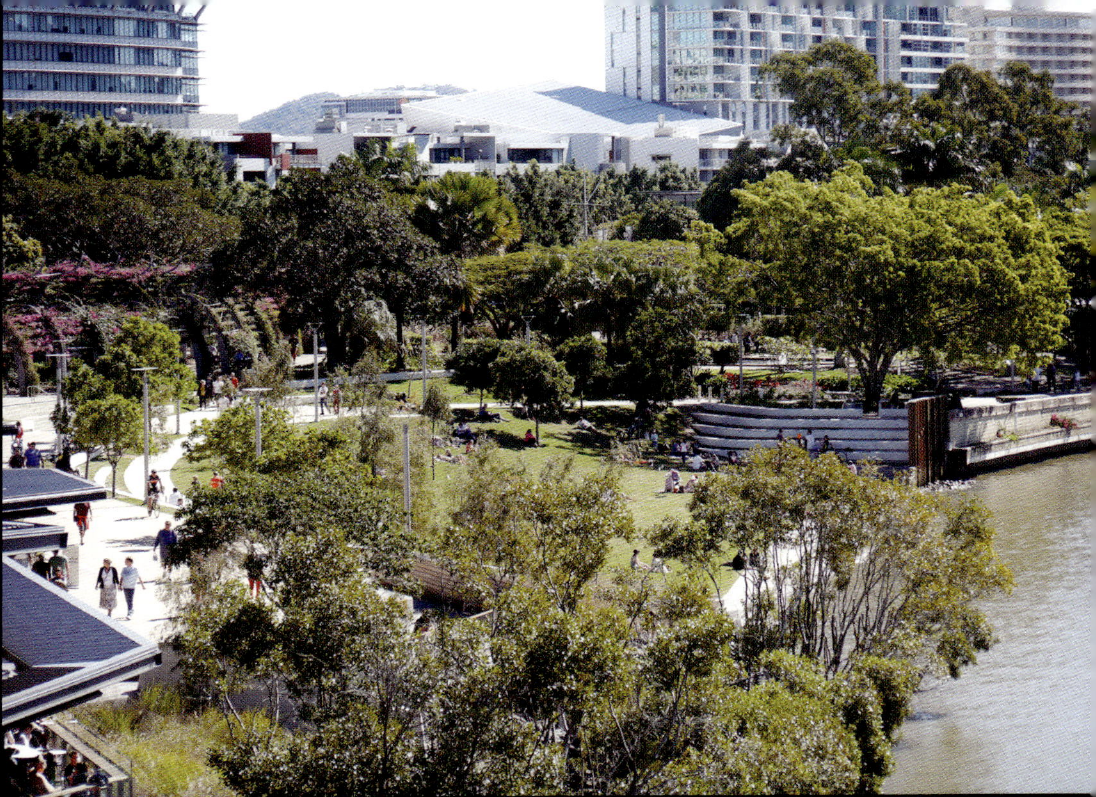
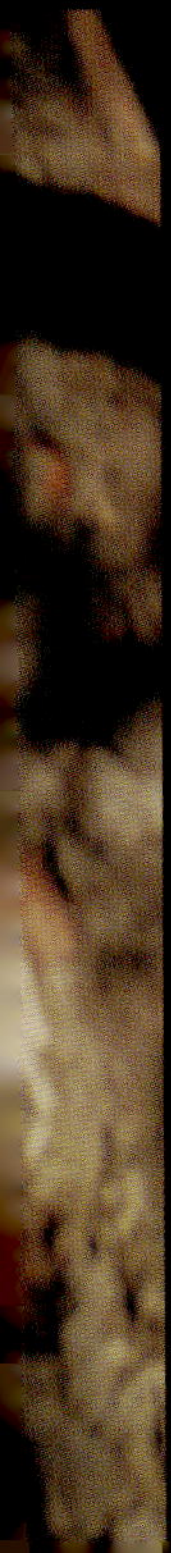
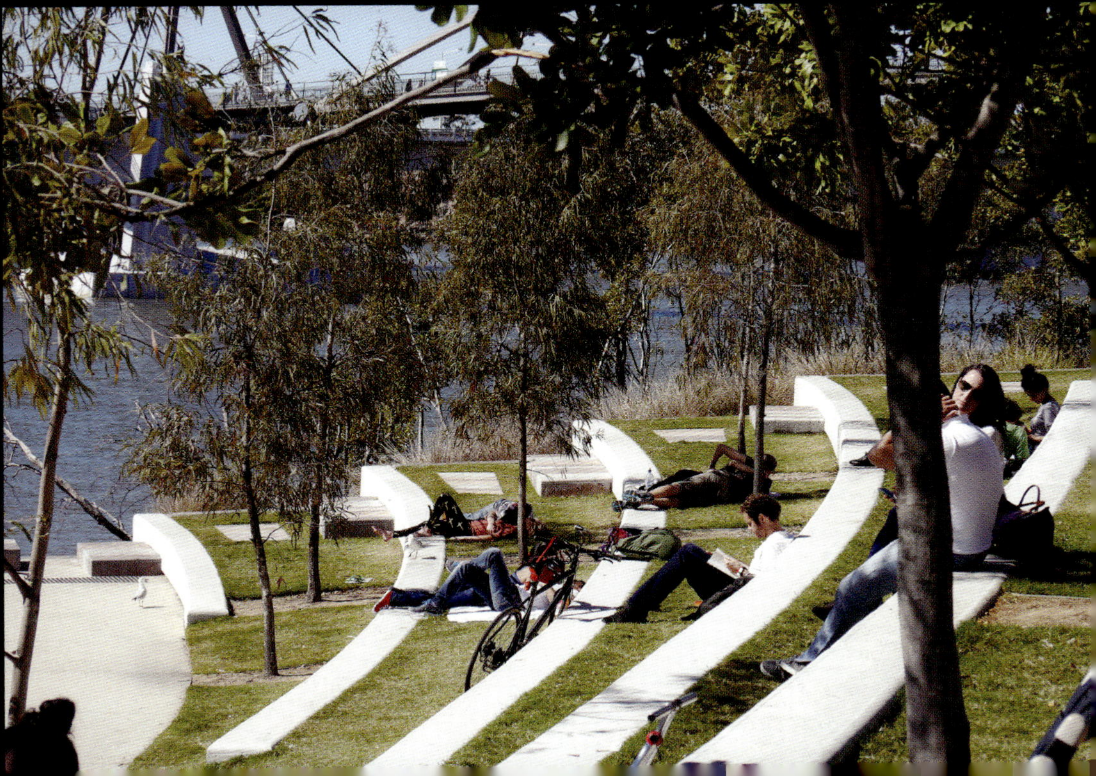

Other couples are having their wedding photos taken, perhaps the ultimate proof that a place has been embraced by its community. At a conference in 2011, the late Spanish architect Luis Mansilla described the moment his friends started sending him copies of local wedding photos taken at MUSAC, the contemporary art museum designed by his practice. His initial mixed feelings soon changed to a sort of proud humility, that people would choose that building for the setting of one of the most important days of their lives.

It is as places become woven into our lives that they become valuable to us. Once a story is attached the place becomes more than simply the assembly of its physical features. Like so many others, my brother will now always think of New Farm Park as the place where his wedding photos were taken. In one of the wonderful pages from the *East London Green Grid Primer*, John Meehan and Neil Davidson relay the story of 92-year-old Ron, who negotiates his motorised wheelchair over bumpy paths to attend the monthly gatherings of the Brookside Fishing Club at 'I think it's called Dagnam Park…'[291] Understanding the stories of place in the first instance, and then responding to them, seems like a good way to ensure ongoing stewardship of our city parks, both existing and future. Linkage parks may be a response to an increasingly fragmented and disconnected world, but as author Robert Macfarlane observes, surely the paths that the earliest humans created, that linked their significant places, that took them from hearth to food to water, following the trails of animals, who in turn followed the ways established by the terrain and geology they traversed, were 'among the earliest acts of human landscaping'.[292]

Our parks must respond to great complexity and contradiction, as they are responding to enormously challenging urban conundrums all over the world.

Our parks must respond to great complexity and contradiction, as they are responding to enormously challenging urban conundrums all over the world.

Yet it is within the challenge that the greatest opportunities lie. Cities are one of the most amazing artefacts the human species creates. City parks have always been bellwethers reflecting our relationship with each other and the natural environment. Green parks created refuge, sanctuary and relied on the uplifting and ennobling power of nature. We must remain vigilant and not take the green park for granted. The tiny, empty playground in my neighbourhood is a reminder that providing some trees and seats is not enough. Brown parks worked with unwanted places encourage us to acknowledge our role in making and re-making our cities. We must remain vigilant here, too, and ensure that our brown parks do not completely eradicate the wild and serendipitous aspects of industrial and marginal land that make them so rich – in some places, providing some trees and seats might be too much. The Future Parks each tell a story, small or large, humble or ambitious, of place and time. It is only because they have responded to the particular that they are able to provide lessons for dealing with universal challenges of globalisation, shrinkage, urbanisation and economic reframing.

Whether as citizens, policy makers or designers, we all can play a role. Enjoy your local park. Take your holiday visitors to the showpiece parks created by your city or region. Require the existing ones be well maintained. Demand that unsuccessful ones are refreshed. Insist that new ones make a contribution that your community needs. Many Philadelphia residents gained enormously once individual abandoned house lots were turfed. New Yorkers living and working in Tribeca have a place to visit and install their artwork, rather than a hoarding-enclosed no-go-zone. Atlantans have a long-term opportunity to improve the health, mobility and housing access for tens of thousands of residents. As they have always done, parks offer a way to think creatively and aspirationally about the public places in our cities, regions and countries. Look outward for ideas, listen inward for the stories of your place. We will all benefit from your Future Park.

e **Endnotes**

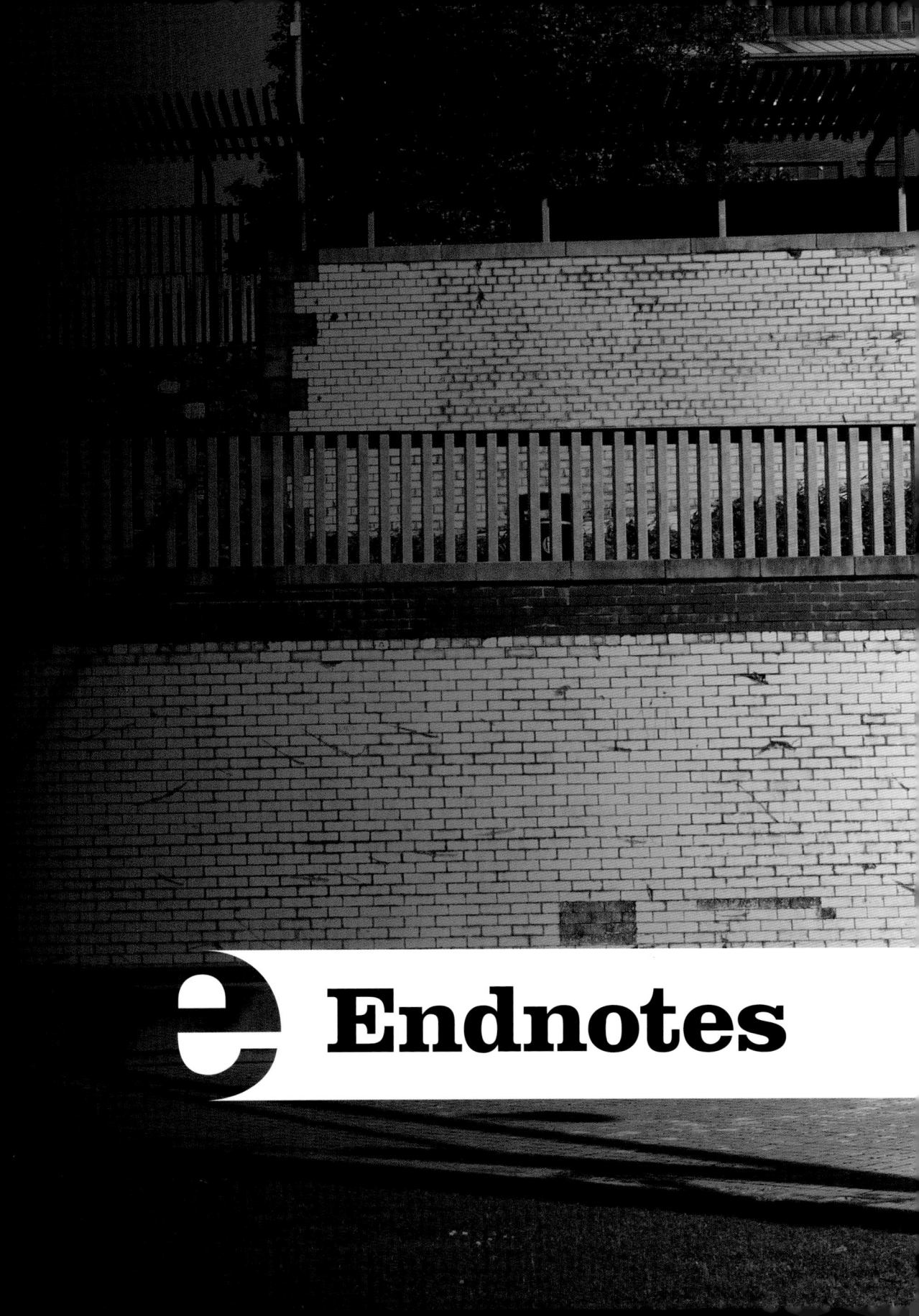

Endnotes

[1] The controversy over Barangaroo is a case in point. Formerly an industrial site, Barangaroo is located in inner-city Sydney, on the eastern bank of Darling Harbour, just around the corner from the Harbour Bridge. An international design competition was held to determine how the site would be redeveloped. The first part of the Barangaroo controversy started after the winner was announced, and then displaced as the preferred developer. The second controversy concerned a proposed new public park at the northern end of the site. The winning scheme, and pretty much all the other finalists, proposed a contemporary park design that reflected both the site's proximity to the central business district and the former industrial usage. This approach did not sit well with the Chairman of the Barangaroo Design Excellence Review Committee and former Australian Prime Minister, Paul Keating. Keating's vision had long been for a 'naturalistic' park, reflecting the sandstone headlands that would have originally existed on the site. In the end Keating was relieved of his post after attacking City of Sydney Mayor Clover Moore as 'an inappropriate person to be lord mayor of this city because she thinks it's a city of villages, she's for low rise, she's for sandal-wearing, muesli-chewing, bike-riding pedestrians without any idea of the metropolitan quality of the city'. The *Sydney Morning Herald* carried extensive coverage of the 'muesli' incident, but at the time of writing Keating had had the last laugh – the headland park is still naturalistic in design. See the following article for example: <http://www.smh.com.au/nsw/keating-lashes-mueslichewer-barangaroo-inquiry-20110505-1each.html>. See the Barangaroo website for details of the park proposal: <http://www.barangaroo.com/>.

[2] The survey was hosted on the Leichhardt Municipal Council website. <http://www.leichhardt.nsw.gov.au/Callan-park.html>. The award-winning master plan by McGregor Coxall can be accessed at <http://www.leichhardt.nsw.gov.au/Callan-Park-Master-Plan.html>.

[3] Adrian McGregor, 'Bionic Urbanism', unpublished paper delivered at the International Federation of Landscape Architects annual conference, Auckland, New Zealand, 12 April 2013.

[4] Wellington Park website: Community Values Survey page. <http://www.wellingtonpark.org.au/survey/>.

[5] For more on the challenges facing Prospect Park see 'Prospect Park: diversity at risk', Chapter 3 in Setha Low, Dana Taplin and Suzanne Scheld's *Rethinking Urban Parks: Public Space and Cultural Diversity*, University of Texas Press, Austin, 2005, pp. 37–68.

[6] Prospect Park website. <http://www.prospectpark.org/environment/wildlife>.

[7] G.M. Moore, *Urban Trees: Worth More Than They Cost*, LA Paper, The Australian Institute of Landscape Architects, 2009.

[8] The apartment is in the Dakota building. Over 30 years after gaining initial notoriety when resident John Lennon was murdered outside his front door, some of the Dakota's residents have recently been airing their dirty laundry in public, with ongoing disputes over potential new residents and the actions of existing ones. <http://ny.curbed.com/archives/2012/07/03/latest_eightroom_dakota_listing_seeks_145_million.php>.

[9] *Valuing Central Park's Contributions to New York City's Economy*, Appleseed, May 2009. Known as The Appleseed Report, this investigation was commissioned by the Central Park Conservancy.

[10] Michael G. Messner, *Olmsted's Ideals Can Help Solve Our Real Estate Mess*, Red Fields to Green Fields website. <http://rftgf.org/joomla/index.php?option=com_content&view=article&id=219>.

[11] Once upon a time we used the term 'cost-cutting' to describe the process of bringing a project back on budget. Today, 'value-management' is king. According to the Institute of Value Management Australia, 'Value Management is the overall name given to a collection of specific principles, techniques and practices which have been proven effective in maximising value to those concerned.' In case that didn't really clear things up 'Value Management is a structured, analytical process which seeks to satisfy "customer" needs by ensuring that all necessary functions are provided at the lowest

total cost, while maintaining the required levels of quality and performance – in other words, to maximise value.' As I said, ... cost-cutting.

[12] *Macquarie Dictionary*, 3rd Edition, Macquarie Dictionary Publishers, Sydney, 2005, p. 1564.

[13] Ed Wall and Tim Waterman, *Basics Landscape Architecture 01 Urban Design*, AVA Publishing VA, Lausanne, 2010, p. 170.

[14] John Brinckerhoff Jackson, The Origin of Parks. In *Discovering the Vernacular Landscape*, Yale University Press, New Haven, 1984, pp. 127–130.

[15] Christopher Alexander, Sara Ishikawa and Murray Silverstein, *A Pattern Language*, Oxford University Press, New York, 1977.

[16] Julia Czerniak, Introduction/Speculating On Size. In *Large Parks*, Julia Czerniak and Geroge Hargreaves (Eds), Princeton Architectural Press, New York, 2007, p. 19.

[17] An excellent starting point is *The Language of Landscape*, Anne Whiston Spirn's richly evocative exploration of 'our native language'. Ann Whiston Spirn, *The Language of Landscape*, Yale University Press, New Haven, 1998.

[18] Galen Cranz, *The Politics of Park Design: A History of Urban Parks in America*, MIT Press, Massachusetts, 1982, p. 246.

[19] This was one of the (many) reasons given over the years to defend the argument that the culture of indigenous Australians was unsophisticated. George Seddon, the eminent Australian lovingly referred to as 'Professor of Everything', so broad were his interests and accomplishments, wrote evocatively of Aboriginal land management in his final book. George Seddon, *The Old Country: Australian Landscapes, Plants and People*, Cambridge University Press, Melbourne, 2005.

[20] For a fascinating account of six very different early gardeners read Paul Fox, *Clearing: Six Colonial Gardeners and Their Landscapes*, The Miegunyah Press, Melbourne, 2004.

[21] Katie Holmes, Susan K. Martin and Kylie Mirmohamadi, *Reading the Garden: The Settlement of Australia*, Melbourne University Press, Melbourne, 2008.

[22] <http://www.crikey.com.au/2012/02/10/latest-circulation-figures-read-all-about-it-or-not/>.

[23] But behind 17 other sporting events. In what may or may not be telling, September 11 coverage by Channels 7, 9 and ABC came in at Number 6 (3.1 million viewers), behind the top-ranking Australian Open final for 2005 (4.01 million). <http://www.smh.com.au/articles/2004/03/30/1080544476965.html>.

[24] <http://www.readersdigest.com.au/australias-most-trusted-people-2008>.

[25] James Robertson, 'What I Drink When … Costa Georgiadis', *The Sydney Morning Herald,* 12 March 2012. <http://www.smh.com.au/executive-style/top-drop/what-i-drink-when–costa-georgiadis-20120317-1vboo.html>.

[26] Website of Reichen and Robert and Associates. <http://www.reichen-robert.fr/>.

[27] Daniel DeSemple, Rio Salado Environmental Restoration Project. In *Proceedings of the Water Environment Federation.* WEFTEC 2006: Session 31 through Session 40, pp. 2839–2852(14). The Water Environment Federation.

[28] Annette Becker and Peter Cachola Schmal (Eds), *Urban Green: European Landscape Design for the 21st Century.* Birkhäuser Architecture, Basel, 2010.

[29] Christian Dobrick, Madrid Rio, Madrid, Spain. In *Urban Green: European Landscape Design for the 21st Century.* Birkhäuser Architecture, Basel, 2010.

[30] Sandra L. Beckett, *Crossover Fiction.* Routledge, New York, 2009, p. 4.

[31] Dan Milmo, After Harry Potter and the prophets of doom. *The Guardian.* <http://www.guardian.co.uk/business/2007/jul/30/books.media/print>.

[32] <http://harrypotter.bloomsbury.com/author>.

[33] <http://www.thehighline.org/blog/2010/04/02/the-high-line-celebrates-its-2000000th-visitor>.

[34] Beth Greenfield, Robert Reid and Ginger Adams Otis (Eds), *New York City.* Lonely Planet Publications, Melbourne, Oakland, London, 2006, pp. 40, 96, 141, 216.

[35] Paul Goldberger, 'Miracle Above Manhattan'. *National Geographic Magazine,* April 2011, pp. 122–137. (This reference was supplied by my dear father, who made a point of requesting this acknowledgement. Thanks, Dad!)

[36] Andrew Blum, 'The Long View'. *Metropolis Magazine Online,* 2008. <http://www.metropolismag.com/story/20081119/the-long-view>.

[37] Robert Sullivan. 'Wall-E Park'. *New York Magazine,* 2008. <http://nymag.com/news/features/52452/>.

[38] <http://www.nytimes.com/2011/05/15/opinion/15Rybczynski.html?_r=1&emc=tnt&tntemail1=y>.

[39] For an enumeration of the financial and tourist success of the Bilbao in its first years of operation see Martin Bailey, 'The Bilbao Effect'. *Forbes*, 2002. <http://www.forbes.com/2002/02/20/0220conn.html>. For a review of the city and the museum a decade after opening see Denny Lee, 'Bilbao, 10 Years Later'. *The New York Times*, 2007. <http://travel.nytimes.com/2007/09/23/travel/23bilbao.html>. For an article in which architect Frank Gehry decries the 'Bilbao Effect' see Ben Hoyle, 'Frank Gehry: the Bilbao Effect is Bulls**t'. *The Times Online*, 2008. <http://entertainment.timesonline.co.uk/tol/arts_and_entertainment/visual_arts/architecture_and_design/article4304855.ece>. The 'Bilbao Effect' of the High Line has been helped by legislative change. As Friends of the High Line advise, "in 2005, the City rezoned the area around the High Line to encourage development while protecting the neighborhood character, existing art galleries, and the High Line. The combination of the rezoning and the park has helped to create one of the fastest growing and most vibrant neighborhoods in New York City. From 2000 to 2010, the population within the rezoned area has grown more than 60 percent. Since 2006, after the rezoning was approved and construction of the High Line began, new building permits in the immediate vicinity of the High Line doubled and at least 29 major development projects have been initiated (19 completed, 10 underway). Those 29 projects account for more than US$2 billion in private investment, 12,000 jobs, 2,558 new residential units, 1,000 hotel rooms, more than 423,000 square feet of new office space and 85,000 square feet of new art gallery space.

[40] Drew Guarini, 'LowLine Creators Reach Initial Fundraising Goal on Kickstarter', *The Huffington Post*, 3 April 2012. <http://www.huffingtonpost.com/2012/04/03/lowline-creators-reach-in_n_1399911.html>.

[41] Janelle Zara, 'Imagining the Lowline' Sheds Light on the Potential for an Underground Park', *Artinfo*, September 15, 2012. <http://artinfo.com/news/story/825684/imagining-the-lowline-sheds-light-on-the-potential-for-an-underground-park>.

[42] Peter Ackroyd, *London Under*. Vintage Books, London, 2011, p.143.

[43] P. Andreas, Promenade Plantée and Viaduc des Arts, Paris France. In *Urban Green: European Landscape Design for the 21st Century*. Birkhauser Architecture, Basel, 2010.

[44] Peter Harnik, *Urban Green: Innovative Parks for Resurgent Cities*. Island Press, Washington, Covelo, London, 2010, p. 98.

[45] The Brisbane Valley Rail Trail currently provides 100 km of trail following the line of a passenger service that ceased operations in 1993. Despite the substantial investment of time, energy and finances by a number of regional councils, the entire trail is remote to most cities and towns in the south-east, although access is available from some small towns bordering the former rail line. More information on Queensland and Australian rail trails is available at the Railtrails Australia website <http://www.railtrails.org.au/>.

[46] <http://www.ci.minneapolis.mn.us/bicycles/midtownfacts.asp>.

[47] *The New Georgia Encyclopedia*. <http://www.georgiaencyclopedia.org/nge/Article.jsp?path=/CitiesCounties/Cities&id=h-2207>.

[48] Atlanta. *The New Georgia Encyclopedia*. <http://www.georgiaencyclopedia.org/nge/Article.jsp?path=/CitiesCounties/Cities&id=h-2207>. To illustrate: At the turn of the twentieth century 15 rail lines crossed the city, bringing 150 arriving trains a day. As World War II approached, road and air networks joined rail to make Atlanta the 'transportation capital of the Southeast'. As the twenty-first century dawned, traffic congestion resulted in an unbroken stretch of 69 smog-alert days, and commute times that were the slowest in the United States. A city of contradictions, Atlanta was both the birthplace of Martin Luther King and the headquarters of the Ku Klux Klan. Residential segregation continues, and although some gentrifying white Atlantans have moved back to the inner city, it remains largely the preserve of a more disadvantaged black population that has never possessed the ability to move to the dramatically expanding suburbs.

[49] EDAW, Urban Collage, Grice & Associates, Huntley Partners, Troutman Sanders LLP and Gravel, Inc. (2005) *Atlanta BeltLine Redevelopment Plan*. Prepared for The Atlanta Development Authority. <http://www.beltline.org/Portals/26/Media/PDF/FinalBeltLineRedevelopmentPlan.pdf>.

[50] ibid. p.1–2.

[51] Kaid Benfield, 'Atlanta BeltLine: the Best Sustainability Project in America?', *The Atlantic Cities*, 4 November, 2011. <http://www.theatlanticcities.com/design/2011/11/atlanta-beltline-best-sustainability-project-america/429/>.

[52] The School of Arts was founded in 1892 and later became a technical school. The School continued in a two-storey building on the corner of Wood and Gregory streets. I went to ballet classes there when I was a child. That building was eventually demolished, and for over 20 years the site has been used as a car park.

[53] Paradise Street was actually named after *Paradise Lost*, by Milton. It is one of a collection of streets in East Mackay named after literary notables. Mackay State High School is in Milton Street, as already mentioned. Nearby streets include Juliet, Othello, Shakespeare and Tennyson.

[54] Mackay Regional Council website. <http://www.mackay.qld.gov.au/community/recreation/bluewater_trail>. This is the trail map that shows the former rail reserve along Paradise and Evan streets as part of the Bluewater Trail: <http://www.mackay.qld.gov.au/__data/assets/pdf_file/0005/91553/Bluewater_Trail_Map.pdf>.

[55] Mark Monmonier, *No Dig No Fly No Go: How Maps Restrict and Control*. The University of Chicago Press, Chicago, 2010, p. 34.

[56] Andrew Michler, 'Architect Ronald Rael Proposes a Green and Socially Viable US Border Fence'. *Inhabitat*, 2011. <http://inhabitat.com/architect-ronald-rael-proposes-a-green-and-socially-viable-us-border-fence/>.

[57] Dave Shiflett, Website of *Bloomberg*, 2010. <http://www.bloomberg.com/news/2010-09-15/idiotic-mexico-border-fence-cost-3-billion-does-nothing-dave-shiflett.html>.

[58] Rebecca Solnit, *Landscapes for Politics*, University of California Press, Berkeley, 2007, p. 93.

[59] Joren Jacobs, Transforming the Sperrgebiet 'trauma landscape', *'scape*, 2008.

[60] Rosia Montana, Even landscapes die out, *'scape*. 1/2008, p. 24.

[61] M. Valentine (translator), *The Path of Remembrance and Comradeship*. Ljubljana Tourism, Ljubljana, Slovenia, 2010.

[62] Translated from <http://www.nationalelandschappen.nl/>.

[63] Saleem H. Ali (Ed.), *Peace Parks*. Massachusetts Institute of Technology, Cambridge, 2007, p. 3.

[64] Belinda Sifford and Charles Chester, Bridging Conservation across La Frontera: An Unfinished Agenda for Peace Parks along the US–Mexico Divide. In Saleem H. Ali (Ed.), *Peace Parks*. Massachusetts Institute of Technology, Cambridge, 2007, pp. 205–226.

[65] Judith LaBelle, Emscher Park, Germany – expanding the definition of a 'park'. In *Crossing Boundaries in Park Management: Proceedings of the 11th Conference on Research and Resource Management in Parks and on Public Lands*. (Ed. D. Harmon), 2001, p. 222. The George Wright Society, Hancock, Michigan.

[66] Claudia Schreckenbach and Christel Teschner, IBA Emscher Park: a beacon approach, dealing with shrinking cities in Germany. Unpublished presentation. Fakultät Architektur Institut für Landschaftsarchitektur, Professur Landschaftsbau, Kent State University Urban Design Collaborative, 2009.

[67] Judith LaBelle, ibid., p. 22.

[68] Lisa Diedrich, Landscape-oriented urbanism. Conference at the symposium *My Norsk Arkitekturpolitikk*. 26–27 May, 2009, Oslo.

[69] United States Environmental Protection Agency *International Brownfields Case Study: Emscher Park, Germany*, 2010. <http://www.epa.gov/brownfields/partners/emscher.html>.

[70] Regionalverband Ruhr Press Release. *The Ruhrgebiet (Ruhr Area) – Somewhere to discover in the heart of Europe*. Press Office. 2004.

[71] Karl Ganser, Art is Wilderness's Closest Neighbour. In *Under the Open Sky: Emscher Landscape Park*. Birkhauser, Basel, 2009, p. 9.

[72] Claudia Schreckenbach and Christel Teschner, ibid.

[73] Karl Ganser, who led the IBA during the decade-long process, clarified that 'The topography of industry is the park's trademark.' As the parkland develops 'Nothing will be demolished, leveled and subsequently covered with soil… Nature is to be given back almost all that was once taken from it…' Karl Ganser, ibid., p. 11.

[74] Christiane Borgelt and Regina Jost, *Zollverein World Heritage Site Essen*, Zollverein Foundation, Stadtwandel Verlag, Berlin, 2009.

[75] Sustainable Cities, *Emscher Park: From dereliction to scenic landscapes*. Sustainable Cities, 2009. <http://sustainablecities.dk>.

[76] The Ruhr Regional Association (*Regionalverban Ruhr – RVR*) would be responsible for the maintenance, construction and further development of the concept, while the water company (Emschergenossenschaft – EG) would be focused on the river, in particular the construction of a 51 km-long underground sewer

pipeline and reconstruction and remediation of the river. Lisa Diedrich, ibid.

[77] Ruhr 2010 website. *RUHR:2010 takes stock*. Press release. <http://www.essen-fuer-das-ruhrgebiet.ruhr2010.de/no_cache/en/press-media/press-information/detailseite/article/ruhr2010-takes-stock.html?tx_ttnews%5BbackPid%5D=631>.

[78] CABE website (permanently archived 2011) Landscape, waterways, buildings and culture. <http://webarchive.nationalarchives.gov.uk/20110118095356/http://www.cabe.org.uk/housing/emscher/projects>.

[79] Internationale Bauausstellung, *New Landscape Lusatia Catalogue/2010*, Jovis, Berlin, 2010, p. 34.

[80] As discussed in the Linkages chapter, the IBA Emscher Landschaftspark ran from 1989 to 1999. An excellent summary of the role, benefit, challenges and future of IBAs is contained in 'Memo on the Future of International Building Exhibitions', Internationale Bauausstellung, *New Landscape Lusatia Catalogue/2010*, Jovis Verlag, Berlin, pp. 274–277. In 2008 Germany's Federal Ministry of Traffic, Construction and Urban Development initiated a broader process to ensure lessons learnt from past successful IBAs could be captured and used to underpin an approach to urban design and development that could be used not just in Germany but across Europe. The goal is to create a network called 'IBA meets IBA'. For more information on IBA meets IBA and the 2007 IBA Hamburg see <http://www.iba-hamburg.de/en/the-iba-story/network-iba-meets-iba.html>.

[81] *Neue Landschaft Lausitz New Landscape Lusatia*, Internationale Bauausstellung (IBA) Furst-Puckler Land (Ed.), Jovis Verlag, Berlin, 2010, p. 23.

[82] *Neue Landschaft Lausitz New Landscape Lusatia*, Internationale Bauausstellung (IBA) Furst-Puckler Land (Ed.), Jovis Verlag, Berlin, 2010.

[83] Gasworks Park in Seattle is considered by many to be the pioneering brownfield, or post-industrial park. Designed by Richard Haag it was one of the first parks in which remnant industrial infrastructure was retained on the site and integrated into the new park.

[84] In April 2012 Yubari, a shrinking Hokkaido city, elected a 31-year old Naomichi Suzuki as Mayor. As reported in the *New York Times*, Yubari's population is 90 per cent lower than during its boomtime in the 1950s and 1960s, and 65 per cent of the remaining residents are aged 65 or over. The story is significant because it flies in the face of traditional Japanese distrust of outsiders (Suzuki came to Yubari as a 26-year-old on a year-long loan from Tokyo Metropolitan Council) and respect for elders (the 70-year-old incumbent stood aside to let the younger man have a free run). <http://www.nytimes.com/2012/04/27/business/global/aging-japanese-town-bets-on-a-young-mayor.html?_r=1>.

[85] Project Office Philipp Oswalt, Case Study Hakodate, 2007. In *Shrinking Cities: Complete Works 3 Japan*, Project Office Philipp Oswalt, Berlin, 2008, pp. 3–32.

[86] Project Office Philipp Oswalt, Working Paper: Case Study Venice, 2006–2007, Shrinking Cities Project. <http://www.shrinkingcities.com/downloads1.0.html?&L=1>.

[87] Thorsten Weichmann, Strategic Flexibility beyond Growth and Shrinkage. In *Cities Growing Smaller*, Cleveland Urban Design Collaborative, Kent State University, Cleveland, 2008, pp. 18–29.

[88] *Towards An Urban Renaissance: Report of the Urban Task Force – Executive Summary*, Department of the Environment, Transport and the Regions, 26 September, 1999. <http://www.eukn.org/United_kingdom/uk_en/E_library/Urban_Policy/Towards_an_urban_renaissance_final_report_of_the_Urban_Task_Force>.

[89] The Australian Bureau of Statistics, *Regional Population Growth Australia, 2010–2011*. <http://www.abs.gov.au/ausstats/abs@.nsf/Products/3218.0~2010-11~Main+Features~Main+Features?OpenDocument#PARALINK4>.

[90] The *State of Australian Cities 2010* report confirmed how urbanised a nation Australia has become, with 75 per cent of our community living in cities with populations greater than 100 000 people. Fewer than 20 per cent of Australians live in smaller communities or rural and regional areas with populations less than 30 000. Department of Infrastructure and Transport, Commonwealth of Australia, Canberra.

[91] <http://www.dfat.gov.au/facts/env_glance.html>.

[92] Robert Stimson, Scott Baum, Patrick Mullins and Kevin O'Connor, Australia's regional cities and towns: modelling community opportunity and vulnerability, *Australasian Journal of Regional Studies*, **7(1)**, 2001, p. 51.

[93] Stimson *et al.*, ibid, p. 52.

[94] *State of Australian Cities 2011*. Major Cities Unit, Department of Infrastructure and Transport, Commonwealth of Australia, Canberra, 2011, p. 19.

[95] *State of Australian Cities 2011*, ibid., p. 52.

[96] Sources vary, positions are tenaciously defended, and there is no absolute proof, but much scholarly debate gives credence to Rome's peak population being around one million people at the height of the Empire. <http://www.princeton.edu/~pswpc/pdfs/scheidel/070706.pdf>.

[97] Jared Diamond, *Collapse: How Societies Choose to Fail or Survive*, Penguin Books, London, 2005, pp. 157–177.

[98] From the website of The Craco Society. <http://thecracosociety.org/index.htm>.

[99] Justin B. Hollander, Karina Pallagst, Terry Schwarz and Frank J. Popper. Planning shrinking cities. *Progress in Planning*, **72(4)**, November 2009, 223–232.

[100] The website of Charters Towers Regional Council. <http://www.charterstowers.qld.gov.au/web/guest/visitors/world_history.shtml>.

[101] Population and Dwelling Profile: Charters Towers Regional Council, The Office of Economic and Statistical Research, Queensland Treasury and Trade, Queensland Government, April 2012. <http://www.oesr.qld.gov.au/products/profiles/pop-housing-profiles-lga/pop-housing-profile-charters-towers.pdf>.

[102] Justin B. Hollander, Karina Pallagst, Terry Schwarz and Frank J. Popper. Planning shrinking cities. Initially published in *Progress in Planning*, **72(4)**, November 2009, 223–232. Downloaded from http://policy.rutgers.edu/faculty/popper/ShrinkingCities.pdf pp. 11–12.

[103] Jennifer Bray, 'Boy, 2, found dead on Irish "ghost estate" after following family dog through fence and drowning in pool of water', *Daily Mail*, 24 February 2012. <http://www.dailymail.co.uk/news/article-2105804/Liam-Keogh-2-dead-Irish-ghost-estate-drowning-pool-water.html?printingPage=true>.

[104] Sarah Goodyear, 'A natural fix for Ireland's "Ghost Estates"', *The Atlantic Cities*, 2 April 2012. <http://www.theatlanticcities.com/housing/2012/04/natural-fix-irelands-ghost-estates/1648/>.

[105] Henry McDonald, 'The Irish Squatters taking on empty homes and a bankrupt system', *The Guardian*, 3 January 2012. <http://www.guardian.co.uk/business/2012/jan/03/ireland-squatters-occupy-homes-nama/>.

[106] *Focus Ireland Annual Report 2010*, Focus Ireland, Dublin, pp. 15–16. Since 1999, these figures showed an increase of 54 per cent in the number of homeless nationwide, and 23 per cent in the numbers waiting for social housing.

[107] Heckle, Harold, 'Spain Ghost Towns Develop From Real Estate Crash', *The Huffington Post*, 16 February 2012. <http://www.huffingtonpost.com/2012/02/16/spain-ghost-towns-real-estate-crash_n_1281032.html?view=print&comm_ref=false>.

[108] *Time* magazine published an online photo essay on Kangbashi with photographs by Michael Christopher Brown. <http://www.time.com/time/photogallery/0,29307,1975397,00.html>.

[109] Bill Powell, 'Inside China's Runaway Building Boom', *Time* magazine online, 5 April 2010. <http://www.time.com/time/magazine/article/0,9171,1975336,00.html>.

[110] J.B. Jackson, An engineered environment, reproduced in *Changing Rural Landscapes*, Ervin H. Zube and Margaret J. Zube (Eds), University of Massachusetts Press, Amherst, 1977, p. 30.

[111] 2004 Shrinking Cities International Research Network (SCIRN). Cited in Karina Pallagst, Shrinking cities: planning challenges from an international perspective. In *Cities Growing Smaller*, Kent State University's Cleveland Urban Design Collaborative, Kent State University, Kent, Ohio, 2008, p. 7.

[112] Project Office Philipp Oswalt, Shrinking cities. In *Shrinking Cities: Complete Works 3 Japan*, Project Office Philipp Oswalt, Berlin, 2008, p. 3.

[113] Justin B. Hollander, Karina Pallagst, Terry Schwarz and Frank J. Popper. Planning shrinking cities. Initially published in *Progress in Planning*, **72(4)**, November 2009, 223–232. Downloaded from http://policy.rutgers.edu/faculty/popper/ShrinkingCities.pdf p. 3.

[114] Artists Romain Meffre and Yves Marchand were, in 2005, among the first to document Detroit's physical decline. The images in their series, *The Ruins of Detroit*, powerfully alerted the American public to the burgeoning problems of urban vacancy and abandonment in the Motor City. In 2011 Meffre contacted *Huffington Post* journalist Hélène Bienvenu about a newly released Swatch watch that appeared to reference a famous Detroit ruin. She wrote about it, and the ongoing fascination for ruin porn on the HuffPost blog <http://www.huffingtonpost.com/helene-bienvenu/detroit-ruin-porn-goes-co_b_1161480.html>. In recent years countless news crews and visitors have added to the portfolio of images of Detroit's abandoned buildings and properties, and just as many commentators have questioned the obsession with images of ruin, and the reluctance to show signs of life that persist in the city that, according to the US Census Bureau, was still home to over 700 000 people in 2011. The most

perfunctory Google search for 'Detroit ruin porn' will easily reveal over one million hits, while half that number result from a search for 'Detroit ruin porn criticism'.

[115] Lorlene Hoyt and André Leroux. *Voices from Forgotten Cities: Innovative Revitalization Coalitions in America's Older Small Cities*, MIT School of Architecture and Planning, Cambridge, 2007.

[116] Alan Mallach and Eric Scorsone, *Long-Term Stress and Systemic Failure: Taking Seriously the Fiscal Crisis of America's Older Cities*, Centre for Community Progress, Flint, 2011, p. 10.

[117] Lorlene Hoyt and André Leroux, ibid., pp. 20–34.

[118] Hoyt and Leroux identify other assets common to many Shrinking Cities in the U.S. including a good, well-connected location, a comfortable city scale, established infrastructure such as roads and parks, distinctive architecture built during boom times, a variety of cultural assets, diversity, affordability and a strong civic identity. Lorlene Hoyt and André Leroux, ibid., p. 16.

[119] More information is available on the City of Philadelphia website. <http://www.phila.gov/qualityoflife/Vacant_Lot_Criteria_.html>.

[120] *City of Saginaw Master Plan*, Draft 24 May 2011, p. 56, superseded by *City of Saginaw Master Plan 2011*, p. 64. <http://www.saginaw-mi.com/pdfs/city-of-saginaw-master-plan-2011.pdf>.

[121] Tobias Armborst, Daniel D'Oca and Georgeen Theodore, 'Improve Your Lot!', *Cities Growing Smaller*, Cleveland Urban Design Collaborative, Kent State University, Cleveland, 2008, pp. 46–64.

[122] Justin B. Hollander, Karina Pallagst, Terry Schwarz and Frank J. Popper, *Planning Shrinking Cities*, pp. 23–25 – same source as for endnote 102.

[123] Brenna Moloney, 'Saginaw: City of Contrasts', *Preservation Nation: The Official Blog of the National Trust for Historic Preservation*, 20 January 2011.

[124] U.S. Census Bureau, State and County Quick Facts, Saginaw (city), Michigan. <http://quickfacts.census.gov/qfd/states/26/2670520.html>.

[125] Alan Mallach and Eric Scorsone, *Long-Term Stress and Systemic Failure: Taking Seriously the Fiscal Crisis of America's Older Cities*, Centre for Community Progress, Flint, 2011, p. 11.

[126] Saginaw Neighborhood Stabilization Program website. <http://www.saginawnsp.com/background/index.php>.

[127] *City of Saginaw Master Plan*, Draft 24 May 2011, pp. 67–70. <http://www.saginaw-mi.com/pdfs/city-of-saginaw-master-plan-2011.pdf>.

[128] Jodi McFarland, 'Our view: with the right approach, Saginaw's 'Green Zone' plan is gaining a sad acceptance', *The Saginaw News*, 21 February 2010. Online edition: <http://www.mlive.com/opinion/saginaw/index.ssf/2010/02/our_view_with_the_right_approa.html>.

[129] *Adapting to Climate Change: Green Infrastructure*, The Australian Institute of Landscape Architects, <http://www.aila.org.au/greeninfrastructure/>.

[130] John Gannon (Ed.), *Reclaiming Vacant Land: A Philadelphia Green Guide*, The Pennsylvania Horticultural Society, Philadelphia, 2002, p. 1.

[131] Diana Balmori is a New York-based landscape architect, educator and provocateur. In 1993 she co-wrote *Redesigning the American Lawn*. She later wrote the introduction for *Edible Estates: Attack on the Front Lawn* (which also featured writings by Michael Pollan, Rosalind Creasy, Lesley Stern and Fritz Haeg), Bellerophon Publications, Inc., New York, 2008.

[132] Diana Balmori, Beauty and the lawn: a break with tradition. In *Edible Estates: Attack on the Front Lawn*, Bellerophon Publications, Inc. New York, 2008, p. 12.

[133] Michael Pollan, Why mow? The case against lawns. In *Edible Estates: Attack on the Front Lawn*, Bellerophon Publications, Inc. New York, 2008, p. 34.

[134] John Gannon (Ed.), *Reclaiming Vacant Land: A Philadelphia Green Guide*, The Pennsylvania Horticultural Society, Philadelphia, 2002, p. 16.

[135] David Lowenthal, Not every prospect pleases, reproduced in *Changing Rural Landscapes*, Ervin H. Zube and Margaret J. Zube (Eds), University of Massachusetts Press, 1977, p. 139.

[136] 'More Green, Less Crime: Rehabilitating Vacant Lots Improves Urban Health and Safety, Penn Study Finds', News Release, Perelman School of Medicine, University of Pennsylvania Health System, 16 November, 2011. <http://www.uphs.upenn.edu/news/News_Releases/2011/11/more-green-crime/>.

[137] Susan Wachter, *The Determinants of Neighborhood Transformation in Philadelphia Identification and Analysis: The New Kensington Study*, The Wharton School, University of Pennsylvania, Spring 2005, p. 2.

[138] Nate Berg, 'The Tricky Politics of Vacant Lots', *The Atlantic Cities*, 24 September 2012. <http://www.theatlanticcities.com/neighborhoods/2012/09/tricky-politics-vacant-lots/3370/>.

[139] *Bioremediation*, CRC Care Fact Sheet 4, The Cooperative Research Centre for Contamination Assessment and Remediation of the Environment, University of South Australia. <http://www.crccare.com/publications/downloads/FS-Bioremediation.pdf>.

[140] T.M. Chaudrey, W.J. Hayes, A.G. Khan and C.S. Khoo, Phytoremediation – focusing on accumulator plants that remediate metal-contaminated soils, *Australasian Journal of Ecotoxicology*, **4**, 1998, p. 38.

[141] *Re-Imagining a More Sustainable Cleveland: Citywide Strategies for Reuse of Vacant Land*, Cleveland Land Lab at the Cleveland Urban Design Collaborative, Kent State University, Cleveland, adopted by the Cleveland City Planning Commission, 19 December 2008, pp. 24–25.

[142] *Re-Imagining a More Sustainable Cleveland:* ibid., p. 24.

[143] University of Queensland website. <http://www.cmlr.uq.edu.au/Research/LeadPathwaysStudy.aspx>.

[144] The story was carried nationally by *ABC News*: <http://www.abc.net.au/news/2010-08-02/study-confirms-mt-isa-lead-poisoning-risk/928728>, and *The Australian*, <http://www.theaustralian.com.au/news/investigations/the-toll-lead-takes-on-isas-infants/story-fn6tcs23-1225925070875>. State media throughout Australia also carried the story. Testing by the Queensland Department of Health in 2006 and 2007 had earlier revealed that 45 out of 400 children between the ages of one and four who were tested, showed elevated blood lead levels. The Press Release that accompanied the release of the study results in 2008 stated, 'The good news is blood lead levels can be naturally reduced by introducing a few practical lifestyle and household measures such as reducing soil exposure, having better diets and keeping dust levels within the house low', which many parents interpreted as an attempt by Queensland Health to minimise its risk and responsibility. The full report is available on the Queensland Health website, <http://www.health.qld.gov.au/ph/documents/tphn/mtisa_leadrpt.pdf>.

[145] T.M. Chaudrey *et al.*, ibid., p. 46.

[146] Telephone conversation with Dr Barry Noller, 24 April 2012. Dr Noller very generously referred me to the extensive research on urban lead contamination undertaken in the United States. He also directed me to the studies showing the effectiveness of apatite in soil amendment.

[147] Michael J. Blaylock, Field demonstrations of phytoremediation of lead-contaminated soils. In *Phytoremediation of Contaminated Soil and Water*, Norman Terry and Gary Banuelos (Eds), CRC Press, Boca Raton, 2000, pp. 13–24.

[148] Samantha Langley-Turnbaugh and L.G. Belanger, 2011. *Phytoremediation of lead in urban residential soils of Portland, Maine*. Soil Survey Horizons *(in press)*. The Abstract for the paper is available at <http://www.nycswcd.net/suitma-2009/abstracts/C%20LANGLEY-TURNBAUGH%20Samantha.pdf>.

[149] Samantha Langley-Turnbaugh, *Urban Soils and Backyard Gardens: Potential Contaminants and Remediation Techniques*, City Farmer, Canada's Office of Urban Agriculture, 18 July 2007.

[150] Kate Orff, *Reviving New York's rivers – with oysters!*, TEDWomen, filmed December 2010, posted January 2011. <http://www.ted.com/talks/kate_orff_oysters_as_architecture.html>. The comments move along at a fast clip and cover the full spectrum from praise to rejection. Kate Orff later led a team that developed 'Oyster-Tecture' for the 2011 exhibition *Rising Currents: Projects for New York's Waterfront* at the Museum of Modern Art, New York. See <http://www.moma.org/explore/inside_out/rising-currents/scape>.

[151] Brisbane City Council has undertaken extensive heat island mapping across the entire local authority area, and used the results to guide priority areas for tree planting. The program was directed by the felicitously named Lyndal Plant, who has spoken widely about the scheme and data supporting its implementation. See, for example, Lyndal Plant, 'Brisbane's Urban Forest and Trends in Selection and Planting', presentation given to the Australian Institute of Landscape Architects, 2008. <http://www.aila.org.au/qld/EVENTS/2008%20Events/renewtrees/cpd/LyndalPlant.pdf>. Council's 2 Million Trees policy was one initiative to help address the urban heat island effect. <http://www.brisbane.qld.gov.au/environment-waste/natural-environment/plants-trees-gardens/brisbanes trees/2-million-trees/index.htm>.

[152] In Australia this approach is called Water Sensitive Urban Design (WSUD). Many state and local authorities now have comprehensive strategies and guidelines for implementing WSUD. See <http://www.wsud.org/> for information on the strategy for implementing WSUD throughout the Sydney Metropolitan Area; Melbourne Water's information at <http://wsud.melbournewater.com.au>; and Water by Design which targets the uptake of WSUD throughout south-east Queensland <http://waterbydesign.com.au>. In the United Kingdom the process is called SUDS – Sustainable Urban Drainage Systems.

[153] *Re-Imagining a More Sustainable Cleveland: Citywide Strategies for Reuse of Vacant Land*, Cleveland Land Lab at the Cleveland Urban Design Collaborative, Kent State University, Cleveland, adopted by the Cleveland City Planning Commission, 19 December, 2008, pp. 20–23.

[154] *Land Revitalization Success Stories 2011*. United States Environmental Protection Agency, Office of Solid Waste and Emergency Response, EPA-560-K-11-001, April 2011, pp. 10–11.

[155] Testimony of Mayor Tom Barrett, Subcommittee on Water Resources and Environment, City of Milwaukee, p. 2. <http://city.milwaukee.gov/TestimonyWaterSubcommittee.pdf>. Long-standing Mayor of Milwaukee, Tom Barrett is currently preparing for his third attempt to become Governor of Wisconsin. In 2009, as his family left a local fair, he was attacked by a pipe-wielding man as he came to the aid of a woman calling for help.

[156] Jeffrey Odefey, Stacey Detwiler, Katie Rousseau, Amy Trice, Roxanne Blackwell, Kevin O'Hara, Mark Buckley, Tom Souhlas, Seth Brown and Pallavi Raviprakash, *Banking on Green: A Look at How Green Infrastructure Can Save Municipalities Money and Provide Economic Benefits Community-Wide*, American Rivers, the Water Environment Federation, the American Society of Landscape Architects and ECONorthwest, April 2012, p. 35. Available at the American Rivers website: <http://www.americanrivers.org/assets/pdfs/reports-and-publications/banking-on-green-report.pdf> and the American Society of Landscape Architects website <http://www.asla.org/ContentDetail.aspx?id=31301>, among other locations.

[157] *Green City Clean Waters: The City of Philadelphia's Program for Combined Sewer Overflow Control*, Philadelphia Water Department, amended 1 June 2011. <http://www.phillywatersheds.org/doc/GCCW_AmendedJune2011_LOWRES-web.pdf>.

[158] Reasons varied. In one instance parents were concerned that children of Latin American descent should not learn how to grow and harvest vegetables, out of concern that it would reinforce the cultural stereotype in which they were viewed as manual labourers, gardeners and field workers.

[159] Kentucky Gardens is one such example. It has a matter-of-fact website setting out rules and regulations (tasks for the 'Compost Work Group' and the like) and listing upcoming events, such as free urban agriculture workshops run by Ohio State University: <http://www.kentuckygardens.com/index.cgi?id=136&p=5084>. Cleveland's community gardens also appear to be frequently mentioned in blogs and articles about the city itself (such as the article 'Winter is the time to start preparing for a community garden', by Roxanne Washington for Cleveland.com: <http://www.cleveland.com/insideout/index.ssf/2008/12/post_4.html>), on other urbanist blogs, and on urban agriculture blogs.

[160] Information on Summer Sprout is available from the Ohio State University Department of Agriculture and Natural Resources. <http://cuyahoga.osu.edu/topics/agriculture-and-natural-resources/community-gardening/summer-sprout>.

[161] Colin Beech, Cleveland community gardens. In *Case Studies of Community Gardens*, David J. Hess and Langdon Winner (Eds), 2005.

[162] Ann Whiston Spirn website. <http://www.annewhistonspirn.com/teacher/mill-creek.html>.

[163] Dominic Vitiello and Michael Nairn, *Community Gardening in Philadelphia: 2008 Harvest Report*, Penn Planning and Urban Studies, University of Pennsylvania, October 2009, p. 3.

[164] The Pennsylvania Horticultural Society does still support community gardens in low-income areas. It focuses on food distribution more comprehensively through its City Harvest scheme.

[165] Dominic Vitiello and Michael Nairn, ibid, p. 37. <http://sites.google.com/site/harvestreportsite//>.

[166] Website of Kansas City Community Gardens. <http://www.kccg.org/>. <http://pressreleases.kcstar.com/release/messages/22208/>. Additional funding has enabled its work to continue, see for example <http://pressreleases.kcstar.com/release/messages/22208/#storylink=cpy>.

[167] Website of Get Growing Kansas City. <http://getgrowingkc.org>/.

[168] Website of Master Gardeners of Greater Kansas City. <http://www.mggkc.org/>.

[169] Resolution No. 120046, Introduction Date 12 January 2012, Effective Date 29 January 2010. Posted on the website of City of Kansas City, MO. <http://cityclerk.kcmo.org/liveweb/Documents/Document.aspx?q=p0vkpSqRcwvF679d7RnPtU1J3bqPWi26pnIvewqSmMMHccPddMgvexNO8QhjybYR>.

[170] Michael A. Pagano and Ann O'M. Bowman, *Vacant Land in Cities: An Urban Resource*, The Brookings Institution, Washington D.C., December 2000, p. 5.

[171] *Preliminary Baseline Data Report: Green Impact Zone of Missouri*, UMKC Center for Economic Information, Kansas City, February 2010, p. 9.

[172] *Gaps in Healthy Food Access in the Kansas City Region*, Mid-America Regional Council Geographic Information Systems, June 2011. <http://www.greenimpactzone.org/Urban_Agriculture/food_access.pdf>.

[173] Website of Grown in Ivanhoe. <http://growninivanhoe.wordpress.com/about/>.

[174] *City of Saginaw Master Plan 2011*. City of Saginaw website <http://.saginaw-mi.com/pdfs/city-of-saginaw-master-plan-2011.pdf>.

[175] Cultivate Kansas City website. <http://www.cultivatekc.org/welcome.html>.

[176] Blue Pike Farm website. <http://bluepikefarm.com/>.

[177] *USDA, Ohio Department of Agriculture, City of Cleveland, OSU Extension Partner on Urban Agriculture Incubator Pilot Project: Project Embodies Gov. Ted Strickland's Ohio Neighborhood Harvest Initiative*, Press Release, Cleveland, 27 October 2010. <http://www.agri.ohio.gov/public_docs/news/2010/10-27-10%20Cleveland%20Urban%20Agriculture%20Incubator%20Pilot%20Program.pdf>.

[178] Mark Lefkowitz, '26-acre urban farm zone in Cleveland to get boost from Will Allen', 9 March 2011. <http://www.gcbl.org/blog/marc-lefkowitz/26-acre-urban-farm-zone-cleveland-get-boost-will-allen>.

[179] Growing Power website. <http://www.growingpower.org/index.htm>.

[180] C. Dunstan, L. Boronyak, E. Langham, N. Ison, J. Usher, C. Cooper and S. White, 2011, *Think Small: The Australian Decentralised Energy Roadmap: Issue 1, December 2011*. CSIRO Intelligent Grid Research Program. Institute for Sustainable Futures, University of Technology Sydney.

[181] *Re-Imagining a More Sustainable Cleveland: Citywide Strategies for Reuse of Vacant Land*, ibid., pp. 29–30.

[182] Bruce Katz, 'Delivering the Next American Economy', speech given at the Buffalo City Forum, 14 March 2012, posted on the website of The Brookings Institution 7 April 2010. <http://www.brookings.edu/speeches/2012/0314_next_economy_katz.aspx?p=1>.

[183] Catherine Tumber, *Small, Gritty and Green*, The MIT Press, Cambridge, 2012, p. 117.

[184] Shrinking Cities Studio Virginia Tech website. <http://shrinkingcities.ncr.vt.edu/strategies/land_banks.html>.

[185] Cuyahoga Land Bank Website. <www.cuyahogalandbank.org>.

[186] Genesee County Land Bank website. <www.thelandbank.org/default.asp>.

[187] Kalamazoo County Land Bank website. <http://www.kalamazoolandbank.org/policies-and-procedures/>.

[188] Dominic Vitiello and Michael Nairn, ibid., p. 45. <http://sites.google.com/site/harvestreportsite//>.

[189] *Red Fields to Green Fields: Atlanta, Cleveland, Denver, Miami, Philadelphia, Wilmington*, presentation by Georgia Institute of Technology, June 2010.

[190] *Re-Imagining Cleveland Vacant Land Re-Use Pattern Book*, Kent State University's Cleveland Urban Design Collaborative and McKnight Associates Ltd, Cleveland, April 2009, p. 4.

[191] Edward Glaeser, *Triumph of the City*, Macmillan, London, 2011, p. 62.

[192] Joseph Schilling, *Blueprint Buffalo – Using Green Infrastructure to Reclaim America's Shrinking Cities*, Virginia Polytechnic University, Alexandria, 2006, p. 155.

[193] The Institute for Sustainable Regional Development, April 2008, *Clermont Preferred Future: Clermont Community Development Strategy*, Central Queensland University, Rockhampton.

[194] Transiting Cities Low Carbon Futures International Design Ideas Competition Interactive Booklet, Updated Monday 24 September 2012. <www.transitingcities.com>.

[195] A 1949 *Sunday Mail* report claimed that 'Of 4200 houses erected last year, 2420 had earth closets. Only 45,000 of the city's 100,000 houses were sewered.' Neil Wiseman, 'Full to the Brim with Dunnies', *The Sunday Mail*, 15 May 2010. <http://www.couriermail.com.au/news/sunday-mail/full-to-the-brim-with-dunnies/story-e6frep3f-1225867130155>.

[196] Fans of trivia may appreciate that Brisbane's major wastewater treatment plant is located at Luggage Point, next to the Brisbane Airport. In 2011 the upgraded Luggage Point Advanced Water Treatment Plant won the 2011 International Water Reuse Project of the Year Award. The Port of Brisbane is directly opposite the treatment plant. It is largely built on reclaimed land that extends further into Moreton Bay each year. Some of the fill used in the reclamation came from excavation for the CLEM7 tunnel, named in honour of the man who sewered Brisbane's loos and paved its streets.

[197] John Snow is regarded as the Father of Epidemiology. Much has been written about his groundbreaking discovery, including Steven Johnson's 2006 book *The Ghost Map*.

[198] Atkins, *Hackney Open Space and Sports Assessment Volume 1: Final Open Space Assessment*, June 2004, Section 5 p. 2.

[199] Hansard 1911. Quoted in <http://quizzicalgaze.blogspot.com/2011/02/winston-churchills-thoughts-on-roller.html>.

[200] <http://stonehog.wordpress.com/2012/01/07/reservoir-tour-maple-leaf-undergrounding-project/>.

[201] This is where it starts getting interesting. According to a Virginia Tech website 'in a mature sand bed, a thin upper sand layer called a Schmutzedecke forms. The Schmutzedecke consists of biologically active microorganisms that break down organic matter while suspended inorganic matter is removed by straining.' <http://www.elaguapotable.com/WT%20-%20Slow%20Sand%20Filtration.htm>.

[202] Moore, Charles (Ed.) *The Improvement of the Park System of the District of Columbia*, Washington, Government Printing Office, 1902, p. 7.

[203] ibid., p. 77.

[204] ibid., p. 101.

[205] C. Millay, Restoring the Lost River of Washington: can a city's hydrologic past inform its future? Master of Landscape Architecture thesis, Virginia Polytechnic Institute and State University, Alexandria, Virginia, 2006. <http://scholar.lib.vt.edu/theses/available/etd-04192006-101151/unrestricted/MillayFinal.pdf>.

[206] Website of the Eli Whitney Museum and Workshop. <http://www.eliwhitney.org>.

[207] William Giles Munson, *The Eli Whitney Gun Factory, 1826–8*, Yale University Art Gallery, Mabel Brady Garvan Collection.

[208] Anne Raver, A Watershed Moment, *Landscape Architecture Magazine*, August 2011, pp. 84–97.

[209] Rebecca Fish Ewan, Uncovered, *Landscape Architecture Magazine*, February 2005, p. 90.

[210] G.R. Herberger Park was named in honour of the man who founded a department store. Among their numerous philanthropic gestures, the Herbergers donated the land on which 31 local parks now stand.

[211] Michael Kohn, Robert Landon and Thomas Kohstamm, *Colombia*, Lonely Planet Publications Pty Ltd, Footscray, 2006, p. 97.

[212] Extracted from the City of Vancouver website. <http://www.cityofvancouver.us/watercenter.asp?waterID=25038>.

[213] Tacoma Weddings website. <http://tacoma.weddings.com/Local/vendordetail.aspx?CategoryCode=CAR&VendorId=258390&MsdVisit=1>.

[214] Bridgette Meinhold, 'Elegant LOTT Clean Water Alliance Building Shows the Sexier Side Of Water Treatment', 24 April 2011. <http://inhabitat.com/elegant-lott-clean-water-alliance-building-shows-the-sexier-side-to-water-treatment>.

[215] <http://cfpub.epa.gov/npdes/cso/demo.cfm>.

[216] BBC *Panorama* website. <http://news.bbc.co.uk/panorama/hi/front_page/newsid_8236000/8236957.stm>.

[217] <http://www.environment.gov.au/water/publications/quality/pubs/sewerage-systems-overflows-paper15.pdf>.

[218] <http://www.portlandonline.com/bes/index.cfm?c=31031&a=41962>.

[219] Nearby neighbours include the community of New Columbia. Located south of the treatment plant, New Columbia was built along 'New Urbanist' principles on the site of a former World War II public housing project. The houses have porches and low-VOC paint finishes; the streets are framed by trees and run-off is captured in integrated rain gardens. It is a beautiful environment with many proud residents who are justifiably upset that media attention focuses almost exclusively on the bleaker aspects of New Columbia: in 2011, a young man was shot in the back after an altercation at a bus stop. He had just returned from visiting his dying mother in hospital.

[220] Foster, M., 'Smell of success', *Landscape Architecture Magazine*, February 2004, p. 22.

[221] From the website of Arlington Arts: <http://www.arlingtonarts.org/cultural-affairs/public-art-in-arlington/recent-and-upcoming-projects.aspx>.

[222] <http://www.kingcounty.gov/environment/brightwater-center/events/Sept17_2011.aspx>.

[223] Claire Enlow, 'Art and infrastructure', *The Seattle Daily Journal of Commerce*, 31 March 1998, p. 3. <http://www.djc.com/special/landscape98/10037858.htm>.

[224] Senator Tom Coburn and Senator John McCain, *Stimulus Checkup: A closer look at 100 projects funded*

by the American Recovery and Reinvestment Act. December 2009, p. 38. <http://www.coburn.senate.gov/public/index.cfm?a=Files.Serve&File_id=a28a4590-10ac-4dc1-bd97-df57b39ed872>.

[225] R. Elkins, 'Tres Rios: from the beginning', *The Kachina News*, **29(1)**, Arizona Water Association, Winter 2012.

[226] Roberts, Sam 200th Birthday For the Map That Made New York, *The New York Times*, March 20, 2011. <http://www.nytimes.com/2011/03/21/nyregion/21grid.html?pagewanted=all&_r=0>

[227] Matthew Coolidge, ibid., p. 10. Matthew Coolidge, *Up River: Man Made Sites of Interest on the Hudson from the Battery to Troy*, The Centre for Land Use Interpretation, Blast Books Inc., New York, 2008, p. 10.

[228] Jeffrey Kastner (Ed.), survey by Brian Wallis, *Land and Environmental Art*, Phaidon, London, 1998 and 2005, p. 160.

[229] Jeffrey Kastner, ibid.

[230] Carol Kino, Stretching her creativity as far as possible, *The New York Times*, 28 November 2012. <http://www.nytimes.com/2012/12/02/arts/design/agnes-denes-stretches-the canvas-as-far-as-can-go.html?pagewanted=all&_r=1&>.

[231] Charles E. Beveridge and Paul Rocheleau, *Frederick Law Olmsted: Designing the American Landscape*, Rizzoli, New York, p. 30.

[232] Jeffrey Kastner, ibid., p. 12.

[233] NYC Parks Department website: <http://www.nycgovparks.org/parksMZ31/history>.

[234] Julia Czerniak and George Hargreaves (Eds), *Large Parks*, Princeton Architectural Press, 2007, p. 35–36.

[235] Jeffrey Kastner, ibid., p. 33.

[236] John K. Grande, *Art Nature Dialogues: Interviews with Environmental Artists*, State University of New York Press, 2004, p. 165. Alan Sonfist also famously once commented that news reports should cover natural phenomena such as the migrations of animals with the same wonder and gravitas as changes in sports results or the stockmarket.

[237] See, for example, this story reporting the reaction of a local Mackay researcher to both the recent 'butchering' of the mango trees that make up the Anzac Memorial Avenue in Pleystowe, west of the city, as well as plans to take cuttings from the remaining trees to re-establish the avenue on another site. Clare Chapman, 'War heroes still belong to Pleystowe', *Daily Mercury*, 24 December 2009. <http://www.dailymercury.com.au/10-brave-boys-still-belong-to-pleystowe/435010>.

[238] *Journal of Landscape Architecture*, autumn 2009, p. 7.

[239] Time Foundation website. <http://www.stichtingtijd.nl/en/articles/15-the-eternal-building-site-of-louis-le-roy>.

[240] Minhazz Majumdar, 'Sculpting from Scrap', *Landscape Architecture*, July 2005, pp. 42–51.

[241] Dia Art Foundation website. <http://www.diacenter.org/contents/page/info/102>.

[242] Frank Edgerton Martin, 'Partners in Art', *Landscape Architecture*, December 2005, p. 62.

[243] Frank Edgerton Martin, ibid., pp. 60–65 outlines the role of landscape architect Brian Tauscher and his design and construction company Artisan Gardens. The Dia Art Foundation does not mention Tauscher's role (or in fact any other consultant or contrator) in realising Irwin's vision, although it does acknowledge the role of architecture firm OpenOffice in achieving the adaptive reuse of the former industrial building.

[244] By 2008, the year of Irwin's official 'retirement', it was estimated that some 12 million visitors had experienced the Central Garden. <http://articles.latimes.com/2008/jul/24/home/hm-irwin24>.

[245] Irwin mentions the criticism of the garden in its early days in his interview in the *LA Times* when the garden was 10-years-old. <http://articles.latimes.com/2008/jul/24/home/hm-irwin24>. Some of the criticism reflects the themes and comments, such as those in <http://www.undergroundgardener.com/red.htm>.

[246] Carol Vogel, 'An Old Box Factory is Haven for New Art', *The New York Times*, April 23 2003. <http://query.nytimes.com/gst/fullpage.html?res=9E0CE0DB113AF930A15757C0A9659C8B63&pagewanted=1>.

[247] Jane Margolies, 'Art and Calm Just Up the Hudson', *The New York Times*, 12 October 2008. <http://travel.nytimes.com/2008/10/12/travel/12HourFrom.html?scp=2&sq=Dia%20Beacon&st=cse>.

[248] The J. Paul Getty Trust. <http://www.getty.edu/about/trust.html>.

[249] The Dia Art Foundation. <http://www.diabeacon.org/exhibitions/introduction/84>.

Endnotes **335**

[250] Susan Hines, 'Ulterior Exterior', *Landscape Architecture*, November 2005, pp. 105–106.

[251] Archinet blog. <http://www.archinect.com/views/view.php?id=10923_0_36_0_c>.

[252] TreeHugger blog. <http://www.treehugger.com/files/2005/03/momas_fake_gard.php>.

[253] Ken Smith, *Ken Smith Landscape Architect*, Random House, New York, 2009, pp. 134–135.

[254] Peter Reed, Groundswell exhibition catalogue.

[255] Ken Smith, ibid., p. 9.

[256] Susan Hines, ibid., p. 109.

[257] Ken Smith, ibid., p. 136.

[258] Jacky Bowring, 'Faking it: Ken Smith in camouflage at MoMA', *Landscape Architecture*, November 2005, p. 148.

[259] Peter Reed, curator of the 2005 MoMA exhibition 'Groundswell' and Ken Smith's client for the roof garden, stated, 'In a densely built urban setting, this garden represents a different notion of what public space can be.' Susan Hines, ibid., p. 106.

[260] Susan Herrington, *On Landscapes*, Routledge, New York, 2010, p. 16.

[261] Other Australians who have participated include Kate Cullity and Ryan Sims, with Taylor Cullity Lethlean Landscape Architects, who interpreted the landscape of the Central Desert in 2005.

[262] Bernard St-Denis and Peter Jacobs, Gardens at the Outer Edge: Métis 2005, *Landscape Architecture*, November 2005, pp. 94–103.

[263] Susan Herrington, ibid., p. 16.

[264] Sharon Zukin, *Naked City*, Oxford University Press, New York, 2009, p. 234.

[265] Mark Ethier, 'Lunch Lady', *Landscape Architecture*, October 2005, p. 42.

[266] Rebar Group website. <http://www.rebargroup.org/projects/victorygarden/>.

[267] Jeffrey Kastner, ibid., p. 142.

[268] Sam Serafy, Brooklyn's Bovine Burlesque, *Landscape Architecture*, November 2005, p. 20.

[269] According to the Nature Capitale website. <http://www.naturecapitale.com/>.

[270] The breathless coverage of the event is shown by articles such as the following. Diane Pham, 'New Zealand train station transformed into green meadow', *inhabitat*, 15 January 2010. <http://inhabitat.com/new-zealand-train-station-transformed-into-green-meadow/>.

[271] Reynolds also called this the 'most shameless' appropriation of the guerilla gardening term, which was applied by the Mayor seemingly because the turf was installed overnight. Richard Reynolds, *On Guerilla Gardening*, Bloomsbury Publishing, London, 2009, p. 24.

[272] Richard Reynolds, ibid., pp. 113–114.

[273] <http://www.news.com.au/entertainment/television/cheering-crowds-count-down-to-oprah-show/story-e6frfmyi-1225970698132>.

[274] <http://www.heraldsun.com.au/archives/old-news-pages/oprah-fans-arrive-for-sydney-opera-house-shows/story-fn795l53-1225970751342>.

[275] Sharon Zukin, ibid., p. 237.

[276] <http://www.theage.com.au/victoria/village-choice-yarraville-takes-road-less-travelled-in-popup-park-20111218-1p0uh.html>.

[277] To be exact, 975 parks, in 162 cities, and 35 countries, according to the PARK(ing) Day website. <http://parkingday.org/>.

[278] Widespread publicity for PARK(ing) Day can be found in varied sources including Australian design blog Object <http://www.object.com.au/springseries/event/sydney-parking/>. New York <http://www.streetfilms.org/parking-day-2008-nyc/> and sustainable design blog Inhabitat <http://inhabitat.com/tag/parking-day/>. Jeff Koons' *Puppy* is one event artwork that has achieved both public popularity and longevity. In fact one is probably the direct result of the other. The gigantic, flower-bedecked puppy seems to tick all the boxes for attracting people: it is enormous but not scary (say, like a Ron Mueck newborn baby), it is happy but not infantile (like Hello Kitty) etc.

[279] Urban Beaches have also been installed in cities as diverse as Berlin, Dublin and Mexico City.

[280] <http://ecohearth.com/eco-blogs/eco-international/823-the-beaches-of-paris-and-the-sustainable-staycation.html>.

[281] New York City Department of Transport, Greenlight for Midtown Evaluation Report, New York, January 2010. Report available at <http://www.nyc.gov/html/dot/downloads/pdf/broadway_report_final2010_web.pdf>.

[282] One strong desire line cut diagonally across the site from the intersection of Adelaide and George streets. This movement is now only possible by walking around the building perimeter to Redacliff Square, or during the day by walking through the building at ground level. The focus of public realm planning was to establish a strong connection from the Queen Street Mall to the Brisbane River. Redacliff Square does achieve this connection, albeit one fragmented by George Street, North Quay and the tunnel portal for the Queen Street busway station.

[283] Susan Herrington, ibid., p. 30.

[284] George Hazelrigg, 'In Kansas City, An Upside to the Economic Downturn – A Productive Landscape', *Landscape Architecture Magazine*, April 2012, pp. 56–62.

[285] Oliver Bishop-Young website. <http://www.oliverbishopyoung.co.uk/conversions.html>.

[286] Richard Reynolds, ibid., p. 61.

[287] Richard Reynolds, ibid., p. 69.

[288] Community gardeners have successfully targeted underused land both private and public, in particular the unused land associated with transport infrastructure corridors. Their endeavours have met with mixed results. Reports from Scotland described a group of guerilla gardeners in Edinburgh who had cleaned up and planted a plot of land beside a railway line, only to find the site padlocked and shut off by the rail company who owned the land, after their efforts had been reported in the local press. <http://www.leisurebuildings.com/blog/garden-sheds-articles/guerilla-gardeners-evicted-by-network-rail/>. In Melbourne, local authorities such as Darebin appear to be taking a 'don't ask, don't tell' approach to the activities of some of the proactive public land gardeners. <http://www.theage.com.au/national/gardening-guerillas-in-our-midst-20081209-6v06.html.>.

[289] <http://www.cityfarmer.info/2011/01/06/25th-anniversary-of-the-destruction-of-the-garden-of-eden-in-new-york-city/>.

[290] John Brinckerhoff Jackson, 'Concluding with Landscapes'. In *Discovering the Vernacular Landscape*, Yale University Press, New Hampshire and London, 1984, p. 147.

[291] *East London Green Grid Primer* Greater London Authority, London, 2006, p. 32.

[292] Macfarlane, Robert, *The Old Ways: A Journey on Foot*, Hamish Hamilton, London, 2012, p. 40.

Appendix

340 future**park**

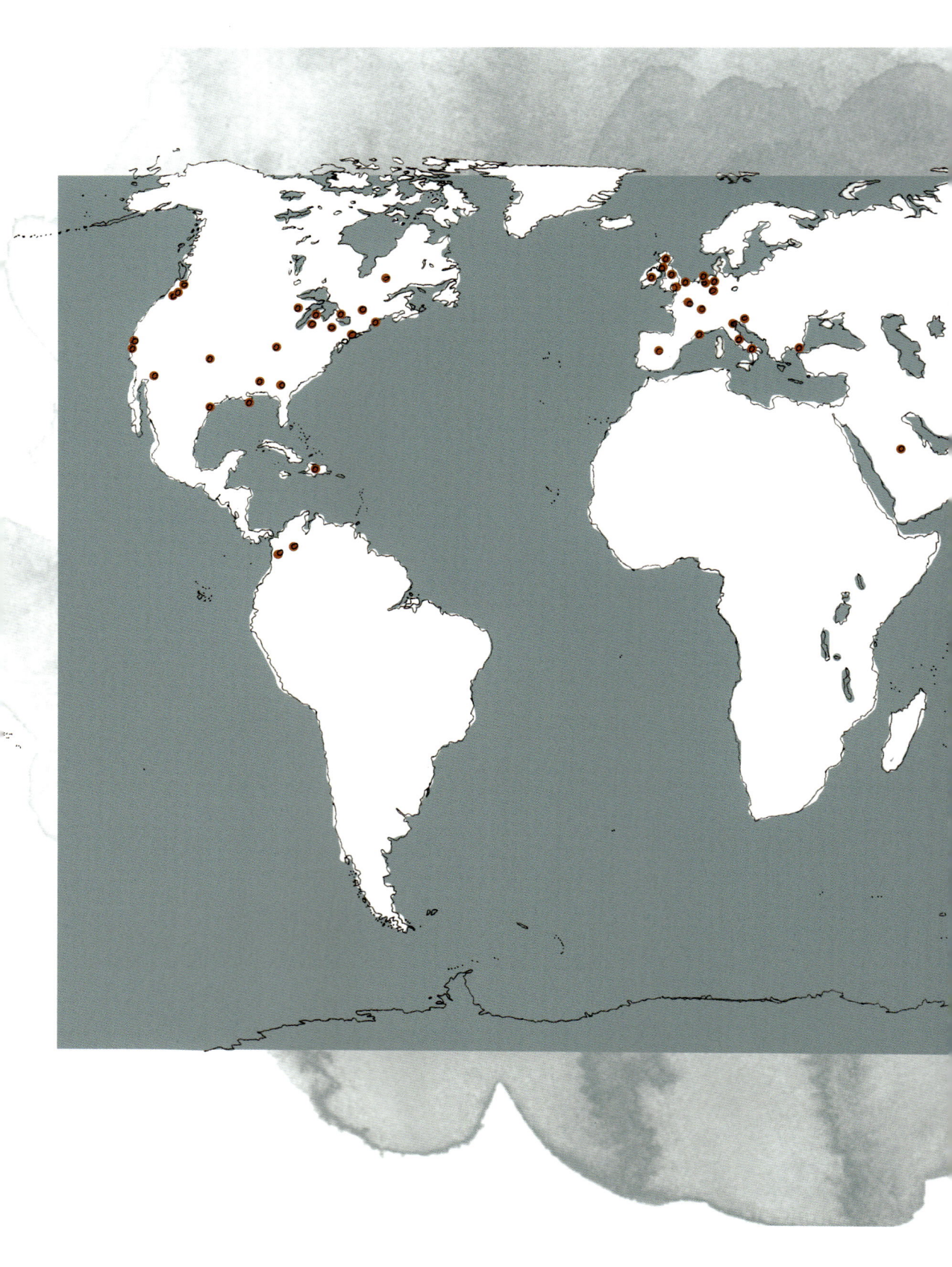

Project distribution

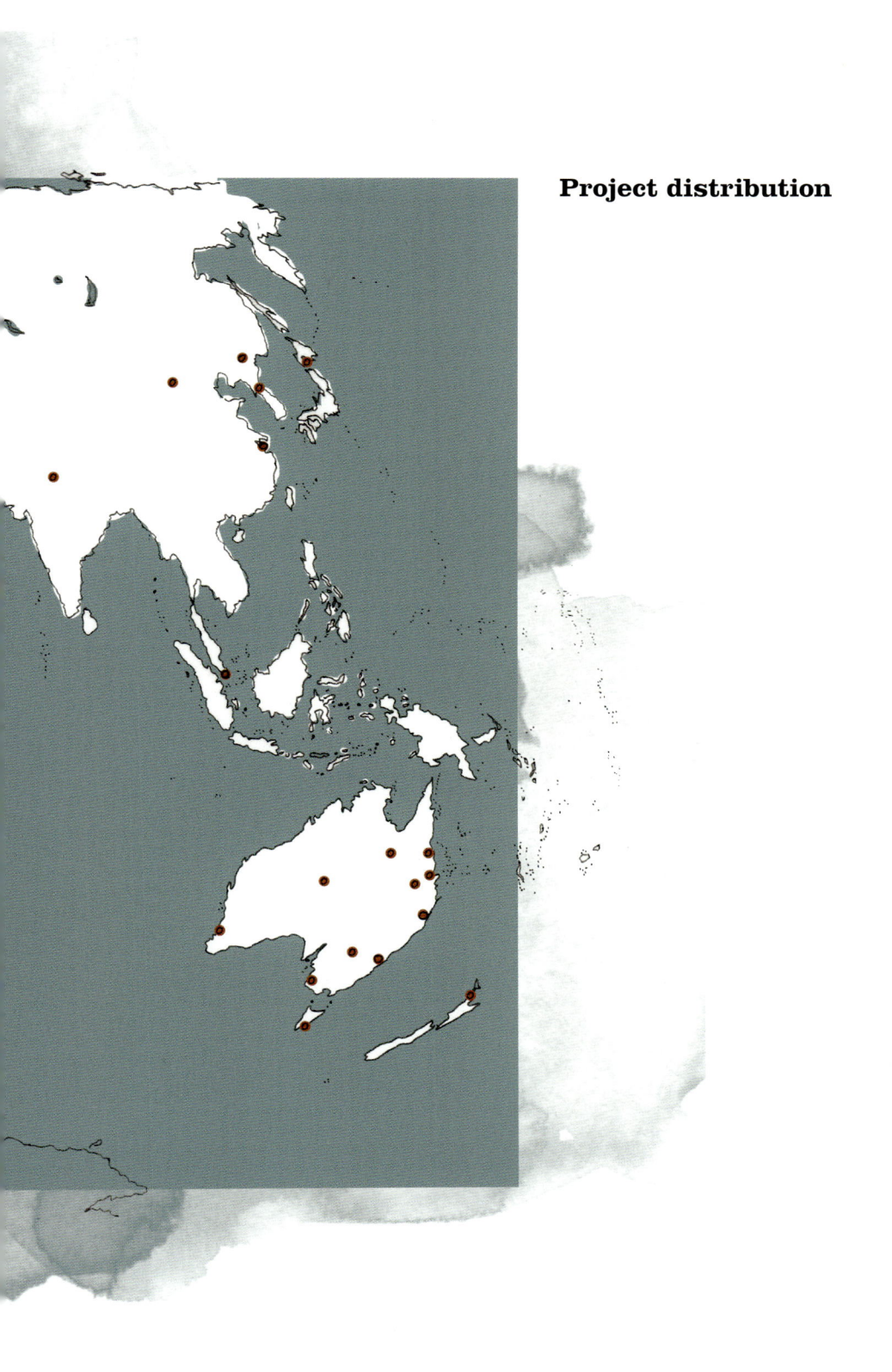

Index

Index

Symbols

18Broadway p. 307, 308

128th Street Community Garden p. 153

7000 Eichen p. 261, 262, 263, 265, 268

A

Abney Park Cemetery p. 178, 180, 181, 182, 184, 185, 186

Abandonment p. 136

Agence Ter p. 105

Alabama p. 128

Albany p. 128, 240, 242, 245

Allen, Will p. 159, 333

Architecture p. 21, 28, 105, 307, 325, 326, 330, 334, 335, 336, 337

Arizona Falls p. 210, 213

Arlington p. 228, 335

Art p. 224, 228, 238, 241, 247, 256, 258, 259, 260, 261, 262, 263, 264, 266, 270, 271, 272, 274, 276, 279, 280, 286, 297, 309, 320, 335

Athlone p. 125

Atlanta p. 64, 65, 66, 70, 78, 164, 174, 175, 176, 326, 333

Atlanta BeltLine p. 64, 326

Australia p. 21, 25, 26, 27, 28, 62, 122, 123, 124, 128, 142, 161, 167, 171, 193, 213, 222, 274, 275, 284, 317, 325, 326, 328, 331

Avenida de Portugal p. 44

B

Backyard Blitz p. 26, 27

Ballast Point Parkland p. 28

Balmori, Diana p. 140, 330

Battery Park p. 257, 258, 262

Beacon p. 191, 268, 270, 271

Belgium p. 153

Benefit p. 16, 17, 18, 81, 138, 139, 141, 145, 165, 171, 190, 202, 213, 252, 283, 321, 328

Berg, Nate p. 141, 331

Berlin p. 82, 122, 327, 328, 329, 337

Better Homes and Gardens p. 26

Beuys, Joseph p. 262, 264, 268

Biofuel p. 161

Bioremediation p. 142, 145, 331

Bioretention p. 147

Birmingham p. 128

Bishop-Young, Oliver p. 308

Blue Pike Farm p. 159, 333

Bluewater Trail p. 72, 73, 74, 76, 327

Bordeaux p. 37

Boston p. 203

Branitzer Park p. 115

Breakfast on the Bridge p. 282, 283, 286

Brightwater Wastewater Treatment Plant p. 236, 237

Brisbane p.11, 13, 41, 62, 171, 195, 289, 296, 312, 314, 315, 317, 318, 326, 331, 334, 337

Brookings Institution p. 161, 333

Brookline Reservoir p. 203

Brooklyn p. 16, 17, 151, 230, 256, 280, 308, 336

Brown and Caldwell p. 238

Brownfield p. 119, 148, 328

Brown parks p. 28, 321

Bruce Dees and Associates p. 220

Bucaramanga p. 213, 214, 215, 216

Buffalo p. 127, 154, 161, 166, 333

Bull, Catherin p. 28

Burke, Don p. 27

Burnham, Daniel p. 199

Buro Happold p. 252

C

CABE (The Commission for Architecture and the Built Environment) p. 105, 328

Callan Park p. 14, 15

Carradah Park p. 28, 29

Castro Commons p. 290, 291, 293

Castro, Lorenzo p. 214

Celtic Tiger p. 125

Cemeteries p. 172, 173, 174, 185

Cemetery p. 163, 172, 174, 175, 176, 178, 180, 181, 182, 184, 185, 186

Central Park p. 17, 20, 21, 185, 201, 273, 280, 284, 324

Central Park Conservancy p. 21, 185, 324

Cescas, Michele p. 214

Chand, Nek p. 266

Chandigarh p. 265, 266

Charters Towers p. 124, 329

Chaumont-sur-Loire p. 274, 277, 278

Chenshan Botanical Garden p. 11

Cheonggyecheon River Park p. 42

Chicago p. 57, 153, 284, 327

China p. 10, 124, 125, 126, 213, 329

Christo and Jeanne-Claude p. 280, 289

Churchill, Winston p. 190

City Farm p. 153

City Harvest p. 158, 332

Civic Center Victory Garden p. 280

Clean economy p. 161

Clean jobs p. 161

Clermont p. 167, 333

Cleveland p. 124, 127, 142, 148, 149, 153, 154, 156, 159, 161, 164, 328, 329, 330, 331, 332, 333

Co-location p. 25, 28, 169, 170, 183, 193, 199, 200, 217, 227, 231, 241, 252, 253, 256, 314

Colombia p. 2, 199, 213, 334

Columbia Boulevard Wastewater Treatment Plant p. 222, 223, 224, 227

Columbia River p. 218, 219, 220, 240

Contamination p. 119, 120, 141, 142, 144, 145, 162, 331

Corner, James p. 53

Corridors p. 38, 44, 51, 62, 175, 210, 262, 337

Country Town Rescue p. 123

Craco p. 124, 329

Craco Peschiera p. 124

Cultivate Kansas City p. 156, 158, 159, 333

Cundall, Peter p. 27

Cuyahoga County Land Bank p. 162

Czerniak, Julia p. 22, 325, 335

D

Danadjieva and Koenig Associates p. 237

Decentralised energy p. 150, 160, 161

Decline p. 62, 111, 122, 123, 126, 128, 130, 132, 136, 163, 165, 329

De-densification p. 131

Definition p. 21, 22, 23, 24, 128, 138, 150, 256, 327

Denes, Agnes p. 257, 258, 259, 264, 316

Detroit p. 127, 128, 129, 130, 131, 133, 154, 165, 166, 199, 329

Detroit's People Mover p. 165

Dia: Beacon p. 268, 270, 271

Diamond, Jared p. 123, 329

Director Park p. 14

Domain, The p. 26

Dominican Republic p. 79

Dresden p. 122

Drummer's Circle p. 17

Duisburg-Nord p. 95, 97, 98, 101, 102

Durie, Jamie p. 27

Dusseldorf p. 37

E

Ecokathedraal p. 264, 265, 266

Economy p. 21, 25, 120, 161, 164, 166, 264, 279, 333

Education p. 18, 166, 185, 219, 220, 237, 252

Emscher p. 91, 92, 93, 94, 95, 105, 117, 119, 166, 316, 327, 328

Emscher Landschaftspark p. 92, 94, 105, 119, 316, 328

Engineering p. 39, 63, 151, 172, 191, 193, 204, 210, 213, 214, 240, 252

Environmental p. 148, 190, 191, 220, 240, 325, 327, 332, 335

Essen p. 104, 105, 106, 108, 111, 327

F

Farris, Julie p. 280

Flint p. 128, 136, 154, 330

Folklife Festival p. 279

Food desert p. 158, 316

Food miles p. 151

Forgotten Cities p. 128, 330

France p. 124, 326

Frankfurt p. 41

Fürst-Pückler-Land p. 117, 119, 124

Fürst von Pückler-Muskau, Hermann Ludwig Heinrich p. 115, 117

G

Garden festival p. 274, 276

Gary p. 128, 331

Genesee County Land Bank p. 162, 333

Georgiadis, Costa p. 27, 325

Geothermal energy p. 161

Germany p. 41, 91, 93, 114, 115, 117, 122, 124, 126, 213, 262, 327, 328

Getty Centre p. 269, 271

Ghent p. 153

Glaeser, Edward p. 165, 333

Glasgow p. 125, 299, 307

Glenatore p.125

Glenwood Green Acres p. 154

Global financial crisis p. 25

Globalisation p. 25

Green Impact Zone p. 157, 158, 333

Green Infrastructure p. 330, 332, 333

Green Light for Midtown p. 295

Green parks p. 28

Green Zone p. 136, 138, 158, 330

GROSS.MAX p. 299

Growing Power p. 159, 160, 333

Guerilla gardening p. 283

H

Habitat p. 18, 23, 39, 147, 185, 237, 246

Hackney p. 181, 183, 185, 334

Haiti p. 79

Hakodate p. 120, 167, 328

Harbin p. 10

Harries, Mags p. 210

Hayes Valley Farm p. 153

Heder, Lajos p. 210

High Line, The p. 18, 19, 53, 57

Historic Fourth Ward Park p. 66, 67, 69

Hobart p. 15

House p. 5, 114, 125, 128, 129, 130, 131, 268, 273, 321, 331, 336

Houston p. 37, 259

Hydroelectric p. 204, 210, 213

I

IBA (Internationale Bauausstellung) p. 93, 95, 105, 117, 119, 124, 166, 327, 328

Iller River Hydroelectric Plant p. 212, 213

India p. 265

Inner Mongolia p. 126

Installation p. 25,81, 98, 255, 256, 257, 258, 260, 261, 262, 263, 266, 267, 272, 274, 276, 279, 283, 287, 289, 293, 301 307, 309, 315

Interboro p. 130, 131, 297

International garden festival p. 274

Ireland p. 125, 329

Irwin, Robert p. 268, 269, 270, 271, 272

Istanbul p. 192, 193

Italy p. 124

J

Jackson, John Brinckerhoff p. 22, 325, 337

Japan p. 120, 328, 329

Jerome, Leonard p. 190

Jerome Park Reservoir p. 190, 203

Jiuzhan Park p. 10

Jones & Jones p. 238

Jordan, Lorna p. 238

K

Kalamazoo County Land Bank p.162, 333

Kangbashi p. 126, 329

Kansas City p. 154, 156, 157, 158, 159, 307, 332, 333, 337

Kansas City Community Gardens p. 156, 158, 332

Kassel p. 262, 263

Kempten p. 212, 213

King Edward Park p. 312, 315

Koolhaas, Rem p. 105

Korea p. 42

L

Lake Whitney Water Treatment Plant p. 207

Land banks p. 162, 163, 166

Landscape architect p. 27, 53, 82, 140, 199, 210, 268, 272, 276, 335

Landscape architecture p. 27, 53, 203, 263, 266, 273, 309

Landschaftspark Duisburg-Nord p. 95, 97, 98, 101, 102

Land trusts p. 162, 166

Langley-Turnbaugh, Dr Samantha p. 145

Latrobe City p. 167

Latz, Peter p. 95

Lawn p. 2, 10, 72, 140, 144, 172, 200, 207, 220, 283, 312, 315, 330

le Roy, Louis G. p. 264

Lead Pathways Study p. 144

Leeds p. 122

Legacy Cities p. 128

Lent Space p. 297, 298, 299, 308, 315

Index **345**

Leyva, Alfonso p. 214

Light rail p. 35, 37

Linkage p. 25, 31, 32, 33, 35, 37, 39, 41, 43, 45, 47, 51, 55, 57, 59, 63, 65, 67, 69, 73, 75, 79, 81, 83, 85, 87, 89, 93, 95, 97, 99, 101, 105, 111, 121, 149, 183, 199, 217, 227, 231, 267, 293, 301, 319, 328

Liverpool p. 122

Ljubljana p. 84, 85, 327

London p. 7, 57, 124, 172, 178, 181, 183, 185, 186, 283, 320, 326, 329, 333, 335, 336, 337

LOTT Clean Water Alliance Regional Services Center p. 220

Lowenthal, David p. 141, 330

Lower Lausitz p. 115, 117, 166

LowLine p. 57, 326

M

Mackay p. 70, 71, 72, 73, 78, 327, 335

Madrid p. 44, 45, 47, 49, 50, 125, 325

Madrid Rio p. 44, 45, 47, 49, 50, 325

Main Riverside Promenade p. 41

Manchester p. 122, 166

Maple Leaf Reservoir p. 191, 192

Martino, Steve p. 210

McGregor Coxall p. 15, 28, 324

McMillan Park p. 200, 201

McMillan Plan p. 199, 200, 201

McMillan Reservoir p. 196, 197, 204

McMillan Sand Filtration Plant p. 196, 197, 198, 200, 203

Melbourne p. 18, 123, 151, 284, 325, 326, 331, 337

Messner, Michael p. 164

Michael Van Valkenburg Associates p.207

Midtown Greenway p. 62, 63

Migration p. 122, 124

Mildam p. 264, 265

Military and political boundaries p. 78

Mill Creek p. 155

Miller Hull Architects p. 208

Millersburg p. 240

Milwaukee p. 148, 159, 160, 332

Minneapolis p. 63

Miss, Mary p. 228, 230

MoMA (Museum of Modern Art) p. 272, 273, 274, 336

MoMA roof garden p. 272

Moriyama and Teshima p. 252

Mount Isa p. 144

Mt Tabor p. 191

Murase Landscape Architects p. 208

Mycoremediation p. 142

N

Nature Capitale p. 282, 289, 336

Netherlands, the p. 86

Newcastle p. 122

New Dutch Waterline p. 86, 88, 316

New Farm Park p. 11, 317, 320

New Haven p. 204, 205, 207, 210, 325

New Orleans p. 128

New Suburbanism p. 131

Newtown Creek Nature Walk p. 230, 234

Newtown Creek Wastewater Treatment Plant p. 228, 230, 233, 236

New York p. 14, 18, 19, 20, 21, 52, 53, 57, 114, 124, 128, 132, 145, 166, 170, 185, 190, 203, 230, 256, 257, 259, 260, 268, 270, 272, 280, 281, 295, 297, 298, 309, 324, 325, 326, 328, 330, 331, 335, 336, 337

Nice p. 37

Noller, Dr Barry p. 144, 331

NYDOT (New York Department of Transport) p. 295

O

Oakland Cemetery p. 174, 175, 176

Obsolescence p. 25, 28, 113,114,119,123, 124,125,127,128,167, 314

OKRA p. 84, 87, 90

Olmsted, Frederick Law p. 16, 21, 199, 200, 203, 335

Olmsted Jr, Frederick Law p. 199, 200

Olympia p. 220

Ordos p. 126

P

Paddington Reservoir Gardens p. 194

Paradox p. 25

Paris p. 21, 35, 37, 58, 59, 256, 276, 282, 286, 287, 289, 326

Paris Plage p. 287, 289

Park p. 2, 6, 7, 10, 11, 14, 15, 16, 17, 20, 21, 22, 24, 25, 26, 27, 28, 32, 35, 37, 41, 42, 44, 46, 53, 55, 57, 66, 69, 72, 84, 86, 95, 115, 117, 121, 129, 140, 141, 145, 162, 172, 175, 185, 191, 192, 193, 194, 199, 200, 202, 208, 209, 210, 213, 214, 215, 216, 217, 219, 220, 222, 223, 224, 228, 233, 234, 236, 240, 247, 249, 252, 256, 257, 258, 259, 260, 261, 264, 265, 268, 270, 271, 279, 280, 284, 286, 287, 290, 296, 298, 299, 301, 307, 308, 309, 312, 313, 314, 315, 316, 317, 318, 321, 324, 326, 327, 328, 336

PARK(ing) Day p. 284, 286, 336

Parklets p. 289

Parque de Arganzuela p. 44, 45

Parque del Agua p. 213, 214, 215, 216

Path of Remembrance and Comradeship p. 84, 327

Pattern Language, A p. 22, 325

Pavement to Parks p. 289, 291, 293, 295

Peace Parks p. 91, 327

Pennsylvania Horticultural Society p. 140, 155, 156, 330, 332

Perth p. 123

Philadelphia p. 2, 57, 130, 140, 141, 150, 154, 155, 156, 158, 163, 316, 321, 330, 332, 333

Philadelphia Green p. 140, 156, 330

Phoenix p. 39, 117, 210, 246, 316

Phytoremediation p. 142, 144, 331

Pierce County Environmental Services Building p. 220

Pittsburgh p. 127, 132, 166

Portland p. 6, 14, 147, 191, 216, 217, 218, 219, 220, 222, 223, 224, 227, 240, 331

Potters Field Park p. 7

Productive landscapes p. 138

Promenade p. 41, 58, 59, 60, 326

Promenade Plantée p. 58, 59, 60, 326

Prospect Park p. 16, 17, 18, 324

Public utilities p. 204, 217, 240, 252

Puentes Cascara p. 46

R

Rael San Fratello p. 81

Rail p. 35, 37, 38, 51, 57, 59, 62, 63, 64, 70, 73, 78, 79, 164, 227, 256, 271, 289, 326, 327, 337

Rail corridor p. 64, 73

Rails to Trails p. 62

Railway p. 62, 70, 71, 72, 270, 283, 337

Rebar p. 280, 284, 336

Reddacliff Place p. 315

Red Fields to Green Fields p. 164, 324, 333

Re-Imagining: A More Sustainable Cleveland p. 148

Renton p. 238

Reservoirs p. 172, 185, 186, 190, 191, 193, 195, 196, 252

Residencial Francisco Hernando housing p. 125

Reynolds, Richard p. 283, 308, 336, 337

Rio Salado p. 39, 41, 210, 246, 325

River edge p. 39, 222

Riverfront p. 11, 41, 42, 44, 161, 217, 219, 220, 234, 270

Riverside p. 172, 314

Riyadh p. 249, 253

Robert F Wagner Jr Park p. 14

Rock Garden p. 265, 266, 268

Roman Limes p. 84

Roma Street Parkland p. 13, 14, 317, 318

Rome p. 123, 328

Roosevelt Reservoir p. 191, 192

Rottenrow Gardens p. 299, 301, 304, 307, 308

Ruhr p. 93, 105, 117, 327

Rust Belt p. 124, 128, 129

S

Saginaw p. 130, 132, 133, 134, 136, 137, 154, 158, 167, 330, 333

Salt River p. 39, 210

Samper, German p.214

San Francisco p. 81, 153, 280, 281, 284, 289, 290, 291, 293, 295

Saudi Arabia p. 249

Schilling, Joseph p.166, 333

Seattle p. 191, 192, 193, 236, 237, 238, 328, 335

Segregation p. 25, 136, 326

Seoul p. 42

Sesena p. 125

Shanghai p. 11, 170

Sheffield p. 122

Shrinkage p. 25, 28, 119, 122, 124, 125, 128, 131, 321

Shrinking cities p. 28, 119, 123, 128, 129, 131, 138, 141, 142, 145, 150, 154, 158, 160, 161, 162, 163, 166, 213, 327, 329

Silos p. 25

Singapore p. 32, 33, 34

Site stabilisation p. 138, 139

Skalak Jr, Carl J. p. 159

Skip Conversion p. 308

Slough Trail p. 223, 224, 227

Slovenia p. 84, 85, 327

Smith, Ken p. 272, 274, 336

Solar power p. 161

Solnit, Rebecca p. 82, 327

Sonfist, Alan p. 259, 260, 261, 262, 264, 309, 335

South Bank p. 41, 317, 318

Southern Ridges p. 32, 33, 34

South Park Blocks p. 6

Spain p. 125, 325, 329

Sperrgebiet p. 82

Spirn, Anne Whiston p. 23, 325

Spring Hill p. 195, 314

Stephen Holl Architects p. 207

St Louis p. 57, 127, 128, 154

Stoke Newington p. 178, 182, 185, 186, 187, 189, 190, 196

Stoke Newington reservoirs p. 190

Stormwater p. 38, 39, 81, 145, 147, 148, 150, 155, 207, 217, 219, 221, 222, 238, 307, 314

Sustainable Border Fence p. 80, 81

Sydney p. 2, 14, 15, 26, 27, 28, 29, 123, 193, 194, 282, 283, 284, 286, 324, 325, 331, 333

Sydney Morning Herald p. 26, 27, 324, 325

T

T3 light rail p. 35, 37

Talking Water Gardens p. 240, 242, 243, 245, 246

Temporary p. 28, 140, 163, 256, 272, 274, 276, 279, 280, 283, 284, 286, 287, 289, 295, 296, 297, 298, 299, 307

Temporary Landscape: A Pasture for an Urban Space p. 280

The Gates p. 280, 281, 284

Time Landscape p. 259, 260, 261, 263, 265, 309

Trafalgar Square p. 283

Trakas, George p. 230, 234

Trees p. 2, 16, 18, 71, 72, 95, 140, 145, 147, 172, 173, 174, 207, 234, 238, 259, 260, 261, 262, 263, 268, 276, 282, 286, 296, 297, 298, 299, 312, 315, 321, 331, 334, 335

Tres Rios p. 246, 247, 249, 335

Trundle p. 123

Tumber, Catherine p. 161, 333

U

Uluru p. 26

UNESCO p. 88, 105

United Kingdom p. 122, 124, 222, 308, 331

United States p. 18, 62, 82, 91, 114, 124, 126, 127, 128, 141, 145, 161, 162, 167, 191, 199, 200, 222, 223, 240, 280, 326, 327, 331, 332

Urban agriculture p. 150, 151, 154, 155, 159, 160, 161, 162, 213, 279, 332

Urban Agriculture Innovation Zone p. 159

Urbanisation p. 25

Urban islands p. 132

US–Mexico border p. 80, 82, 91

Utrecht p. 84

V

Vacancy p. 119, 132, 136, 329

Value p. 16, 18, 21, 27, 136, 141, 148, 166, 185, 223, 240, 258, 314, 325

Vancouver p. 219, 220, 334

Vaux, Calvert p. 16

Venice p. 120, 121, 167, 328

W

Wadi Hanifa p. 249, 252, 253

Wall, Ed p. 21, 325

Washington D.C. p. 196, 204, 279, 333

Water Pollution Control Laboratory p. 216, 217, 219, 220

Water Pollution Control Plant p. 228

Water Resources Education Center p. 219, 220

Waterman, Tim p. 21, 325

Watershed p. 155, 218, 334

Waterton–Glacier International Peace Park p. 90, 91

Waterworks Gardens p. 238

Watts, Dr Isaac p. 178

Weil, Gad p. 282

Wellington Park p. 15, 16, 324

West 8 p. 44

West Point p. 236, 237

Wetland p. 205, 207, 220, 238, 240, 246, 252

Wheatfield: A Confrontation p. 258, 259

Whitney Jr, Eli p. 204, 205, 207

Willamette River Water Treatment Plant Park p. 208

Wilsonville p. 208

Wind turbines p. 161, 204, 213

WSUD (Water Sensitive Urban Design) p. 147, 148, 150, 331

WWII (World War II) p. 86

Y

Yerebatan (Basilica) Cistern p. 192, 193

Youngstown p. 128, 154, 162

Z

Zollverein p. 104, 105, 106, 108, 111, 327

Zukin, Sharon p. 279, 284, 336

Index **347**

Places

A
Australia p. 21, 25, 26, 27, 28, 62, 122, 123, 124, 128, 142, 161, 167, 171, 193, 213, 222, 274, 275, 284, 317, 325, 326, 328, 331
- Ballast Point Parkland p. 28
- Brisbane p. 11, 13, 41, 62, 171, 195, 289, 296, 312, 314, 315, 317, 318, 326, 331, 334, 337
- Callan Park p. 14, 15
- Charters Towers p. 124, 329
- Clermont p. 167, 333
- Hobart p. 15
- Latrobe City p. 167
- Mackay p. 70, 71, 72, 73, 78, 327, 335
- Melbourne p. 18, 123, 151, 284, 325, 326, 331, 337
- Mount Isa p. 144
- Perth p. 123
- Spring Hill p. 195, 314
- Sydney p. 2, 14, 15, 26, 27, 28, 29, 123, 193, 194, 282, 283, 284, 286, 324, 325, 331, 333
- Trundle p. 123
- Uluru p. 26

B
Belgium p. 153
- Ghent p. 153

C
China p. 10, 124, 125, 126, 213, 329
- Harbin p. 10
- Kangbashi p. 126, 329
- Inner Mongolia p. 126
- Ordos p. 126
- Shanghai p. 11, 170
Colombia p. 2, 199, 213, 334
- Bucaramanga p. 213, 214, 215, 216

D
Dominican Republic p. 79

F
France p. 124, 326
- Bordeaux p. 37
- Chaumont-sur-Loire p. 274, 277, 278
- Nice p. 37
- Paris p. 21, 35, 37, 58, 59, 256, 276, 282, 286, 287, 289, 326

G
Germany p. 41, 91, 93, 114, 115, 117, 122, 124, 126, 213, 262, 327, 328
- Berlin p. 82, 122, 327, 328, 329, 337
- Dresden p. 122
- Duisburg-Nord p. 95, 97, 98, 101, 102
- Dusseldorf p. 37
- Emscher p. 91, 92, 93, 94, 95, 105, 117, 119, 166, 316, 327, 328
- Essen p. 104, 105, 106, 108, 111, 327
- Frankfurt p. 41
- Kassel p. 262, 263
- Kempten p. 212, 213
- Lower Lausitz p. 115, 117, 166
- Ruhr p. 93, 105, 117, 327
- Zollverein p. 104, 105, 106, 108, 111, 327

H
Haiti p. 79

I
India p. 265
- Chandigarh p. 265, 266
Ireland p. 125, 329
- Athlone p. 125
- Glenatore p. 125
Italy p. 124
- Craco p. 124, 329
- Craco Peschiera p. 124
- Rome p. 123, 328
- Venice p. 120, 121, 167, 328

J
Japan p. 120, 328, 329
- Hakodate p. 120, 167, 328

K
Korea, South p. 42
- Seoul p. 42

N
Netherlands p. 86
- Mildam p. 264, 265
- Utrecht p. 84
New Zealand
- Auckland p. 283

S
Saudi Arabia p. 249
- Riyadh p. 249, 253
Singapore p. 32, 33, 34
Slovenia p. 84, 85, 327
- Ljubljana p. 84, 85, 327
Spain p. 125, 325, 329
- Madrid p. 44, 45, 47, 49, 50, 125, 325
- Sesena p. 125

T
Turkey
- Istanbul p. 192, 193

U
United Kingdom p. 122, 124, 222, 308, 331
- Birmingham p. 128
- Glasgow p. 125, 299, 307
- Hackney p. 181, 183, 185, 334
- Leeds p. 122
- Liverpool p. 122
- London p. 7, 57, 124, 172, 178, 181, 183, 185, 186, 283, 320, 326, 329, 333, 335, 336, 337
- Manchester p. 122, 166
- Newcastle p. 122
- Sheffield p. 122
- Stoke Newington p. 178, 182, 185, 186, 187, 189, 190, 196
United States p. 18, 62, 82, 91, 114, 124, 126, 127, 128, 141, 145, 161, 162, 167, 191, 199, 200, 222, 223, 240, 280, 326, 327, 331, 332
- Alabama p. 128
- Albany p. 128, 240, 242, 245
- Arlington p. 228, 335
- Atlanta p. 64, 65, 66, 70, 78, 164, 174, 175, 176, 326, 333
- Battery Park p. 257, 258, 262
- Beacon p. 191, 268, 270, 271
- Boston p. 203
- Brooklyn p. 16, 17, 151, 230, 256, 280, 308, 336
- Buffalo p. 127, 154, 161, 166, 333

Chicago p. 57, 153, 284, 327

Cleveland p. 124, 127, 142, 148, 149, 153, 154, 156, 159, 161, 164, 328, 329, 330, 331, 332, 333

Columbia River p. 218, 219, 220, 240

Detroit p. 127, 128, 129, 130, 131, 133, 154, 165, 166, 199, 329

Flint p. 128, 136, 154, 330

Gary p. 128, 331

Kansas City p. 154, 156, 157, 158, 159, 307, 332, 333, 337

Houston p. 37, 259

Mill Creek p. 155

Millersburg p. 240

Milwaukee p. 148, 159, 160, 332

Minneapolis p. 63

Mt Tabor p. 191

New Haven p. 204, 205, 207, 210, 325

New Orleans p. 128

New York p. 14, 18, 19, 20, 21, 52, 53, 57, 114, 124, 128, 132, 145, 166, 170, 185, 190, 203, 230, 256, 257, 259, 260, 268, 270, 272, 280, 281, 295, 297, 298, 309, 324, 325, 326, 328, 330, 331, 335, 336, 337

Olympia p. 220

Philadelphia p. 2, 57, 130, 140, 141, 150, 154, 155, 156, 158, 163, 316, 321, 330, 332, 333

Phoenix p. 39, 117, 210, 246, 316

Pittsburgh p. 127, 132, 166

Portland p. 6, 14, 147, 191, 216, 217, 218, 219, 220, 222, 223, 224, 227, 240, 331

Renton p. 238

Rust Belt p. 124, 128, 129

Saginaw p. 130, 132, 133, 134, 136, 137, 154, 158, 167, 330, 333

Salt River p. 39, 210

San Francisco p. 81, 153, 280, 281, 284, 289, 290, 291, 293, 295

Seattle p. 191, 192, 193, 236, 237, 238, 328, 335

St Louis p. 57, 127, 128, 154

Vancouver p. 219, 220, 334

Washington D.C. p. 196, 204, 279, 333

Wilsonville p. 208

Youngstown p. 128, 154, 162

Projects

Symbols

18Broadway p. 307, 308

128th Street Community Garden p. 153

7000 *Eichen* p. 261, 262, 263, 265, 268

A

Abney Park Cemetery p. 178, 180, 181, 182, 184, 185, 186

Arizona Falls p. 210, 213

Atlanta BeltLine p. 64, 326

Avenida de Portugal p. 44

B

Blue Pike Farm p. 159, 333

Bluewater Trail p. 72, 73, 74, 76, 327

Branitzer Park p. 115

Breakfast on the Bridge p. 282, 283, 286

Brightwater Wastewater Treatment Plant p. 236, 237

Britomart p. 283

Brookline Reservoir p. 203

C

Carradah Park p. 28, 29

Castro Commons p. 290, 291, 293

Central Park p. 17, 20, 21, 185, 201, 273, 280, 284, 324

Chenshan Botanical Garden p. 11

Cheonggyecheon River Park p. 42

City Farm p. 153

City Harvest p. 158, 332

Civic Center Victory Garden p. 280

Columbia Boulevard Wastewater Treatment Plant p. 222, 223, 224, 227

Country Town Rescue p. 123

D

Dia: Beacon p. 268, 270, 271

Director Park p. 14

Domain, The p. 26

Drummer's Circle p. 17

E

Ecokathedraal p. 264, 265, 266

Emscher Landschaftspark p. 92, 94, 105, 119, 316, 328

F

Folklife Festival p. 279

Fürst-Pückler-Land p. 117, 119, 124

G

Gates, The p. 280, 281, 284

Getty Centre p. 269, 271

Glenwood Green Acres p. 154

Green Impact Zone p. 157, 158, 333

Green Light for Midtown p. 295

Green Zone p. 136, 138, 158, 330

Growing Power p. 159, 160, 333

H

Hayes Valley Farm p. 153

High Line, The p. 18, 19, 53, 57

Historic Fourth Ward Park p. 66, 67, 69

I

IBA p. 93, 95, 105, 117, 119, 124, 166, 327, 328

Iller River Hydroelectric Plant p. 212, 213

J

Jerome Park Reservoir p. 190, 203

Jiuzhan Park p. 10

K

Kangbashi p. 126, 329

Kansas City Community Gardens p. 156, 158, 332

King Edward Park p. 312, 315

L

Lake Whitney Water Treatment Plant p. 207

Landschaftspark Duisburg-Nord p. 95, 97, 98, 101, 102

Lent Space p. 297, 298, 299, 308, 315

LOTT Clean Water Alliance Regional Services Center p. 220

LowLine p. 57, 326

M

Madrid Rio p. 44, 45, 47, 49, 50, 325

Main Riverside Promenade p. 41

Maple Leaf Reservoir p. 191, 192

McMillan Park p. 200, 201

McMillan Plan p. 199, 200, 201

McMillan Reservoir p. 196, 197, 204

McMillan Sand Filtration Plant p. 196, 197, 198, 200, 203

Midtown Greenway p. 62, 63

MoMA p. 272, 273, 274, 336

MoMA roof garden p. 272

N

Nature Capitale p. 282, 289, 336

New Dutch Waterline p. 86, 88, 316

New Farm Park p. 11, 317, 320

New Suburbanism p. 131

Newtown Creek Nature Walk p. 230, 234

Newtown Creek Wastewater Treatment Plant p. 228, 230, 233, 236

O

Oakland Cemetery p. 174, 175, 176

P

Paddington Reservoir Gardens p. 194

Paris Plage p. 287, 289

PARK(ing) Day p. 284, 286, 336

Parque de Arganzuela p. 44, 45

Parque del Agua p. 213, 214, 215, 216

Path of Remembrance and Comradeship p. 84, 327

Pavement to Parks p. 289, 291, 293, 295

Philadelphia Green p. 140, 156, 330

Pierce County Environmental Services Building p. 220

Potters Field Park p. 7

Promenade Plantée p. 58, 59, 60, 326

Prospect Park p. 16, 17, 18, 324

Puentes Cascara p. 46

R

Reddacliff Place p. 315

Red Fields to Green Fields p. 164, 324, 333

Re-Imagining: A More Sustainable Cleveland p. 148

Residencial Francisco Hernando housing p. 125

Rio Salado p. 39, 41, 210, 246, 325

Robert F Wagner Jr Park p. 14

Rock Garden p. 265, 266, 268

Roman Limes p. 84

Roma Street Parkland p. 13, 14, 317, 318

Roosevelt Reservoir p. 191, 192

Rottenrow Gardens p. 299, 301, 304, 307, 308

S

Skip Conversion p. 308

Slough Trail p. 223, 224, 227

South Bank p. 41, 317, 318

Southern Ridges p. 32, 33, 34

South Park Blocks p. 6

Sperrgebiet p. 82

Stoke Newington reservoirs p. 190

Sustainable Border Fence p. 80, 81

T

T3 light rail p. 35, 37

Talking Water Gardens p. 240, 242, 243, 245, 246

Temporary Landscape: A Pasture for an Urban Space p. 280

Time Landscape p. 259, 260, 261, 263, 265, 309

Trafalgar Square p. 283

Tres Rios p. 246, 247, 249, 335

W

Wadi Hanifa p. 249, 252, 253

Water Pollution Control Laboratory p. 216, 217, 219, 220

Water Pollution Control Plant p. 228

Water Resources Education Center p. 219, 220

Waterton–Glacier International Peace Park p. 90, 91

Waterworks Gardens p. 238

Wellington Park p. 15, 16, 324

West Point p. 236, 237

Wheatfield: A Confrontation p. 258, 259

Willamette River Water Treatment Plant Park p. 208

Y

Yerebatan (Basilica) Cistern p. 192, 193

Index **351**

People

A
Agence Ter p. 105
Allen, Will p. 159, 333

B
Balmori, Diana p. 140, 330
Berg, Nate p. 141, 331
Beuys, Joseph p. 262, 264, 268
Bishop-Young, Oliver p. 308
Brown and Caldwell p. 238
Bruce Dees and Associates p. 220
Bull, Catherin p. 28
Burke, Don p. 27
Burnham, Daniel p. 199
Buro Happold p. 252

C
Castro, Lorenzo p. 214
Cescas, Michele p. 214
Chand, Nek p. 266
Christo and Jeanne-Claude p. 280, 289
Churchill, Winston p. 190
Corner, James p. 53
Cundall, Peter p. 27
Czerniak, Julia p. 22, 325, 335

D
Danadjieva and Koenig Associates p. 237
Denes, Agnes p. 257, 258, 259, 264, 316
Diamond, Jared p. 123, 329
Durie, Jamie p. 27

F
Farris, Julie p. 280
Fürst von Pückler-Muskau, Hermann Ludwig Heinrich p. 115, 117

G
Georgiadis, Costa p. 27, 325

Glaeser, Edward p. 165, 333
GROSS.MAX p. 299

H
Harries, Mags p. 210
Heder, Lajos p. 210

I
Interboro p. 130, 131, 297
Irwin, Robert p. 268, 269, 270, 271, 272

J
Jackson, John Brinckerhoff p. 22, 325, 337
Jerome, Leonard p. 190
Jones & Jones p. 238
Jordan, Lorna p. 238

K
Koolhaas, Rem p. 105

L
Langley-Turnbaugh, Dr Samantha p. 145
Latz, Peter p. 95
le Roy, Louis G. p. 264
Leyva, Alfonso p. 214
Lowenthal, David p. 141, 330

M
Martino, Steve p. 210
McGregor Coxall p. 15, 28, 324
Messner, Michael p. 164
Michael Van Valkenburg Associates p. 207
Miller Hull Architects p. 208
Miss, Mary p. 228, 230
Moriyama and Teshima p. 252
Murase Landscape Architects p. 208

N
Noller, Dr Barry p. 144, 331

O
OKRA p. 84, 87, 90
Olmsted, Frederick Law p. 16, 21, 199, 200, 203, 335
Olmsted Jr, Frederick Law p. 199, 200

R
Rael San Fratello p. 81
Rebar p. 280, 284, 336
Reynolds, Richard p. 283, 308, 336, 337

S
Samper, German p. 214
Schilling, Joseph p. 166, 333
Skalak Jr, Carl J. p. 159
Smith, Ken p. 272, 274, 336
Solnit, Rebecca p. 82, 327
Sonfist, Alan p. 259, 260, 261, 262, 264, 309, 335
Spirn, Anne Whiston p. 23, 325
Stephen Holl Architects p. 207

T
Trakas, George p. 230, 234
Tumber, Catherine p. 161, 333

V
Vaux, Calvert p. 16

W
Wall, Ed p. 21, 325
Waterman, Tim p. 21, 325
Watts, Dr Isaac p. 178
Weil, Gad p. 282
West 8 p. 44
Whitney Jr, Eli p. 204, 205, 207

Z
Zukin, Sharon p. 279, 284, 336